THE REAL SHROPSHIRE
ORGANIZATION

THE REAL SHROPSHIRE ORGANIZATION

The untold Truth behind the alleged heroin organization protected by Baltimore Police Detectives

ANTONIO SHROPSHIRE

Published in the United States by TMC Publications.

Library of Congress Cataloging-in-Publication Date has been applied for.

Name: Antonio Shropshire, Author

Title: The Real Shropshire Organization: The Untold Truth

Description: First edition, Baltimore: TMC Publications, 2021

Identifiers: ISBN 978-1-7370283-0-7 (Soft cover) ISBN 978-1-7370283-1-4 (eBook)

Subject: Antonio Shropshire, 1985 Baltimore (Md.)
Drug Traffic – Baltimore –
Conspiracy to distribute – Baltimore –
Violence – Baltimore –
Criminality – How to evade law enforcement –
Religion – Bible, Quran –
Corruption – Police, Prosecutors – Baltimore
Relationships – Men/Women –
Effects of slavery – oppression on people of color

This book may be purchased in bulk for any reason. Please contact TMC Publications by email at antonioshropshire85@gmail.com

Author's Note

The account of events laid out in this book are all non-fiction and are derived from my personal experience. This is my opinion. I have reviewed discovery and trial transcripts of my case, federal case law, motions filed by different attorneys and affidavits/applications for search warrants. Also, derived from the books written by Baynard Woods and Brandon Soderberg "I got a Monster" and Justin Fenton's "We Own This City". There are conflicting versions of events. Of course the government will always have their side of events and will sometimes mislead anyone to believe they are true. Due to the lack of resources, which is due to my incarceration, I'm not able to provide a full lay out of how I came to the conclusions laid out in this book. If there are any disputes, please reach out to me so we can resolve them in a respectful manner.

TABLE OF CONTENTS

FOREWORD

"The Real Shropshire Organization" is an inside look into the pros and cons of the game. Not by some lame clown perpetrating the fraud as if he has firsthand experience on something he knows nothing about, or has never experienced. But it is from the perspective of a bonafide, solid, stand up man. He not only lived what he is talking about, but continues to stand firm in the madness called White Supremacy. Not often do we get an inside look into the game from a man who lived it and didn't RAT. This book can be a blessing or a curse; it all depends on how you receive it. We know that perception drives our reality; therefore, I suggest that you read "The Real Shropshire Organization" with an open but keen mind. Read the book in its entirety. That way you'll get the full gist of what Brother Brill is conveying to you.

Brother Brill was knee deep in the game, but he is in no way glorifying the game. What Brill does in "The Real Shropshire Organization" actually exposes the makers of the game and games that these people (corrupt government officers including law enforcement) play. Yeah! Those who make and enforce the rules can, at any moment, "change the game" and break the rules to their benefit. Often to the detriment of black people, people of color in general and even poor white people. One of the key points that Brother Brill makes in "The Real Shropshire Organization" is that most people in the so called game either don't have an end game or don't make it to their desired end game.

The game more often than not, puts an abrupt end to those who play it. And there is several ways that happens: 1) Death by the streets; 2) The mental death that comes with the over consumption and glorification of material objects at the expense of sound reason and all who is directly or vicariously affected by the ignorance of those who play the game, and or 3) DEATH BY RATS. Death by rats is the worst kind of death because RATS, which is an acronym for Raping Alluding The System, take an unwritten oath to uphold the laws of the street but break both the laws of the street and the laws passed by Congress.

And so called law enforcement (i.e. police, detectives, F.B.I agents, prosecutors, Judges and even Congress) condone criminality as long as the ones committing the criminal acts agree to cooperate. RATS are given a license to steal, kill, lie, cheat, rape and rob and they are given all kinds of benefits for being the "WHORES THAT THEY ARE". Both RATS and law enforcement are hypocrites. As Brother Brill skillfully points out in this book, some police (i.e. law enforcement officers) goal is not necessarily to uphold the law and stop criminality, but as it relates to the hood, break as many young black men as they can. Leaving the ghetto in disarray and in the process instilling distrust and hatred as well as jealousy among black people for each other. The beautiful thing about "The Real Shropshire Organization" is that Brother Brill has one epiphany after another and realizes that the game itself is a carefully devised plan, an orchestrated scheme designed by diabolical minds who have never set foot in the hood but is the unseen hand behind most of the madness that goes on in the hood.

That is one of the many reasons why this book, "The Real Shropshire Organization" is a must read. When we don't know that which we think we know, we are a danger to ourselves. When we know we know, that which we don't know, we are a danger to ourselves and others. However, when we know we know, that which we do know, we must ourselves be what we know. In other words, we have to take a step back and carefully examine and challenge everything that we have accepted as our truths, even our names because we've been enslaved, misinformed, false-indoctrinated, miseducated and led astray.

That is the number one reason why black people, young black men in particular, can put the label "game" on criminality, when criminality in and of itself has never been, and will never be a black man's game. And when we find ourselves caught up in the game that they created and get a good glimpse into their system, we realize that it may have been a game to us, but those people aren't playing. The only commonality between, let's say football or basketball and criminality, is the numbers (sentences) that these people pass to us like balls. You see, Brill doesn't have it all figured out, but he figured out enough to be able to offer insight and guidance that can lead a fur tile mind in the right direction. Read the book: The Real Shropshire Organization, and be enlightened.

Respectfully,
Master Djhuiti Menes

INTRODUCTION

One day in March of 2018, I was at a federal holdover spot in Oklahoma waiting to be taken to F.C.I (Federal Correctional Institution) Beckley in West Virginia. During that day, I heard the officer yell, "Shropshire you have mail." I had just come from C.D.F (Chesapeake Detention Facility), the only federal pretrial spot in Baltimore. My only focus was to prepare for my direct appeal from the conviction that had me at this federal holdover, which was conspiracy to distribute heroin. After seeing how things played out during my 12-day jury trial, I became fascinated with federal law and then became determined to give this 25 years back to the people who gave it to me.

Since I had been at the holdover, every morning at 6 in the morning, I was the first on the law computer. The way I saw it was, either I was going to let those people destroy me or I was going to fight back. Then I asked myself, "How could I have been so blind to what's been happening to others for years?" Did I think those things couldn't and wouldn't happen to me? I must have thought that! Even when I knew they must have been investigating me, I still didn't stop. I remember sitting in the car talking to Heads, from Pennsylvania Ave in West Baltimore, saying, "I'm in too deep to stop."

So as I looked at the mail I got from the older white officer, who told me to build my credit while I was in, I saw the name Jessica Lussenhop, which had a Washington, D.C address. I opened the mail and Lussenhop was a journalist for the BBC news. She explained that she was doing a story on the G.T.T.F, which was Baltimore City Police Department's elite gun recovery unit, who in fact broke records for the most gun arrests and gun recoveries. They also broke the law they swear to protect, and were federally indicted for robbing drug dealers, stealing their money and selling their drugs to other dealers, amongst other crimes. I responded to Lussenhop who said, "the story is already done," but still wanted to hear my side if I was willing to tell it. So after 3 weeks in Oklahoma, I arrived at F.C.I Beckley on April 11, 2018. Three months later, I received a letter from Baltimore Sun journalist Justin Fenton:

"How are you? I am a reporter with The Baltimore Sun who is writing a book about the dirty cops on the gun trace task force. I would like to talk to you about how some of the stuff went down. I'm sure the story is more complex than what the public knows."

Then came a letter from Baynard Woods weeks later:

"I am a writer with a colleague on a book about the G.T.T.F case, that obviously intersects considerably with yours. Gondo had a lot to say about your business but I'd love to give you the chance to tell your side of things."

I just wondered, "What was so important about my side of the story, for these people to be reaching out to me?" I guess my case really was tied to the G.T.T.F's case because of Gondo's alleged role. It wasn't until I started to really analyze my life's story to figure out why I chose this life, just to realize that the life chose me. Then I realized that I was blind, and it was not my fault that life is the way it is for people of color. I saw how things could have been different for me if I had conscious people around me that knew what needed to be brought to the youth's attention, the youth I once was. So I thought and thought, and wondered why Fenton said what he said in his next letter, dated June 3, 2019:

"I know you probably don't want to talk about yourself but I would really like the chance to be able to make you a three dimensional person and explain your own story."

Which in turn made me think I needed to tell my story, then came another letter from Woods:

"I also have very deep suspicions about the way they say the investigation came together, that is, I think similar to yours. And it is possible that the scenario is reversed. You might be able to help me figure that out."

I thought, "Who would want to hear my story?" I sat back and reminisced about my story. Memories about all the foolish guys (like myself) that risked everything like their family, children, wives and their freedom playing in them streets. I said to myself, "Them niggas won't hear me because their blindfold hasn't been lifted yet." Then I thought about the youth. I thought about how I did not want them to go through what I've been through. So I wrote a letter to Brandon Scott, who was a councilman at the time. I particularly liked him because he spoke up for communities in the city and is now the Mayor of Baltimore.

Anyway, I was explaining to him that something had to be done for the youth of Baltimore, who are the future of Baltimore. I couldn't stop thinking about my life and federal law. At that point, I couldn't stop writing. I told myself, "I'm going to write my own book about my own life and the way I see things!"

LAST 3 DAYS OF FREEDOM

know it's some days of your life that you just can't forget. Like when you lost your virginity or when you damn near burned your mother's house down thinking you can cook. I'm sure it's plenty of days you did some dumb shit and you think about it often. Well, my last three days of freedom is something I will never forget. Honestly, how could you forget that? For me, the shit plays back like film even though it was 1,640 days ago.

It was a rainy Wednesday, November 30, 2016 and I was awakened by a morning kiss from Kelly. Damn, I was never asked to describe Kelly before but let me tell you about her. Let's see, she's a 5'7" redbone. Slim, nice tits, with a round ass, long hair and slick mouth. She has a swag like no other, an attitude like Keisha off "Belly" that can talk an Eskimo out of his coat. I was dealing with the shit for 13 years at the time. We had our son, Slick Tone, when we both were 22 and have been together ever since. "We gone Brillet! Hit me when you get up!" She was leaving for work and always dropped Tone off to school. Kelly is a successful beautician, who's had her own salon, Studiofix, for a decade now. Tone was 9 going on 13 and I was your neighborhood kingpin.

I grabbed the ringing phone from the nightstand and heard, "Yo, Brill, where you at?" It was my little man D-bo. "I'm just getting up; I'm going to hit you soon as I get around the way." I flipped open 5 other phones to check for missed calls. I used to have to cut the ringer off on most, if not all, my phones. Hell Kell, who got the name from raising hell, use to hate when they started ringing simultaneously. I got in the shower and was out the door. I walked to the gas station down the street from my house to get some backwoods. I then ordered an Uber from the iPhone that nobody I did business with (or family) had the number to. That phone was for emails, chasing the gram, out of towners, legitimate business, and bitches. I had just rented a spot on Park Ave in Baltimore's ChinaTown. I was going to make it a cafe' called "Cafe 3-1-2." I was on red alert and moved like I had a warrant for my arrest. Little did I know, I did.

I knew somebody was hot on my ass because on August 4, 2015 I was going to meet someone I thought was cool and because I didn't really know the wild nigga, I always played it safe. That day, I got there first to peep the scene out, then told him where to go. Soon as the guy came down the block, I noticed this gold SUV that I always used to see in my neighborhood and the SUV driver had his phone out as if he was recording something. I always thought the lightly tinted SUV was the police. So when I saw it at the bottom of the street where I'm about to sell dope to somebody, and we weren't in my neighborhood, I knew that it was a cop.

They didn't know what I was driving, so I pulled off smoothly, went somewhere and broke every phone. That same somebody later identified as Maryland State Trooper Neil Miranda, who I sold 10 grams to on July 15th, 2015. He made me think someday I would have to pay the price for it. On March 31, 2016, I found a G.P.S. tracker on my car. October 11, 2016, Baltimore City Police hit my house. On November 25, 2016 (Thanksgiving night around 1am), I left my house and was about to walk through the alley. But a car rode past my street that caught my attention. As I walked through the dark ass alley, the same car turned in the alley from the next street over.

Damn near hit me speeding through. The car pulled to the end of the alley, sat there for a minute, then turned up my street. My rental was parked at the top of the street so I ran to the car to try to catch who was driving it. It's crazy because had I walked out the house a second too late, I would have missed everything. Luckily, the driver caught every light and I was able to catch up. It was somebody with a hoodie on. I looked harder and couldn't believe my eyes. It was the same Baltimore City Narcotic Detective that raided my house in October.

Later identified as Robert Hankard. I thought about why he would be coming past my house on Thanksgiving night. Then it hit me! He was looking for my 2016 Honda Accord Touring that he kept asking me about. I later found out that he had a warrant, signed by Judge Berry Williams, to place a G.P.S on my car. I guess he didn't get the memo that I parked my cars on the next block over and walked through the alley he almost hit me in.

An overweight older white man pulled up driving a Honda CR-V. "Hello," I said. I always like to talk to people I don't know, you just never know what they might say. After he asked how I was doing this morning, I asked "so how long you been an Uber driver" he said "oh not long, I had to get this new car first, my crazy wife crashed the older model CR-V we had a month ago." It made me think about the older white lady that hit my Honda and three other cars on my block a few months ago. She was driving a damn Honda CR-V.

I called D-bo, "Yo where you at?" I asked. "My man just got in an accident. I'm going to go pick him up then come meet you." It wasn't nothing but a 13-minute drive, if that, from the gas station to my rental which was parked a block over from my grandmother's house. Soon as I pulled up, I thought about this dumb ass coke I had in my car from the night before. I was doing my man from Cedonia (a neighborhood in Northeast Baltimore) a favor. I only sold dope, smack, boy, heroin, but I knew niggas that had bricks of cane. If I fucked with you, I would get it for you. My man wanted 9 ounces so I went and got it.

My timing is always crazy, so I just dropped him off the coke and told him I'll get the money later. When I went to get the money that Tuesday night (the 29th), he said he cooked up 62 grams and it was something he didn't like about it. He paid me for the 62 grams and gave me the rest back. I called my man who shit it was and he brushed me off because he was doing something else. That night, I was trying to meet Heads and Georgie at Outback Steakhouse so I put the coke in my grandmother's backyard. After Kelly cursed me out about not getting her something from Outback, I realized my man never called me back. I couldn't leave the coke in my grandmother's grill overnight, so I pulled a block over from her house and caught an Uber home.

I sat in the car contemplating what I was going to do with the coke. Before I smoke in the morning (weed of course) I had to eat something, but I could never eat. I started drinking Ensure in the morning instead. That weed will fuck you up on the low. I reached in the backseat to find I had no more

Ensures. I got a text message that read, "Good Morning!" I saw who it was and said "Oh shit!" It was from Neisha. She was a light skinned cupcake I met down at Ruth Chris Steakhouse (that Monday, the 28th). She seemed nice, damn sure looked good and had this nice ass coat, jacket whatever you want to call it, which was what caught my attention.

I was with Amy who was sitting in the car. She was a girl from just outside my neighborhood who I knew for 15 plus years. Amy was my home girl, well a girl I was dealing with. You know, keep shit at her apartment, fuck her and pay half her bills. But it was more than that, we were actually good friends. Amy hit me that night saying she wanted to hang out and get something to eat. All I ever want to eat is "The Chris" so I said "let's go to Ruth Chris." Amy looked at me like I was crazy. "Now you know…" which was short for, you know motherfucking well you got a girlfriend and everybody and their mother be at Ruth Chris!

The Chris in Baltimore is very, very popular when it comes to the urban people. I immediately laughed. "It's Monday night, ain't nobody going to be there," I said as I brushed her off. We pulled up and told Amy to sit tight while I saw who was in there. I went in through the back way. There's a hotel right next door and if you walk in there's a door that will lead you right into the bar area of Ruth Chris. I walked in like I owned the joint. Shit, I'm down there 3 times a week. The fucking bar area was jumping. I couldn't believe it. I guess everybody was over all the Thanksgiving food because everybody was there.

The first people I saw were Zora & Diamond at the booth closest to the door sitting with some old head. I know they were on bullshit with the old head. The middle booth was empty. Ty & Shirley was at the last booth with two niggas. The Y.B.S. boys were at one of the bar tables. I remember seeing Ali (Rest In Peace King) and some other guys I didn't know. Y.B.S. stands for Young Ballers Shining. They are a group of guys from West Baltimore. Not sure if you heard of Lor Scoota but he was a talented Baltimore rapper who was gunned down leaving a "Stop the Violence" event at Morgan State University in June 2015. I was there with my son, when Lor Scoota got killed. People like The Game, Meek Mill, P. Diddy Combs and many more took to social media to pay their respects. Lor Scoota is and will always be Y.B.S. Rest in Peace, young king!

4

This one couple was at one of the other tables, two D.C. girls were at one end of the bar and Neisha was at the other end. I left out and told Amy, "It's banging in there. You want to go somewhere else or get it to go?" She laughed and said, "I told your dumb ass! Get the food to go." I laughed and went back in and sat at the bar next to the two D.C girls. I forgot what Amy got, but I ordered two orders of chopped fried lobster, Au Gratin potatoes and a Patron margarita (Cadillac style, hold the salt). I made small talk with the D.C. girls and asked where they were from. I knew they weren't from around here. One of them said D.C. I wasn't feeling them so I moved down the bar to where the girl with the nice ass coat was sitting.

I hit her with my famous line, "How many boyfriends you got?" She smiled, as they all do. I told her my name was Tony and that I didn't know if I liked the coat more or her. We talked until my food came and I got a text message from Ty with the mad emoji face. I laughed and thought fuck she mad for, she over there on a whole date. Zora & Diamond were leaving and they both said "Hey Brill!" at the same time. (Tereze Pinkey B.K.A. Zora ended up getting killed on June 23, 2017. Rest in Peace baby girl). I finished my drink and asked for the bill. I secretly told the bartender to give me Neisha's check as well. We exchanged numbers and I left.

On the way out the door, Monument Street Mike said "Brill, what's up?" I was surprised because I didn't see him when I first came in to survey the spot. Mike was from Monument Street in East Baltimore and that was my man. I don't know how I missed him sitting up there with Ty & Shirley. Probably because I was too busy trying not to get caught up with some shit I ain't have no business doing. I faked like I saw him and said "What's up Mike, I ain't want to bother you boys." Then I smiled and walked out the door. Ty was sitting at the booth looking like she was thinking, "Damn, Brill know every fucking body." Got a text from Neisha minutes later, "You think you slick, thanks for the food." Me and Amy just sat in the car eating and talking shit. Her crazy ass always cursing me out because we don't be fucking like that. She had the nerve to tell me she only let me use her apartment because she thought we would fuck more. I couldn't help but laugh.

Later, Ty called talking shit about me being all in Neisha face and how they got something going on over some nigga they both dealing with. Ty said "I know you got her number, we both like the same kind of guys." I played dumb. "We were just talking." Ty cool though, that's my road dawg. She be having me tripping. She was telling me that she saw me and Rocko (good friend of mine) at Euphoria (a night club in Canton Industrial part of Baltimore). "I didn't see you," I said. "But I saw y'all and your girl Neisha was there too." So when I got the text from Neisha, I was tripping.

At this point, I had no place to go and was scared to death to pull off with that coke. I called her to see what was up with her. We talked for like 20 minutes, she was cool, the kind of cool when something is familiar. I asked her, "You a Pisces?" She laughed as if I was telling a joke and replied, "Yea, how you know?" I don't recall what I said but I know because I get this funny feeling when I talk to a female that's a Pisces. I've been dealing with female Pisces all my life as if that's the only sign that's attracted to me. Kelly is a Pisces, Ty is a Pisces and my girlfriend before Kelly, Krystal is a Pisces. Plus, I met other girls that were Pisces, so I know when a girl is Pisces. Neisha asked me what I had planned for today. I told her my man Lou was coming home that day and I'm going to the bar to buy up all the Rose'.

Lou had been locked up for the last 6 months for a D.U.I. he caught going to the Horseshoe casino. How the fuck you catch a D.U.I. *going* to the casino? Most people catch theirs *leaving* the casino. Like how Michael Phelps got his leaving Maryland Live! Casino in 2014. I was happy he was coming home and was trying to go get him, but one of his female friends was already going to go get him.

"Make sure you bring me one," Neisha said in a sexy ass voice. "You already" (Baltimore slang which means you already know). I started to think again where to put this coke. I can't ride with it like the 15 grams of heroin I had for my little man D-bo. 188 grams isn't easy to hide if I was to get stopped. It was too early to call one of my little men that lived in the area. Amy's spot was downtown Baltimore so it didn't make sense to go all the way down there when I had to take the coke back to my man who would be in the Northeast area. I wanted to smoke but had to get the Ensures first, so I said "fuck it" and pulled off.

Soon as I got to the corner of the Alameda & Belvedere (which is northeast Baltimore where I'm from), I saw this white man in a rental car. I knew it was a rental because I rented many in my day and since shit been crazy I think everybody is the police. I said to myself, let me hurry up and get these Ensures and park this bitch until I get in touch with my man to give him this dumbass coke back. As I was pulling in the Alameda shopping center, I got a call from Kelly. Nobody really had a number on me, so a lot of people used to call her to tell me to call them. Anybody I talked to that was family, I had a phone just for them. If you worked for me, I had a one-on-one phone for us to talk on. I will explain one-on-one phones in a different chapter. Because of my connection to Kelly, and the fact she had the same number 20 years, I got her a one-on-one phone. I don't recall who it was that she said had called for me, but we started talking about the Miami trip I had just paid for and I told her Rocko was meeting us down there. It was Art Basel weekend down Miami and we always went. She said something about us meeting for lunch once she got done with her client, and I said, "Just hit me when you ready."

By then I had double parked in front of the Rite Aid and I went in to grab a six pack of Ensures. When I was coming out I saw two white guys exiting a white 4 Runner with dark ass tinted windows. I knew they were police; the tint always gives them away every time. So I walked past my car and noticed they were walking towards me, but for some reason I thought they weren't. Before I knew it, they both grabbed me and the fat one (Baltimore County detective Scott Kilpatrick) said "Baltimore County Police." I thought, "Fuck they want? I don't be in Baltimore County." "Antonio Shropshire, you have a federal arrest warrant."

I couldn't believe it, then before I knew it, five different cars pulled up out of nowhere. All I could think about was that dumbass coke. They started to pull everything out my pockets which was nothing but the key, money and phones. "Damn you come out of the house with this kind of money on you," I heard one of them say. It was nothing but $5,000. It was raining so I flipped my hoodie on by bending over, one of them snatched it off. I looked at him like, damn what you so mad about? They took the keys and found the 188 grams of coke and the 15 grams of dope I had in the newspaper I was going to read. They put me in the passenger seat of the 4 Runner, the fat one got in the back, the big head one that looked like Jimmy Neutron (later identified as lead case agent Corporal David Mcdougall, a DEA task force officer) got in

7

the driver seat. He put all my phones in a bag, all 7 of them, then called Hertz Rental Car Company. "This is the DEA. We have one of your cars here at Alameda Shopping center and you can come get it." You could tell they both were happier than a faggy with a bag of dicks. Jimmy said, "What's the fastest way downtown Brill?" I smiled and said "83 South."

Before we could make it out the shopping center Jimmy said, "Do you want to call Kelly?" I laughed and replied, "Yeah." One thing about me, all I do is smile and laugh at everything, all day long. Good or bad, best believe you will always see a smile on my face. I guess humor is relevant in every moment of life. As once said by the great Maurizio Cattelna, "Smiling is what saves you from taking yourself too seriously and keeps in mind where you came from." "What's the number?" he asked. I replied, "443-7#% and before I could say the rest he said "#%71" and looked at me with this "*I know everything about you, Brill,*" look on his face. Kelly answered, already hearing the news from Travis (a childhood friend more like family).

Somebody called him and said, "the feds grabbed Brill," and he called Kelly. "This is DEA Task Force Officer McDougall. We have Brill. If you want, you can come down to the federal court house on Lombard Street." So of course, they were dying to ask me questions. The fat one was sitting on the edge of his seat like a kid going for a ride in his father's new truck. The first question was "Where did you stay last night? We saw Kelly take Tone to school this morning, but you never came out?" I replied, "You must have just missed me, didn't you see my car there?" "We know you park your car on the next block over and walk through the alley." I was tripping when he said Kelly and Tone names like he knew them for years. But when he said I parked on the next block over, it really fucked me up. "We didn't bother to follow you down Dallas a few weeks ago." I replied, "You should have came down there to see the game." The Cowgirls were nice that year. It was Dak Prescott & Ezekiel Elliott first year and they were on a roll. They had to see the Ravens so you know everybody from Baltimore went down there to paint Dallas black and purple. It was me, Rocko, Georgie, Head and a few others.

Jimmy then asked, "Why was Ivan at your house the day he got locked up?" Ivan Brown was a friend from my neighborhood who is now serving a 10-year federal sentence after Jimmy raided his apartment and found more than a half of a kilogram of heroin hidden in a pet carrier. It was so crazy because I was waiting for Ivan to come meet me. I didn't talk to a lot of people over the phone, so Ivan and I talked through Snapchat. We met at my house and I told Ivan to be at the spot at 1:30. I was supposed to compress that same dope they locked his ass up with. I told Ivan if he was not there at 1:30, I'm gone. 1:35 rolled around, I sent him "1:30" on Snapchat and left. When I heard what happened, I couldn't believe it.

I was dying to ask Ivan who it was that locked him up and what happened. If I had known it was Harford County Police, I would have done things differently. Some of the money I made came from Harford County Maryland so I would have started to put shit together. What would have happened if they caught me compressing that shit for him? I would have been sick as a cancer patient. They must have had a G.P.S. tracker on his car. Of course I wanted to know how they knew that, but I played cool and said, "We were playing Madden for money. How about this, you ask a question then I ask a question." He said "Ok, what's your question?" "How did you know where I was?" "We saw your big head ass riding down The Alameda." I knew he wasn't lying.

The police have many ways of tracking down criminals. One of the popular ways was to ping your phone if they have your number. When your phone is pinged, the police rely on principles of triangulation to track the phone. A cell phone uses cell towers to evaluate the signal strength of the phone once the phone communicates with one or more cell towers. The police use triangulation software to find the phone's strongest signal to estimate the geographic position of the phone on a 3 dimensional plane, known as ping. The police can find out generally what neighborhood down to the block of the user of the phone, either in real time or recent history.

I was well aware of how the ping worked and was worried about that happening to me. I was very analytic about things when it came to my safety, so I never took any phones in any apartment I used if it wasn't a one-on-one phone. If Jimmy had any of the 7 phones that rang the whole ride tapped or pinged, his big head ass would have known I was still in the house and we wouldn't have just missed each other. His question was, "How did you know the G.P.S was on your car?"

I never knew who put it there, but I was meeting my man Flip over Belair Rd and I saw this SUV with tinted windows that beeped the horn at me because I was blocking traffic on a one-way street. A few hours later, I was in Druid Hill Park (West Baltimore) and that same truck pulled up, parked for a few minutes then left but came back an hour or so later. We were in the park for hours smoking and joking, fucking with bitches working out and shit.

I learned and trained myself to check for G.P.S trackers and I was just at the shop literally a week before checking for a G.P.S. Once I seen that SUV pull up, I knew they were on my ass and there either was a G.P.S on my car or they were on one of my phones. In the park that day, it was me, Heads, Rico, L, and Big Head Boogie. I told them that I think that truck is on me so when I leave, if they pull off, call me. Soon as I got down by the pool, Heads called and said "They on you shawty, and as soon as you got down by the pool they pulled off."

I pulled to the BP gas station on 28th street next to the Burger King, bought some Backwoods, broke every flip phone I had then threw them in the trash and pulled off. My man Rico was scared to death so I dropped him off and parked three blocks over from Hertz on Reisterstown Rd. I told them to give me whatever they had. The next day I had Heads drop me off to my car and I went to the shop and found the G.P.S. All I told Jimmy was I saw the same SUV twice and it made me check. I had paid the old head Howard to put the G.P.S on somebody's car.

At the time (April 2016), I had an apartment at The Quarters in Towson in one of Zora's cousins' names. Zora and her cousins were about money and I paid like I weighed like KK and them. I called Zora's cousin, told her I'll pay her to drive the rental to New York and I drove the Honda that had the G.P.S on up there to my cousin that lived in Brooklyn on Kings Highway. I had some men up there that was going to do something for me anyway, so this was the perfect time to do it. One of Zora's cousins stole my $800 Bugatti glasses and my $1000 police scanner, they were mad because I didn't pay them what they wanted. She thought I had them drive drugs or something up there. I told her that she would have driven drugs back from New York and not to New York.

Fat ass Kilpatrick told me two stories during the ride. The first was when they were raiding an apartment at The Quarters. He said he saw me and somebody running (my man Rico) out the building. I was tripping because I remembered that shit. I had got on the elevator with 3 D.E.A agents that day after I realized they wasn't on me with 300 grams of dope. I had a guy at Towson Mall right across the street from The Quarters waiting on me that wanted it and I couldn't miss that little money.

The second story his fat ass couldn't stop laughing while trying to explain it to me. When he was able to get it out he said, "When you thought you were burning, that was the funniest shit." I had to laugh at that one because I remember that shit too. "You were scared as shit thinking you burned Kelly," he said. I cried laughing because I was scared to death. I had called the hospital 100 times trying to get the results. "Your face was big as shit," he said. I thought about how they had to have my iPhone tapped. How else would he have known that and to say my face was big as shit.

Me and my guys always call each other big face and when shit happens we say "Your face was big as shit." Thank God it was just a U.T.I (urinary tract infection). I would have really been sick though. Kelly would have killed me. Shit, she still may try after she reads this book! I only got some head and if that bitch would have burned me off the head, she would have been a hot mouth bitch for real.

After the funniest police ride ever, we were pulling up at the Edward Garmatz United States Courthouse in downtown Baltimore. I asked, "what y'all going to do with the drugs?" Jimmy replied, "What do you think we're going to do with them?" "Give them to one of your informants and tell them to give you the money and buy your wives something nice for Christmas," I said snidely. We all laughed. I just knew I was charged with somebody. Maybe my little men in the North. My man with the bricks of cane. The people from New York, Atlanta or Baltimore who I got the dope from. I wasn't sure at this point.

I asked Jimmy, "Who am I charged with?" He said nobody. As soon as the Marshal's brought me into the courtroom for my initial appearance in front of Magistrate Judge Stephanie Gallagher, I saw Kelly and Rocko. I was told my charges, conspiracy to distribute a kilogram or more of heroin, and was given a copy of the second superseding indictment. I looked at it in disbelief like why am I charged with them and started to wreck my brain on whose name this is redacted in the indictment. I looked at fat ass and Jimmy, and they both were smiling. Right then and there I knew it was all bad.

It's a Lang Thang

You ever heard October babies rule the world? Well I'm an October baby and proud of it. Born on that 30th day, 1:05am at St. Joseph Hospital in Towson, Maryland. My grandmother Marie "OG" Lang plays 150 on the lotto tip because I was born at 1:05. According to my lovely mother Deneen "Big Neen" Lang, she didn't want to know what she was having and I came out dry as a prune and quiet as a church mouse. My auntie Monica "Moni" Lang, (who everybody thought we were brother and sister because of our close relationship) said that me being quiet as a mouse didn't last long and that I put the T in Terrible Twos, Three's, Four's, and Five's. My father, Shawn Shropshire, (who I heard was a lady's man) wasn't around as a father should be.

I wouldn't say I was a lady's man, but I see where my issues with being faithful came from. I got that nigga blood in me, I got his looks, his charm and smart ass mouth. All that's missing is the drugs in me. I remember OG Marie (who's favorite movie is the "Godfather" and why I gave her that nickname), told me she was on her way to The Alameda Shopping Center pushing me in the stroller and ran into my father's mother Margurite "Maggy" Addison (who lived on the next block over). "What's this I hear my son has a little boy by your daughter?" From my understanding, oh Shawn wasn't trying to hear I was his son and Margurite felt differently after looking at me sitting in the stroller. My aunt always had jokes and used to tell me the mailman was my father and I see why she used to play like that. My aunt is the sweetest lady you ever meet and loves to joke. I would be lying to say I remember the early part of my childhood. All I know is 1985 was that year!

My mother had two brothers: Ronald "Grumpy" Lang (the oldest) and Rodney Lang, and three sisters: Moni, Veronica, and Rhonda. My grandfather Ronald "Ron" Lang Sr. was the man of the house and didn't take no shit. I remember one day me and my best friend Melvin (better known as Furl) were playing Monopoly and he was on the house phone. My grandfather came in, took the phone, hung it up and said, "Y'all can't do both." Furl couldn't believe it. I thought, 'Yeah that's Ron for you." When I was growing up, my neighborhood wasn't the hood and it's still not the hood. I'm sure people's opinion about what is hood is different, but the best way to describe my neighborhood is to say it's a low middle class neighborhood. A payment from being the hood. It's like once I was old enough to really see how things went, I started to see the neighborhood turn into something I don't remember it being as a kid. Northeast made me, but drug dealers raised me.

My mother and other family were from 28th & Harford Rd area in Northeast/East Baltimore. My grandfather (Ron) was from East Baltimore, the hood for real. I wouldn't say my family was poor or rich. I would say they had enough to put food on the table, but that was about it. I always had a roof over my head, and clothes on my back. Everybody lived check to check and it didn't cut it for me as I got older. My uncle Rodney treated me like a son, and went to prison when I was 3 or 4 and came home when I was like 12-13. I remember the trips to different federal institutions with my family to visit him. Seeing different pictures from back then, I guess things were sweet. Unc was getting money.

I can't say I remember my mother really having money. She without a doubt was a great mother, with a heart of gold, always putting me first. My mother never was on drugs and never had a drinking problem. I wouldn't say I had the best of things growing up even, as the only child. All my clothes came from Gallo's (the ten-dollar store) and as I got older, Shoe City and Eddie Bauer. I saw pictures of me with Jordan's on, but I think that was when Unc was home.

I didn't have a bad childhood, never was in the dark or had to eat syrup sandwiches, or pick roaches out of the cereal box. I wouldn't dare sit here and say I went through no shit like that. I do remember my boom box I got for Christmas one year had to go back to Rent-A-Center. Couldn't say I was happy about that. My family had just enough to get the job done and raised me with morals and respect. Moni told me when I was 7, I got in my grandfather's truck, put the truck in drive and hit Mrs. Johnson's car. She always said I was bad as shit.

My education wasn't the best at all. I spent most of my school years in special education, which everybody called it D.E.C when I was growing up. "Dummies Eating Chicken." "Dummies Eating Crayons". You name it, I heard it. My mother always said it was because I missed a lot of school because I had my tonsils taken out. I believe it was her holding me back, mixed with a behavior problem. I was taken out of special education in the 8th grade. I went to three elementary schools and got kicked out of one, two middle schools and got kicked out of one and two high schools and you guessed it, was kicked out of one. And on top of all that, I never graduated. What the fuck did D.E.C stand for though? I'm sure that was some made up shit?

High school is when I first started selling drugs. I remember 10th grade I had the weed banging, back when ounces of Reggie was $60. I was going to Northern High School, but we called it "Northern Get High." I wasn't popular and didn't play sports. I was the quiet, stayed to myself type until somebody pissed me off. I remember having an attitude problem, almost like something was wrong with me, and always left (when somebody made fun of me or pissed me off) with thoughts of trying to hurt them. High school for me was bandanna's and Army fatigues with the butters or black suede Tim's. I got put out of Northern for shooting dice with my man Bert. I guess they were tired of our shit.

I then went to Harbor City High School when it was on Saratoga & Schroder in West Baltimore a few months after I got kicked out of Northern and after my grandmother's house was raided. I end up staying over B.C.D.C (Baltimore City Detention Center) L section for robbery and attempted murder, which was in 2001. My uncle Rodney paid my $100,000 bail after not having one for 45 days, that was my first and only time sitting over the jail. Soon after I started going to Harbor City High School, I was in the 11th grade. I still remember why I dropped out of high school until this day.

It was 12th grade year and between me wanting money, looking up to drug dealers trying to figure out who I am, all the dope that I saw being sold, rap music, and the fact I hated my school schedule, school was the last thing on my mind. My schedule was Spanish 1 and 2, music, biology, and physics. I had all my math, social studies, and had all my English's. The hard part of high school was over, I don't know what I was thinking about. Northern was so fucked up, they gave me chemistry first, not biology. The music teacher was the Spanish teacher and I couldn't understand anything she said, the shit was crazy. I always wish I could go back in time.

Growing up I remember my mother only having two boyfriends, Joe and Dana. We lived with Joe when I was young as shit. Joe had a daughter named Dina, she was at least 5-6 years older and even after my mother and Joe broke up, me and Dina always called each other brother and sister. Dina's daughter Bryona is my baby and she calls me uncle Brill. My mother and Dana met in 1997 and were together until 2006. Shit they were married; how could I forget that. Of course growing up as a little boy, you looked up to whatever man was around. I use to always want to ride with Dana and really listen to the music. He was the one who put me down with Wu-Tang, Mobb Deep, Nas, Az, Biggie Smalls, and the list goes on.

Dana had a Toyota Camry with the BBS's on it and the big speaker in the trunk. My mother used to tell me to go open the door for him when we lived at my grandmother's house and I used to go out front and dance to the music as he parked his car. I always loved music. I'm surprised that I didn't become an artist. I truly remember when I was younger, my mother played the shit out of Anita Baker. My uncle Grumpy was into all kinds of music, so I felt, growing up, I had an ear for music. One of the reasons why I always pushed guys from Baltimore who did music, was because I loved music.

I don't know where my father was at and it wasn't until my late 20's when we got cool, real cool. I remember going over Margurite's house on the holidays and my father used to be there. Until this day, I still think about how my father wasn't around and the impact it had on my life. When I used to ride with Dana, he used to go to people's houses, go in and come out. I always stayed in the car and didn't care because I just wanted to listen to the music; I always loved the music. After many rides I realized Dana was a drug dealer. I never saw any drugs or drug transactions, but I put two and two together.

As years went on, I wanted different things and I would ask Dana. It was always the same answer, "I have to go to the bank." He was a tight as fist pussy, if you ever heard that before. After a while, I saw he was a liar, cool as shit though, but didn't come up off no money. I remember stealing from him and wearing his clothes. It was weed I used to steal. I would damn near give it away, and after a while I didn't care what he thought. I grew up with Furl and Boo (childhood friends) and we thought we were the toughest mothafuckas alive and we would have fucked him up. I remember he had a nine millimeter with a lemon squeeze and one New Year's Eve he let me shoot that shit, I was young as shit. But as I got a little older I used to take it and carry it around without him knowing. Dana wasn't that bad at all, and even after we got locked up with the gun, he never said nothing about the missing gun or weed. He gave me my first two cars, so that made up for everything. I got my license and it was over.

Our family Reunion at Gunpowder State Park will always be something I will remember. All the soft ball games, my family was always the shit to me. I think my family stopped doing them. I always think we have to get them back going. Being in prison opens the mind to what's important, which is family. I didn't know too much about my family, like background information. From the looks of things, the Lang family was tight-knit and was there for each other. It's crazy because I don't remember too much of what all was going on in my younger days. I know my mother did in fact keep me sheltered when I was younger, so I was really behind in a lot of things.

I do remember my mother never putting me in sports, etc. I wondered why she didn't allow me to experience the things other kids my age experienced. From what I could see, she was always worried about something happening. I believe when I did jump off the porch and kept getting arrested, it was because she thought the shit into existence. Well of course I was doing shit I should not have been doing. But you know how people say "You talked the shit up." It's like she thought the shit up. I don't know, but I do know I wished I listened to her. Momma knows best is a factual statement.

I wouldn't say I was a bad son; I just wasn't the best son. It took for me to come to prison to realize how thorough and real my mother was. I love our relationship now, we are so much closer and I understand everything she says now. I just wish I wasn't so blind when I was home. What trips me out until this day is how my mother is a super-fast talker and gets hype as shit when she feels a way, and me and my son are the same way. I can't do anything but laugh when she starts talking fast and cursing. She don't take no shit and I laugh so hard because I see where I get it all from. It's so funny because she used to always say, "What you bored, tired and disgusted?" As I got older I became "bored, tired and disgusted" with my life causing me to be unhappy. So I always laugh because she saw what took me 16 years to realize.

I was in my teens when I learned Shropshire is no kin to my bloodline. Of course none of our names are kin to our bloodline because we all have our slave masters last name, (my opinion) but I have my grandmother's then husband's name, Shropshire. My father's father name was McCoy and I never met my grandfather, but I heard they were from West Baltimore. Now that I see things clearly, I just want to learn more about my family, and one day I met that side of the (McCoy) family, we share the same blood line.

TONY IN THE RED CAR

While I was going to Northern, one of my classmates told me he could get me dope to sell if I had somewhere to sell it. This was 11th grade and I was going with Krystal at the time. She was short, cute with a phat ass. But had a hell of a mouth on her, snappy too, like a little female pit-bull. I thought she was the one, but she broke my heart. It's something about them Pisces women, they are crazy as shit. The last I heard Krystal was an FBI Agent in Los Angeles, but who knows. Anyway, her older brother Big Weez A.K.A Hot took a liking to me. They were from Old York and Willow (an area in northeast, a few miles from my neighborhood) which was a crack cocaine strip. So I asked Weez if I could bring the dope around there.

Weez practically ran the 600 block of Willow, so once he gave me the green light, it was a go. I teamed up with a few people from around there, got the dope from my classmate's uncle and we opened up shop on York Road in Willow. The block was booming but not for dope but crack, so things didn't last long. That was my first time selling dope and damn sure wasn't my last. I was already selling crack off my paper around my way, so I was already on the wrong path.

My best friend Furl and our man Bo got convicted of a home invasion and got sentenced to 15 years. Before that I used to go out to Cedonia with Furl to hang out there, so when Furl got locked up, his cousin Damoe took me under his wing. Before you knew it, I was out Cedonia selling crack, and Waycross and Moores run was the block. I was again on somebody else's ticket and those crack heads were coming through all night. It was just what

I needed to start my rise to the top. If I wasn't out Cedonia, I was hanging around my way at the Alameda Shopping Center.

I used to always run into this dark skin kid named Nick. Well we both were kids, he was just a little younger than me. Nick was from Ramblewood and the Alameda, and Chinquapin Park was what divided our sides from each other. I knew Nick, but not that well, so as we would see each other more often we would kick it for a few then part ways. It wasn't long before we started hanging together and I started hanging with him on Ramblewood. Then you had my man Terrance, he was from Hillen Rd, right across Loch Raven Blvd. This had to be around 2002. My dumb ass was supposed to have graduated in 2003, but I made other plans. I said fuck school and dropped out to sell dope full time. It's October 13, 2020 and as I think about my thoughts back then, I must have been crazy.

So after I made the life decision to jump off the Empire State building, I thought about a cool name to call myself and Tony in the red car wasn't it. What I didn't think about was how I really planned it all, down to the name Brill. Everything I planned I did, but what I didn't realize was I drew a road map that led me straight to a federal correctional institution from high school. My mother had a red Chevrolet Cavalier and I used to always drive it, so everybody from Ramblewood used to call me Tony in the red car. It's really funny as shit, because it's a dude that's here with me at F.C.I McDowell, from Baltimore named "Big Bunk," who used to hang around Ramblewood.

When he sees me in the yard, he calls me Tony in the red car. Anyway, I thought every dope boy needed an alias to go by. I don't know where I was but I was watching Enemy of the State with Will Smith. I watched it and thought damn that Brill is a slick motherfucka so I started calling myself Brill. Lilly Daskal said "Life is not about finding yourself, life is about creating yourself." Enemy of the State, was a 1998 film by Tony Scott, Brill was played by Gene Hackman, who was a former spy that realized he was working for the wrong side. Brill's character was always a few steps ahead and knew what he was involved in.

Krystal really started to call me Brill and then everybody started to call me that. How could I forget that on Valentine's Day, Kelly and Krystal got into a fight in front of Krystal's house. Travis (a childhood friend, more like family) was with me. He saw Kelly and her home girl knocking on the wrong house as we all got in my mother's car. Krystal didn't see Kelly. We got in the car parked up the street. So when Krystal saw Kelly she jumped out the car and ran down the street. The shit was crazy as shit. Travis was laughing like shit and I ain't know what to do. Krystal fought Kelly and her home girl.

Anyway, not only do I call myself Brill, I tried to move and think like him. I started to think two steps ahead of the game when it came to the dope game. I remember I started to learn how the police moved and what they did when they were investigating. I made it my business to learn everything I could about law enforcement. How else was I supposed to become the dope dealing version of Brill?

I started to meet some guys from Ramblewood from being out there with Nick. Some of them I knew of, but didn't know. I can't describe Nick no other way than saying he acted rogue, lawless and didn't give a fuck about shit. I used to say, "Damn you heard about yo?" Nick G or Ross, what they called him because he reminded you of Rick Ross, would say "Better them than me," so that was his attitude. Nick ass stayed locked up, so somehow I got cool with Lou, who we called Kyle at the time. It's too many guys from Ramblewood to name but as I hung out there, I got cool with them all. As time went on I got smarter and made more money. I stayed online reading about different cases, learning what other guys' downfalls were.

As I used to be out in Cedonia, I used to see my big cousin Darryl "Swo" Lang, known out Cedonia as Swo Daddy. Darryl was known in the family as D, and I used to always see him going to his mother's house (my great aunt) who lived in Cedonia. I used to see him coming down Waycross in his 2003 Mercedes Benz S500, I used to call it "the whale." This had to be late 2003 or early 2004 and every time I saw my cousin D I made sure he saw me. He used to stop and holla at me but not too often. You could always catch him with his dog "Snoop'" which was an American Staffordshire terrier. I always used to assume "Swo" sold drugs but of course never saw it with my own two eyes.

He was at every family event looking like money, and I used to hit him up for money that he always gladly gave. I remember one time he was at my grandmother's house for an event and he saw me and said, "You not going to freshen up?" These were my super thuggin days when army fatigues, boots and a bandanna was the dress code. I started to see him more and more out Cedonia and I don't know how we hooked up but we did and my standing on the block days were over. Him and my uncle Rodney were really tight so I guess he felt he could trust me. His license was suspended so who better to drive for you then your little cousin. You should have seen me pushing the whale.

I always thought I was the shit but now you couldn't tell me nothing. Before my man Furl went to prison we used to play with the gun. Whatever needed to be done kind of thing, so it was him who I learned my basic gun training from, I would call it. So back in my "Cedonia" days, I was a young ruthless mothafucka that would have killed you. So there were times "D" would come get me and I have the joint on me (Baltimore slang for gun). "D" would never say anything but he loved that kind of shit. "D" was a smooth, well dressed, slick talking mothafucka, that you knew was the boss when he came around, funny as shit, and had all the jokes in the world. I remember one time I had to go to court and I didn't know any better so I put on what I wore to prom smh. Man let me tell you, when "D" saw me in that shit, he cried laughing literally. Then hit one of them moves you would see the Temptations do. I was the laughing stock for weeks and "D" kept the jokes coming. We were blood cousins but didn't know each other that well, so the time we spent together we were really able to build.

I still would hang out "Cedonia" during that time and I picked up the phone hustle from out there. I started to put a few crack heads on my phone from out there. Before that, I was using the pager, beeper, whatever one you want to call it. When I was with "big cuz" I started to see he was really somebody and the respect people had for him was real. I had my mind made up from the word go, so everything "D" did or said I took notes. He would introduce me as his cousin to whoever he would meet. A lot of people knew my uncle Rodney (who already had his own name) so he would say this is Rodney's sister, Deneen's son, Tony. In my neighborhood I used to sell crack and everybody either knew me for me, or it was because of who my uncle Rodney was. You would hear a lot of "that's Rodney Lang nephew" so when it came to my neighborhood, it's been a wrap.

Unc already had it sewed up. Back before Unc went to federal prison I was told all you would hear was Rodney Lang, Darryl Lang and Grumpy Lang (my other uncle whose name was Ronald). Everybody thought my name was Tony Lang (Tony being short for Antonio). But it was "D" who I spent the most time with. During that time Unc taught me a lot but I could tell that ain't what he wanted for me. Not saying "D" wanted it for me either but that's how the shit ended up happening. "D" really started teaching me the do's and don'ts about the drug game, and showed me a bigger view. Taught me how to apply myself and exposed me to the finer things. The next time I started selling dope was dope that I begged for him to give me. I used to get 10 grams at a time and I sold $20 bags. At $85 a gram, I was bagging up $200 off each gram. I started to meet white college kids in my neighborhood who wanted to buy dope, but it was this one older white guy name the wizard that brought me all the money.

As weeks went by, I was selling at least 10 grams day, at $850 for the dope and a $1150 profit. I was off to the races. Every morning D used to come get me and he ended up getting his license back so that told me it wasn't just about me driving him around. I believe it was something in me that he saw that made him keep me around. He taught me damn near everything I know about the dope game. My first time counting over $100,000 was with him, shit that may have been $200,000 that time. Of course not a coin was mine but he needed my help counting it. He seen me counting and said, "what the fuck is you doing, who taught you how to count money?" He showed me the right way to count, and always would give me a few hundred after.

I was just happy to be a fly on the wall. I then was taught how to cut the wrappers of the bricks, cut the dope and what to do with the wrappers after, it was the training from him that made me the boss I became. Anybody that knows about me going to Sabatinos (a restaurant in Baltimore's little Italy) to get the pan fried shrimp knows I used to say "I'm going to break bread." Well "D" took me down there to Sabatinos and ordered me the pan fried shrimp and grabbed the fresh bread by one end and told me to grab the other end and pull. "This is what you call breaking bread," he said. "D" always was on some mobster shit and always played by the rules. My first steak at Ruth Chris Steakhouse was with him. There used to be this fat Latin that came to "D" house and always told me jokes and bought me Boost Mobile phone cards.

You remember the Boost phones, right? Well I was the one that went to the Latina truck to grab them bricks. As time went on, it was nothing for my phone to do 10-15 grams a day, all $20 bags. At 19 years old making damn near $1500 a day profit, running with Big cuz who was a boss, you couldn't tell me nothing. So as I learned daily and took notes, I saw what it was like to be the boss and how a boss was supposed to move and think. The days I was with D, class was in session without a doubt. I wanted to be around cuz more, but I still had to do my little one, two, so I didn't have the time.

The people I was meeting and the shit I was learning being around cuz was key. If one day I wanted to drive a $100,000 Benz and become a boss. So I started thinking and did some math. I'm not sure what the math came to, but I had room to pay somebody to sell the dope for me while I was out with cuz. I went around my way and started asking around to see who was trying to get some money. It was easy money too. All you had to do was answer the phone and go meet people who had no problem paying it. After asking around, Kyle accepted and it was easy money. I don't think anything happened, but that didn't last too long.

Kyle was a born leader, mastermind type nigga, a cash cow, who later got the name Lou from Lou- Lou on "Paid in Full", you know Ace's plug. Of course I got somebody else to do it and I rode with big cuz. While all of this was happening, I was pulling up at Kelly's mother house with roses I bought from the Mexicans on the corner. Everybody knew I loved me some Kelly. Years went on and it was at least now 2006 and business was booming. I came up with the idea to sell half grams of heroin for $70 and they loved it. I don't think there's nobody to dispute this, but I laid the foundation for the dope game in my area northeast Baltimore. I brought that phone game around there that I picked up from Cedonia and put my twist on it. I put everybody on with the prepaid Verizon phones, I was the one to start that wave.

I could go on forever about Darryl Lang, all my big dreams came from running with him. I wouldn't be who I am today without the knowledge from him. So of course I loved Kelly but I got caught cheating often. I just can't figure out why I used to cheat but I was dealing with this one girl. I can't remember her damn name but she was just a little older and worked the front desk at the Best Inn Hotel. Anybody from Northeast knows about the Best

Inn at the top of Frankford (a street in Cedonia). All the guys from Cedonia and the surrounding area played that hotel. It was cheap and the staff didn't give a fuck what you did. My man Bert made $50,000 plus out of that hotel selling weed, and it was many others. Getting a bag out of that hotel. Anyway, the girl who worked the front desk, niggas use to be on her line.

At any given time, Cedonia niggas would have 5-10 different rooms, so I was there often. I'm sure I wasn't the only one, but she loved the shit out of me. One night, around 2-3 in the morning, I should have been home but I was over her house. My phone was on silent and at some point I checked it and had damn near 30 missed calls. Of course most were from Kelly and then I saw my mother had called and my uncle Rodney too. I knew something was wrong if Unc called me 3 in the morning, so I called Unc back first. "They got em, they killed D," he said. I couldn't believe it. I say that a lot in this book, and if I said it, I meant it.

I drove past his house and the shit was yellow taped off. I was sick, and the next day I was out with a Ruger P90 looking for answers. The word was he was coming in the house and somebody came in behind him. It was a lot I didn't understand, it's always people on the corner across the street from his house. My theory is if y'all outside (the guys on the corner) and y'all see somebody standing around or somebody in a car that y'all don't know, y'all do nothing? Since when was that a rule on the block? It's no way nobody saw nothing. I mean these guys are always out there.

I believe that it was the guys who lived in that area. "D" was smart, too smart for his own good and it's no way he didn't see some guys in a car on the side of his house. Or some guys he didn't know from the neighborhood standing around. Either somebody kicked the door (I don't remember the family saying it was a forced entry), or he saw the guys hanging around on the corner and thought they were the guys who were from around there and came in behind him. Some days later I got one of the older dudes number who was one of the main guys around there named Mo and we met. He knew D, they were around the same age.

Everybody that was around D knew I used to be with him every day. I asked Mo if he heard anything and he said no. I already knew that's what he was going to say any way because he was from around there and who am I for him to tell me some shit about guys he knew all his life. I wanted him to know that I had questions, I'm sure he already knew there were going to be people who wanted answers. For years I felt some kind of way, because you the OG (original gangster) around this Marble Hall part of North East Baltimore and you knew nothing. A female friend of mine's house got broken into around my way and I used to be around her house often.

Our kids used to play together. She asked me about it and I really didn't know anything about it, but she felt differently. She said "How is this your hood and you don't know nothing?" So I had to change the way I felt about Mo knowing what happened. Until this day, it's still a mystery. The type of caliber dude D was, he had no business living around there.

To Darryl "Swo" Lang what's up Cuz, missed you like shit over the years. I still remember going to your gravesite to get advice from you. I tell my son about you all the time. Things went South a few years back, I am now sitting in a prison cell fighting for my freedom. I didn't see this coming. All I want to do now is stop the up and coming from following the path. You know we all love and miss you and soon as I get out, I am bringing Tone to come see you.

GAMBLED WITH MY LIFE

S ince I could remember, you could catch me at a dice game, and before I sold drugs, I was shooting dice. I wish I knew who taught me how to shoot dice. I would choke the shit out of them for teaching me. I fucked up thousands on top of thousands. It all started shooting a dollar and betting a dollar and dollar (for the non-gamblers that's betting the combination, 6,8 9,5 or 10, 4). I grew up shooting dice with my childhood friends Boo, Fat Marvin, and Furl. We shot dice in the alley until Miss Johnson called the police. Damn that's when I didn't have a care in the world.

My son trips me out talking about shooting dice. Lord knows I have to get home to him, and I'll be telling him to stop, further explaining gambling made my life a lot harder than it had to be. He probably learned from YouTube or some shit like that. Being from Baltimore everybody knows selling dope was a sure way to get rich, and I guess an even quicker way to get killed or end up in prison. It was now 2007 and I had the half grams of dope booming. The hurt I felt from losing Big cuz was slowly leaving and I was eating like shit. My man BZ from Cedonia, had a brother from "the Blvd," which is a number of blocks in one of the deadest parts of East Baltimore which everybody calls "Down da Hill." So a few of us used to hang down there.

Oliver and Montford was the block, this had to be 2006. Anybody that's familiar with the area and is of age heard of the infamous LT (Rest In Peace). Snoop from the Wire is from Oliver and we all used to hang out there. Long story short, my man B is from around there and as I hung out there we got cool. We got even more cool when he was on the box (home confinement) at his girl house who lived around my way. I would pull around there often and we built from there. B ended up getting killed (rest in peace) but it was him who put me with my man until this very day, that gave me the best dope I ever had in my life. That's how I went from 0 to 100 real quick.

Back to 2007, I ran through multiple people who worked for me and I was now fucking with Twan a.k.a Antoine Washington, who was from Ramblewood. I took a liking to shawty and never was the one to not put niggas on. So I taught Twan everything I knew. I wanted everybody around me to eat, and everybody ate. Kelly got pregnant, and I rose in the dope trade in North East Baltimore. The $1150 profit went to $2000, $3000, $4000 and so forth. The more money I made, the more I fucked it up gambling. Shooting dice was a daily thing and all the real gamblers from East Baltimore knew me, Whitey, Green Mount Ty, Buddy, Elbow, Rivers, Nose, just to name a few. The most I lost in one night was $15,000. The most I won was $25,000. I remember losing $10,000, three nights in a row. Gambling fucked my life up and I know I lost at least $200,000 in my 14 years of gambling.

I was in fact a degenerate gambler and had it not been for gambling, I know I would have done something with the money (started businesses) and would be worth a half of a ticket ($500,000). Anyway, one day in February in 2008, we was shooting dice at Nick's apartment. There were a dozen of us there and had to be at least $50,000 there, and I had lost $10,000 the night before. I knew I had my money back and was winning. So I was betting this one guy $200 on somebody's point. Let's say this guy's name is Doritos. Something happened with the shooter and the fader (the person that's betting the shooter) and I called off my bet with Doritos. But instead of picking up my 10 $20 bills, I grab Doritos two $100 bills. Doritos had gotten into it with UTZ about an hour before, and Doritos left and came back, but nobody thought nothing of it.

We were all friends I thought, plus everybody ran in and out. So Doritos jumped in my face about his two $100 bills. I was young, 22 years old, 6 feet tall and weighed 275 pounds. I pushed Doritos, little did I know Doritos had a gun and pointed it at me. I ran in the kitchen and heard two things, Twan yelling "Doritos put that got damn gun down" and one shot. Chris aka Snoop (a childhood friend, more like family, we call each other cousins) and I hopped in my 2004 LS 430 and hauled ass to Good Samaritan hospital in North East

Baltimore. I gave Snoop all my money, phones and walked in the ER. I felt like I was hit in my leg, they cut my pants and boxers off, told me to stand up, I looked and saw my balls were the size of oranges. The bullet went through the thin ass kitchen wall, through my left leg, through both testicles and out my right leg.

I had surgery and Dr. Christian Alezivzatos came in and said, "I was able to put everything back together, but your days of having kids are over." I was the blind leading the blind and didn't even give a fuck, I don't feel that way anymore. I am hurt about not being able to have more kids, I always wanted a daughter. Baby Tone was four months when this happened and I'm blessed to have him as my son. During that time, we were renting a $1500 a month single-family home, me, Kelly and baby Tone. So I spent time healing. I remember I had paid for Vegas around that time and me and Kelly went. I enjoyed myself out there, balls in a sling and all. I had a guy or two secretly on Doritos ass but he was nowhere to be found.

During that time, you either heard two things, "Doritos blew Brills ball's off" or "that nigga Brill eating like a mothafucka." I knew if something was to happen to Doritos ass I would have been the first nigga down homicide. Either somebody would have got locked up and told what they knew or somebody would have got the bright idea to tell on me to try to get the money I was getting. It was now July 2008 and it was time to step it up, so I called Big Sam, who was at the time working at Auto Showcase on Northern Parkway in Northwest Baltimore. I had bought a Lexus GS from him before and Kelly bought a Lexus truck. "Yo, I'm trying to get something for the summer, what you got for me?" As I asked Big Sam, who said, "Come on over, you know I got you." I went over there the next morning around 9 and left around noon. In a 2006 BMW 750 LI, gold joint. I traded in my Lexus LS 430 and gave him a few thousand.

That bitch was like a spaceship. I didn't even know how to put the shit in drive, Sam had to show me. I parked on my grandmother's block, hopped back in the rental, and trapped it down the rest of the day. When night time came around, I went home, took a shower, put that shit on and was out the door. My little home girls were calling, I told them to meet me on my block, showed them the 750, and talked shit until Lou and Twan pulled up. My then homeboy Chauncey had a Black 750 LI so we were back to back on the way to the bowling alley party out Merritt Blvd in Baltimore County. When we got there the parking lot looked weak as shit.

After spinning the lot like three times, my man, Big Head Boogie, from Park Heights (North West Baltimore) hit me on the boost mobile chirp, "Yo where you at? Rick Ross down Club One." I hit Chauncey on his chirp, "Yo Rick Ross down Club One." "This shit phoney, what you trying to do?" Chauncey said he was staying. Me, Lou and Twan hauled ass downtown. Club One was jumping. My man big head was fucking with Snoop from The Wire heavy. And Rick Ross just had her in his video, so he got with her soon as he got to town. I hit Big Head and his shit was busy. You remember when the Boost used to be busy when somebody sent you an alert?

I didn't get in touch with him, so we went and ordered our bottles of Rose' and enjoyed the show. Ross killed that shit, we left out and headed to the parking lot to see I left the headlights on. That motherfucker was a spaceship for real, I didn't know how to work it. We jumped in and weren't ready to go home so we headed towards down da hill. My man Boo was behind us and we were at the light on Eager and Aisquith, right on the side of Latrobe projects, (in east Baltimore) I was rolling a blunt. I saw this silver Grand AM pull up on the side of us looking, but they were across the yellow line, so I thought it was somebody we knew.

The nigga in the back pointed his gun and started shooting. I pulled off and felt like I was hit in the back. I heard Boo bust through the chirp" that's #$*#* and them." At some point two things crossed my mind, how the fuck I get shot in the car I just bought and I thought we were OK with #$*#* and them. I pulled up to John Hopkins Hospital in East Baltimore, the ER was on Monument Street. Then I gave Lou the Buffalo I had on me (Baltimore slang for a lot of money). Had to be like $8500, some shit like that, got out and walked towards the ER. Lou yelled "Yo how the fuck you put it in drive?"

I went back to show him then walked in the ER. They put me through the CAT scan. The doctor came in and said, "the bullet is in you, right behind your heart. You're lucky you're a big boy. It's saved your life; we're going to leave it there. It would be too risky to go in to get it". It wasn't long before a female detective from Eastern District named Taylor came to my room asking what happened. I told her my name was Michael Johnson and I was at the light and somebody started shooting. I'm sure she did not buy it before Kelly came asking for Antonio Shropshire.

Detective Taylor was black, looked to be at least 40, had a scar on her face if I'm not mistaken. New Orleans accent if I recall currently, and was tough as they came. I guess I rubbed her the wrong way as I do 60% of the people I meet, so I was taken by force to Eastern District for questioning. That lady drilled me for hours about what happened. I guess she felt something was off about my story. I even gave her the car to confirm my story but it wasn't enough. Maybe it was the fact I got shot five months earlier, was 22 years old driving a $60,000 used BMW registered in my name or maybe she thought she knew something different from what I was telling her. She told me "this isn't northeast District, Mr. Shropshire, and I'm going to get to the bottom of what happened." From there I went to Central bookings for allegedly assaulting a male nurse when they were trying to get me to calm down. I was on probation for a 2004 crack charge and after being shot back to back everybody had questions.

The fact I failed to be cooperative in both investigations made me the bad guy quickly. The first story I told the detective from the Northeast district whose name was Taylor (also) was a lie. I told him I was walking down "The Alameda" and heard shots, I'm sure he didn't buy it. I only had to see my probation agent once a month, so when I strolled in they called me in the back where the big bosses meet. A lady came in and said "So this is Mr. Shropshire? I heard a lot about you sir." I said "you can't believe all that you hear." She asked, "what are you into out there?" I said, "just the wrong place at the wrong time." "Twice?" she said. I was lost for words.

She then explained that I will be placed on V.P.U and if I miss a visit there will be a "no bail" warrant issued for my arrest. She told me to have a good day then walked out. VPU was some new shit that was an extreme form of probation that went by the name Violence Prevention Unit and you had to report twice a week. Business was going good as usual in my part of Northeast, but I started to see unidentified faces and vehicles. The female detective "Taylor" went to Kelly's job starting shit with her.

At the time, Kelly was working at Xcetra Beauty Salon that was at the Alameda Shopping Center. One day me and Travis (childhood friend who worked for me at the time) got pulled over by an unmarked Dodge Caravan. A plain clothes detective by the name of Craig Jester said I ran a stop sign. He got my license, registration and went back to the car. Minutes later 4 to 5 unmarked cars pulled up and they all got out and came to each window of the rental car I was driving. One of them said "Why do you keep getting shot?" I explain the wrong place, wrong time theory for the 10th time that nobody was buying then someone said step out the car as he pulled on the door handle.

They searched Trav and sat him down on the curb but told me to stand. Each officer, all plain clothes detectives, did their own search of the car. So what are you in a gang and you beefing he said. I told him I'm not in a gang, either it's the wrong place, wrong time or I'm somebody's target and just don't know it yet. After the small talk, one guy walked up out of nowhere and said, "we are on to you and whatever it is you doing you need to stop." I would guess the 9+ thousand I had in my pockets didn't leave a good impression with Baltimore's finest.

All of this was within weeks of me being shot the second time. I started doing some asking around and I was told that these officers were OCD (Organized Crime Division). Whoever they were, they were on my side of northeast Baltimore and they made it clear that I was the target. I started to analyze the whole thing in this heat came from nobody but that damn lady Detective Taylor. I don't recall how I know but the two detectives had more in common than just the same last name. They were fucking married! I said what are the odds of that being the case.

That's what that comment about Northeast District doing their job was about, I bet you. I didn't do shit but get the packs (drugs) when my guys called which was like every 1 to 2 days so I just stayed out the neighborhood. Weeks later I was going to meet my then buddy Chauncey at his father's house, which was in the neighborhood. This was August 2008 and the NBA All-Star game was in Arizona that February 2009. Me and Yo were going to fly out there to talk to a few club managers about renting a club to have a party during All-Star weekend. We wanted to make some money! I was in touch with a few managers and they were waiting on us. I pulled up to his father's house and told him I was outside. I was in a rental van, and was on the laptop checking the prices of some flights to Arizona.

Before I knew it, 30 minutes went by so I called him. He told me he was taking a shit and he was coming. As soon as he got in the van, a dude I was waiting for called. I pulled off and met the guy around the corner. He got in and I pulled off. I was buying a pound of Purple Haze for a friend of mine that needed a hand. I pulled back to the guy's car, he got out and I pulled back in front of Chauncey's fathers house. Seconds later, a marked police ride passes with just the lights on. Yo said I got this thing on me and he got out of the car all one motion. I thought he was talking about the joint (gun). So I got out of the van with the laptop in my hand. Before I could take two steps, a car pulled up. Someone jumped out, gun drawn and yelled, "Don't fucking move."

I looked at the gunman and realized it was the same detective that told me, "Whatever it is that you're doing, you need to stop," later identified as detective Ivo Louvado. Seconds later, another unmarked car pulled up. I looked and saw Yo in the trunk of his 750 not paying attention to what happened in the blink of an eye. By the time he realized what was going on, it was too late. They sat both of us on the curb and asked "What's in the van?" I replied, "Whatever is in the van, he don't have nothing to do with it." "You going to sign something saying that?" I yelled "NO!" They got the keys and went to the van, got the pound of weed and asked "Who lives here?" Like a fool, Chauncey said he did and they went into his pockets and pulled out $20,000. I sat there thinking, "Fuck Yo was about to do with that?" I thought that must have been the thing he was talking about. They raided his father's house and found a glock-19. We both were arrested and taken to Eastern District.

At the scene, there were many detectives. Amongst them were Jester, Wayne Jenkins, Louvado and others. All who were members of the unit O.C.D at the time. I knew how things worked when dealing with these types of detectives. I have studied them for years, even if I did sign something saying he had nothing to do with the weed, they were still going to do what they were going to do. And him having that money on him didn't help the situation. So I knew the next thing they were going to do was hit any house they knew about. I had shit at my house but wasn't sure what all they knew about me. He put us in a holding cell with this old ass man, we all were handcuffed.

I asked the old man if he had a phone and luckily he did. I went in his pocket, got the phone, put it back together and called Kelly. I told her what happened and to get the stuff under the bed (M-15) and the kitchen draw (Glock 40) and what's underneath the sink (50 grams of heroin). They never went to my house, so they didn't know where I live and they didn't go past my grandmother house which is the address I used all my life. We went to central booking, I was charged with the weed and he was charged with the weed and the Glock 19. I had a $250,000 bail, his was $750,000.

I told him I was out of here and asked what he wanted me to do. He asked me to take money to his lawyer. I paid the $7,500 to get out and took money to his lawyer. "Yo" blamed everything on me and started talking bad about me to everybody. The feds picked his case up and Yo got 10 years. I beat the case in state court.

Detective Ivo Louvado joined the Baltimore Police Department in November of 1999. It wasn't until 2008 when he was promoted to Detective. In January of 2010, Louvado was assigned as a task force officer for the A.T.F (Bureau of Alcohol, Tobacco, Firearms, and Explosives). It was in fact what Louvado did six months after he arrested me and Chauncey that got him in deep shit in March of 2020. In February of 2009, Detectives Louvado, Jenkins, Keith Gladstone, Jester and Victor Romero, all members of O.C.D, were investigating Trenell Murphy, in the 1400 block of Ellamont street. During which 41 kilograms were found in a nearby truck and Murphy was charged.

Somewhere during the transport of the 41 bricks to E.C.U (Evidence Control Unit), 3 additional bricks were discovered. Louvado and two others, agreed to give the 3 bricks to an informant and split the proceeds. Ultimately Louvado received $10,000 in drug proceeds from the sale of the cocaine. The F.B.I interviewed Louvado about the cocaine on May 30, 2018, in which he concealed and covered up material facts. Louvado and Romero were both charged with lying about the February 2009 incident.

I wouldn't be surprised if Jester (who debriefed an informant with Baltimore County task force officer Steve Leimbach on April 21, 2015 in reference to information about me, in the investigation behind why I'm in prison today) was involved in the acts with Louvado and others. It's said, by attorneys, that the two other officers were Gladstone and Jenkins. If you haven't learned anything, you should know that the government and the state and the officers that investigate for them, are not to be trusted. Some people sided with Chauncey (his friends) and the people that know the whole story sided with me.

Either of these things happened that day, (1) the nigga I bought the weed from set me up, (2) they just so happen to be watching the area I picked him up at, (3) they was following me or (4) they was watching Yo father house and was on him. Between the time they pulled me and Trav over and the day me and Chauncey got locked up, me and Twan was riding down the block that everybody knows Chauncey bitch lives on. Everybody knows he be stashing shit at her house.

We saw Detective Craig Jester climbing his ass in the back of that same Dodge Caravan. We called Chauncey as soon as we saw Jester and told him. What you think Jester was doing? Surveillance! On who? Chauncey, if you ask me. That's what Jester was doing and either four of those options could be what happened. According to the charge papers they saw what kind of car the weed seller was driving, and what street I picked him up on. Only thing they had wrong was that I sold him the weed and not the other way around.

I had about $7000 on me before I bought the weed. It's very possible that they were watching him and I got caught up in his shit. When Yo went to prison I didn't fuck with him and only because Kelly said "you can't leave him hanging," I did Christmas for his children for like 4 years straight. He would be in touch with Kelly and she did whatever he needed done as far as legwork and I still gave him money when Kelly used to say something to me about it. I told Kelly that nigga ain't never do shit for me, put no money up to none of the bails me and Nick was catching left and right so guess what?

Yo end up coming home in 2017 or 2018 and it was still "Fuck Brill!" He was still talking shit about me. I told Kelly that nigga wasn't shit, and we should not have did shit for him. He got to the point, I guess he was so hell-bent on getting back at me, that he made the comment that he should fuck Kelly. Of course I was locked up for this charge when he came home. I even heard him and Boo got together saying shit about me. Two girl mouth ass niggas sitting around talking about me. I told Kelly what that nigga said, only because she was going so hard for that nigga after I told her he wasn't shit.

So the girl Neisha (not Neisha from Ruth Chris) was having a grand opening for her shop "Amour Feti" and Kelly got into it with Chauncey. How it was put to me, Kelly popped off on Chauncey for running his mouth. I heard what happened and just thought Kelly's ass is crazy. Anyway I guess they wanted me off the street, so they violated my probation because I got convicted of driving on a suspended license and sentenced me to prison for a year on December 23, 2008.

Mistake of Driving a Motherfucking Honda

It was the beginning of a cold November in 2014 and I'm sure I was just coming off some birthday fun. I don't know where my little man was because I had the phone when one of my sales called. "Hey Brill I'm trying to sell my car." My antennas went up quick and I replied with veins damn near detonating out my neck, "What that Honda?" He said, "Yeah, I just have to go to the M.V.A to get the title." I said, "how much you want for it? "Just give me $1500 Brill." I felt bad, because I knew having a dope habit was a motherfucka, but I thought shit why let another motherfucka get over? "I want it, where you at?" I said. He replied, "I have to first get the title."

Don't worry about it, I know somebody at M.V.A who will get us in and out. I was hot on his ass before he could call somebody else. I knew he was sick as one of the bats out of Wuhan, China so I went and got him a gram to get well. He had a 2004 or 2005 Honda Accord V-6, green joint and $1500 was a steal of a lifetime. I never was the get over type because I learned that people who think they got the long end of the stick, I saw their luck turn into shit. So I could have really talked him into taking half dope and half cash, but I said naw, I'm going to give him $1500 on the nose and let him make his own decisions.

Baltimore has to be the city of the Hondas. I mean don't get it fucked up, we ride big shit too, it's just something about them Hondas. They are good work vehicles; the only thing is they attract a hell of a lot of police attention. I really couldn't believe he only wanted $1500 for his car. I could have really cleaned it up, got it inspected and told somebody to give me $2500 and pay me another $2500 in instalments. At the time I was driving a rental (shit I'm always in a rental) even when I had a car. Most people in my line of work drove rentals.

We went to the M.V.A., I gave him the $1500 and sent him on his way. Of course he bought a gram or two and I didn't turn down his money. Shit I think I gave him a break on the price. I went to my favorite tag and title spot with my mother's license and insurance info, got some tags and was out the door. First things first is always get an oil change when you buy a used car, even if they tell you they just got it changed. So since it's only one way to ride, the next spot was the tint place. "Heavy on the tint please, and don't forget to hit the windshield." The joint was forest green and I got my man Barnard to clean the joint up for me. I was wheeling and dealing and being wavy in something new was a must, so I didn't tell nobody what I was driving.

During the time my son was going to UMAR boxing gym over west Baltimore on North Ave. They had an after school program where the kids would do their homework, then teach them how to box. Every sport I put my son in he hated; football wasn't good, in basketball he missed all his shots, and baseball he was slow as shit. So I don't have to tell you that boxing didn't last long. I guess he was like his father; the owner of the team, not the player. I used to get calls from guys in my neighborhood, at least on three occasions, asking who that was in the green Honda. One day my little man hit me asking, "Yo, who the fuck is that in the green Honda hitting hard around the way?" I laughed out loud, "chill boi, that's me". He said, "I was about to flip that bitch a few times".

It wasn't long before I got blitzed coming out of my Grandmother's alley. It had been a week and a half since I had the car and I had just come from my new apartment on St. Paul Street. I was there bagging up a quick 100 grams for my guys to distribute. 50 grams in 10 gram bags, 30 grams in 5 gram bags, 10 grams in gram bags, and 10 grams in half of gram bags. I pulled around my way to meet my guys but didn't want to pull up with all that shit. I didn't have a spot around there, so I used whoever's house who was trying to get some money. My little man from my block was cool and trustworthy, so I got him one on one and we were in business. I give him the 80 grams to hold just until I could get up with my other little man and I pulled off. As I pulled into my Grandmother alley and pulled to the top, I saw a heavily tinted Chrysler Sebring coming down the block. The car blocked me into the point that I couldn't turn onto the block, the only way was to go in reverse.

Two black Knockers hopped out (plain clothed narcotics detectives) dressed in jeans, hoodies, bullet proof vests, and track shoes. Both came to the driver window and the one with the New York accent pulled on my door handle. Before I could say or do anything the other one saw the plastic bag from the other 20 grams I was on my way to take to my man sitting in the cup holder. As they grabbed me out of the car I heard, "that's Brill put him in the car, y'all get in his car and follow me." I've never been kidnapped before but I'm sure it felt just like that.

They put the cuffs on and put me in the back of the Sebring. I looked and it was no other than Baltimore City's finest, Detective Wayne Jenkins. He was known in Baltimore for locking niggas up and dope shops would close when niggas heard he was around. Jenkins was out to look up all the big fish and as Lou said, "He is like a pit-bull with the pink thing hanging out." Jenkins said, "Hey Brill I got you today," I was even at the wrong place at the wrong time or he came looking for me. It's not too much of nothing going on, on my Grandmother's side of the Alameda, so why was he riding through.

Driving a Honda with tinted windows in Baltimore was a magnet for police activity. He pulled around the corner and said, "What's up Brill, what's going on"? I said, "Just another day in the neighborhood, what's up with you?" He said, "this is the first time I caught you dirty (with drugs), what you want to do about it?" I knew what he meant, but I was trying to get time to think of a way out of this, so I said, "What are you trying to do about it?" I was really mad as shit because I started to give my little man the 20 grams to give to my other little man, but I didn't want him to know he was holding shit for me. The less a person knows, the less a person can tell. I was already on probation for the six grams Detective Daniel Hersl planted on me.

I was driving my white 2009 Acura RL bearing Maryland tag A237406; registered in Kelly name, travelling eastbound in the 1300 block of E. Biddle St. on May 21, 2012, at approximately 9:35pm. I saw the lights behind me and I had nothing but some weed on me so I pulled over. Sergeant Burns and

Hersl working in plain clothes in an unmarked car came to my driver window. Of course they smelled the weed so they told me to step out. While the other two dickheads searched the car, Hersl had me at the back of the car running my information through the KGA dispatcher.

They found $2,257 of U.S currency in the center console and a scale with tan-ish powder residue on the back passenger seat. Hersl asked if I had any drugs or guns on me. I said I had weed and handed it to them. Hersl started asking questions about murders in the area and an argument broke out. Hersl wasn't trying to hear I wasn't from East Baltimore so I wouldn't know anything going on in East Baltimore. He got mad and planted six grams on me, told the court he found it in my boxers and booked me for distribution of heroin and they gave me a $450,000 bail because I was already out on bail from an October 2,2011 house raid. I paid the $10,000 because sitting over the jail when you got a bail was not an option. I had to think quickly. I knew Jenkins was a rotten Motherfucker.

So I wanted him to say give him money when I asked him what he was trying to do about it. "Well Brill, you're going to have to tell me something," he said. "Come on Jenkins, you know I don't be on no shit like that", I said. There's stories of Jenkins letting people go after he found drugs, plus he wasn't all that bad.

One night I was walking up Northwood Drive and he pulled up by himself and put the spotlight on me and said "King Tut." I knew a few King Tuts and I was neither one. He must have looked again and said, "Brill, what you doing walking this time of night, you need a ride"? I was on my way to catch a hack and I had about 8 grams on me that I knew he wouldn't find. Plus, I thought if I said no, it would make me look like I was hiding something. So I replied, "Yes." He said, "Come on" and he took me like a mile away and I walked the rest of the way. He was cool; he made jokes about how dumb guys around my way was and asked me when I was going to stop selling drugs. So I thought, let me act like I'm going to tell him something to see what happens. "What you want to know?" "Do you know Blue-Black?" he asked without hesitation. I didn't know Blue-Black from any other way but from shooting dice with him and from being with Richie-Rod who I know personally.

Their crew was on fire around this time. I remember I was listening to this police scanner and I heard the police following a guy who had a Jeep SRT, and I knew Nug who be with Richie-Rod, and Blue-Black had one. So my man Georgie knew Nug's girl or somebody and we met Richie- Rod and them at the Windsor Inn. I told them where they had came from and that the police were following them. Anyway, I responded "What, Blue-Black from West Baltimore?" Jenkins' face lit up like a Christmas tree and said "Yeah, you give me his number and I will let you go". I told Jenkins "I can get it, give me your number and I will call you when I get it". Jenkins looked at me as if he knew I was blowing haze smoke up his ass and said "Brill if you get in trouble call me".

Jenkins gave me his number, took the money I had and the dope and let me go. I was happy as a mothafucka. I had run-ins with him all the time, either he chased me and I got away or I wasn't dirty, but that day was different. I never told on anyone in my life and if he wasn't going to buy what I was selling, I guess I wouldn't pass GO and would have gone straight down the bookings, because telling isn't an option. So now I needed another rental. I thought to myself why did I even take the one I already had back. Oh yea, because I had to pay for it and pay the person who got it for me.

I called my go to lady for whatever I needed. "Hey baby, you trying to get me a rental? I'll pay you." Kelly is like my best friend; I could ask her for anything. "Hell no, I ain't fucking with you," she said. I knew that's what she was going to say but I had to try my arm. I figured if I offered her this money, I would end up paying the next girl. I fucked up a lot of rentals in my day, mostly police chases that ended in a crash and me getting away. Out of the many places to rent from, Kelly was banned at more than half fucking with me. I cnd up saying fuck a rental and just played it super safe due to this fact: Jenkins knew what I was driving. Lor Scoota had Jeff drop "Still in the Trenches Vol 2" and I had that bumping. The Horseshoe Casino had not too long ago opened up and that shit was jumping all night. It wasn't long before I became a regular down there, and was down there every night. It was now the 17th, 18th or 19th, of November, I really wish I could remember, but it was boxing matches going on at the Baltimore Arena.

Tone was into boxing so we went down to watch the fights. It was raining all that night and I was drinking all that day. Me and Tone ended up seeing the people from Umar boxing gym, I'm sure somebody from their gym was fighting. We had a good time, watched a couple matches and even saw the girls beat the shit out of each other. After the fight, Kelly came downtown to meet me to pick up Tone and I was off to the Horseshoe. This wasn't the usual time I went but I thought, let me see if I could go down here early and win something.

If I wasn't playing Blackjack, I was at the craps table. So I tried my arm at the craps table and was betting $500 on the don't pass line and everybody was missing. I know it wasn't no later than 11pm when I met Kelly and I didn't remember seeing anyone worth remembering there that night. When I seen I had damn near $5000 in chips, I cashed out and got the fuck outta there. After I sat in the car counting damn near $9000, next stop was Norma Jeans. I don't know what I started with, but I know I didn't have no more than $4000 on me.

Out of all the strip clubs in Baltimore, Norma Jeans is by far the best. I didn't go to Norma's to throw away money. Norma's was like a club, hang out spot, so I went on pass. I would say we went down there 4-5 times a week, and when I pulled up, it was 1:30am on the nose. Soon as the lights came at 1:45am, I remember getting a text message "the street blocked off I can't get through." It was my home girl who was in town for the Thanksgiving holiday and you know she had to holla at a real nigga. "Meet me at the 7-11. I'm bout to come around there now," I replied. I pulled around there and told her I was out front in a green Honda.

She was dark skinned, short, cute with a phat ass, and a pretty smile. I loved short girls, so she got in talking shit as always and I was so drunk. Somebody must of sold me this half of gallon of patron, because I don't know how the fuck I ended up with it. All I know is I poured endless cups that day, and she poured her a cup. We were cool, not on no fucking shit or nothing like that. So we were talking shit for about 15 minutes and I asked what she was about to do, but not in a way to insinuate anything, just in a making conversation way. I don't know what she had on her mind, but she said" I'm going with you." I was fucked up when she said that, damn near spit the Patron out. We weren't on that type of time so I was flabbergasted, so me being the un-faithful dog I was, call the veterinarian, I pulled off.

East Baltimore is nothing but a hop, skip and a jump from downtown and before I knew it, I was pulling into the infamous BP gas station on Orleans and Gay street, an area that is very familiar with crime. My apartment on St. Paul Street, 2227 St. Paul to be exact, was the next stop however, as soon as I pulled into the BP I heard like 5 gun shots. All in one motion without ever stopping, I was pulling out of the BP even quicker. As I turned right onto Orleans Street I heard 7-8 more shots, then felt I was hit. The girl I was with couldn't believe it and neither could I. The only thing I thought about was if I died in this car with this bitch, Kelly is going to kill me.

Johns Hopkins Hospital was like a half of a mile down the street, shit maybe 1/3 of a mile. I looked in the rear view mirror and I seen one car behind me, a White Honda Accord, so I put my famous driving skills to work in got the fuck outta there. I pulled up to the ER on Monument Street and told her to "Get out, I will be ok." She was crying, scared to death, and got out. I called Kelly and told her I was shot and I'm at Johns Hopkins. I got out and walked up to the door and saw a sign that said the ER has moved to Orleans Street. I must have been in a fucked up, confused state of mind, because I knew the ER was now on Orleans Street. I got back in the car and went up Monument Street and turned right on Wolf Street (which is a one way travelling west) and pulled in the fucking main entrance of the hospital, which is on Wolf.

I had to be out of my fucking mind to pull to the main entrance. I got back in the car and made a right on Wolf, damn near running head on to other cars, made the right on Orleans and pulled up to the ER. Before I knew it I was on the CAT Scan machine asking if I was going to die. I must of went out because I woke up in I.C.U with tubes down my throat. Kelly and my man Georgie was there asking "What the fuck happened?" You know Baltimore's finest wasn't too far behind asking the same thing. I didn't tell Kelly or any of my friends I was with that girl. None of my friends can hold water, and it's like Kelly tricks them out for info on me often. The funniest shit ever is I told the Detective who the girl was and he said "I locked her ass up before for stealing." I laughed as hard as I could and said "Yeah that's her".

I stayed in the hospital for almost a week, during that time my man Ryan A.K.A Rocko B.K.A 2RAWTHEDON made a rap video in the booth and came to show me. I was happy as shit because I was one of the guys who pushed him to do music. I got hit once in the back (again) and they had to take some intestines out and repair my lung. I was discharged the same day Dirt Bike Dev got killed (Rest In Peace, young king) which was November 23, 2014. I didn't know little homie but I heard a lot about him. After Rocko helped me to Kelly's truck, I was going to get my haircut by my barber of 14 years, Dee from Cedonia. So as we went up Belair Rd, we saw one of the blocks yellow taped off. It was the scene of where Dev got shot and killed. I made it home just in time for Thanksgiving and Tone was asking all kinds of questions.

I always hated having to lie to him, if I wasn't lying to him about what I did for a living it was why I was in the hospital. All I thought about was what the fuck happened, where that shit came from. I thought who I seen at the Horseshoe and Norma's and nobody came to mind. All I could think about was they were shooting at somebody else. I was in a fucked up side of town and right next to the BP was P.V.G (Pleasant View Gardens) which is the hood inside of a hood. I never felt the girl had something to do with it because her only motive would have been robbery, and that wasn't no robbery.

Plus, we were cool as shit and I always gave her whatever she asked me for not to mention she was in the car with me. The detective had 6 phones, the $9000, my police scanner and the car was on hold. I had to at least act like I was willing to cooperate to get my stuff back sooner than later. They let the car off hold, so I went with my mother to go get it from the pound, me and my man Bert. We checked the car to see how many bullet holes it had, it was only one.

I heard at least 12 shots so that really made me think that shit wasn't for me. At first we couldn't even find any holes, then I looked at the back tag and there it was. The shit went through the tag, through the backseat then through the driver seat. We took the car to CarMax and them tight motherfuckers gave me $3000 for the car. They said if the car didn't have a bullet hole and smell like weed they would've given us some more. Me and Bert blew that bitch down all the way to CarMax. Of course my mother was driving her car, I told you that the car was worth $5000 easy. A week or so went by and I was called to Eastern District police station. As I walked in I bumped into Hersl. "Look who it is Mr. Take One for the Team" Hersl said, talking to the detective he walked with down the hall. I took what he said as me taking probation for the dope he planted on me.

As I walked in the office I heard from across the room "Mr. Shropshire you're a very lucky man." The detective said "Come on in have a seat. How are you?" I was still thinking about the funny shit Hersl said on the way in. "I'm doing good, thanks for asking "Have you heard anything?" The detective asked, "I haven't heard anything and I reached out to some guys on that side of town as well." "I did notice one bullet hole in the car, but heard at least 12 shots, I don't think it was for me." "Oh well Mr. Shropshire, I disagree sir," he replied as he looked at me with this funny face. "See we are homicide detectives and we know who you are and due to your status in the northeast area, we believe it was a hit." I thought damn, here we go again this makes my third time getting shot.

Third time having to wrestle with these damn detectives. He continued. "You have multiple phones, a police scanner and over $8000 in cash. We are not worried about what you do for a living; we are worried about who shot you." He gave me everything I had back and said "Do you remember seeing any white cars that night?," then proceeded to show me a video. It was of three guys leaving Club Oxygen on Calvert Street, one block over from the 7-11, which was two blocks over from Norma Jeans and they looked to be in a rush. "Do you know any of these men?" he said. It was a clear video of the men, which had to be footage taken from the club that night.

I didn't know any of the men, and told him I had never seen them before. He then showed me a photo array of six men. I didn't know any of them but the third guy looked familiar I thought to myself. Then he showed me a photo of the guys talking outside of three cars. They were driving a white BMW 3 series, a white Nissan Altima and a white Hyundai Santa Fe. I said to myself, "Damn it was an Altima, not an Accord". Then thought damn How the fuck did he get all of this. Then explained, "Somebody saw you at Norma Jeans and called those three guys who just so happen to be blocks over." I thought hell no, I wasn't there but 15 minutes' tops!

Plus, nobody I would have had a problem with knew I was driving that car. "While you were at 7-Eleven, three cars circled the block multiple times until you pulled off." I thought again somebody would have had to either see me get out of that car or get in. I parked right in front of Normas and went right in and when I came out, got right in the car. It's no way somebody saw me that quick. "When you pulled off one car was in front of you, one was on the side of you and the third was behind you and he followed you all the way to the gas station. Mr. Shropshire, those guys were trying to ambush you." Then I thought again, all of them shots but only one hit the car. Everything he said damn near helped convince me and I was impressed how he put everything together. But he didn't know I just bought that car less than two weeks before I was shot, and nobody knew I was driving it. I acted surprised and told the detective I'll keep an ear out if I hear something and got the fuck outta there.

I saw on Instagram that the girl Chanel was selling a Celine bag so I called her down to the apartment on St. Paul so I could buy it from her for Kelly. After all, Kelly has always been there for me so I thought I would get it to show my appreciation. I was still healing and couldn't move around like that, so after Chanel left, a few guys I did business with came by then I got a call. "Boy, where the fuck you at? Your dummy ass stay in some shit." It was Amy, funny ass shit as always. I told her where I was at and she pulled up. She was just coming to holla at a nigga, told me I need to sit my dumb ass down.

I told her what happened and she was just as confused as I was. We always stayed in touch with each other, if I didn't have my apartment I could always use her spot. So as we were talking shit, she looked at me with this Oh my god I just thought of something look. "Do you know Snook?" I replied "What Snook? Y.B.S Snook?" "No Edmondson Village Snook." I personally know Y.B.S. Snook, but only heard of Edmondson Village Snook, and the things I heard about him was the worse you could hear about a nigga in the street. "I don't know him but I heard a lot of fucked up shit about him."

Me and Amy use to do what we did, but everybody knew Kelly was my girlfriend so it wasn't unusual for Amy to talk to me about the niggas she dealt with from time to time. The word through Baltimore is that "EDMONDSON VILLAGE SNOOK" was a fucking rat. I can't stamp it because I haven't seen any paperwork, but everybody heard the same. I didn't even have to say nothing, Amy already knows. "My home girl told me that he been shot so many times because he told on some niggas." I said "Yeah, I heard the same thing" but what she said next blew my mind. "He got the same kind of green Honda you got, same tags and dark ass tints." I can't believe she said that, and before I could say it she said "I think they thought you was him!" I thought ain't no fucking question them niggas thought I was him.

After a while what that detective was saying kind of made me think somebody saw me just that quick and ordered me up. Now I 100% believe that those guys thought I was Snook, nothing leads to anything else. I thought about all the scenarios but not in a mistaken identity way. All roads lead to them thinking I was Snook. Somebody saw my Honda and thought it was Snook's Honda and called the guys around there, and they saw me parked on the corner and waited. I know this guy Snook got me beat on getting shot at least 2-3 times. I remember he got shot in front of Club Mirage one night which was a very popular nightclub in downtown Baltimore, just a mile up the road from the 7-Eleven I was at. I cursed Kelly out about not getting me a rental. I'm sure once she reads this book she going to curse me out but fuck it. It's the untold truth.

It's time I tell the truth for a change, I ended up getting a white 2015 Honda Accord touring "YBS Dip" had a white Honda Accord as well. I remember we used to be at the same club (not together) and there used to be notes on my car of bitches talking shit thinking I was him. So one day I seen him out front of the club and he gave me a note and said "this was on my car, it's for you." I read the note and we both busted out laughing hard as shit. Only if he knew I got shot behind somebody thinking I was somebody else driving a mothafucking Honda.

THE CHESAPEAKE BUILDING

As I was escorted out of Judge Gallagher's courtroom, I looked at Kelly and she looked how a concerned wife would look. I was placed in a holding cell with a slim light skin guy who said he was woken by 7 U.S Marshals who had an arrest warrant for violating his probation. I wasn't in a talking mood and didn't say anything. The look on my face was of a man who had a million questions. The big question was how the fuck I get charged with Twan and Munch AKA Alexander Campbell? After wrecking my brain about why, how, where, and when did I conspire with them to distribute heroin between 2010–2016, I started to think, I read the Indictment 367 times trying to figure this shit out and I came to the same conclusion.

I didn't work with them during that time. I know Lou was like "What the fuck!" when he heard the news! He was just getting released, maybe at the same time as I sat in the cell damn near going crazy. Everything came rushing back to me, the undercover buy, all the unmarked cars I saw daily, the G.P.S I found, the Baltimore city gun and drug charges. I just shook my head because I fucking told myself all that shit was going to catch up with me some day. I had to lay it down and the cold ass steel bench looked like a great place to do it. "Shropshire, time to go!" I heard the Marshal say. I woke up lost, confused, and wished I was in my dream. The ride C.D.F (Chesapeake Detention Facility) was sicken, and as we pulled up I said "I'm at the got damn Chesapeake building." Every time my man Nick said or did some dumb shit I always said, "you must be trying to go to the Chesapeake building."

For years C.D.F was the Maryland Correctional Adjustment Center known as Supermax, that housed Maryland's Death Row Inmates. Supermax was built in 1988, and is located at 401 East Madison Street in Baltimore's Eastside. It wasn't until June 2010 when the State Of Maryland received a contract with the Federal Government to solely house federal pretrial detainees. Of course the federal detainees were not subject to the 23 hours a day. Monday through Friday lock down and 24 hours a day on Saturday and Sunday conditions that the 1988 jail was built for. The facility, I like how they use the word facility instead of jail, is now operated by the Maryland Department Of Public Safety and Correctional Services. Everybody in Baltimore knew C.D.F was where you went when the Feds grab you. So to be out front waiting for the garage gate to open up, all I thought was how I use to always ask Nick "What you trying to be down the Chesapeake building?" The gate opened in the Marshall pulled in smoothly and man was I pissed.

They took me in and I had to sit in the metal detector chair. I guess they are trying to make sure you don't have nothing up your ass who knows. It wasn't long before I heard, "Brill what the fuck." It was the nigga Woods from around Northwood Shopping Center which is right across the street from Morgan State University about 2-3 miles from my neighborhood. "All man I don't know what the fuck is going on." I replied to Woods. He said "See if you can get down to C-unit where I'm at."

I was given a pair of white Payless shoes and a brand new maroon prison outfit, and one free call, so I called Kelly. I'll be lying to say I remember what we talked about, I'm sure it was about what was going on which I had no clue. After my I.D. was printed, that said my nickname was Brill on the back, I was taken to E-unit. C.D.F has six units, A-F. Each unit has four pods that house up to 48 inmates, that's 12 cells up and down stairs. One of the pods on E was for new inmates, you know, to get classified to see your security level, take your blood etc. I walked in the pod and asked who was next on the phone. There weren't many guys there, so after I set up my name and shit for the phone, I called Kelly.

I couldn't do anything but notice this one guy who was joyful, too joyful to be at Supermax. I had to ask what was up with him and he said "I was just at Lee County (Federal Penitentiary in Virginia) and I'm back on a new trial." His name was Nelly A.K.A G-Code, not sure where he was from, I was told he was from Liberty heights & Garrison, in northwest Baltimore, but he said he was hanging around Harford Road in East Baltimore, Zone 18 as my Harford Road niggas call it. Nelly said he got caught up on the Mondawmin Mall indictment, which was a reverse sting operation. Some nigga who was the plug got caught with a Rv full of bricks and got the bright idea to call Nelly and others to Mondawmin to act like he was going to sell them the bricks.

One by one the feds locked their ass up as they pulled up. I actually heard about the Mondawmin shit, it was a big thing. We ended up knowing some of the same people so we talked until it was time to lock in. He asked me about my case and I really had no idea. I can't thank Nelly enough because it was him who unconsciously opened my eyes to what I would have been blind to. He showed me how to work the law computer and said don't let them people trick me. He showed me what to look for, how to study my case and the law. He said the lawyer will come down in about two months and say this and that and not to trust him.

As days went on, guys were getting classified and going to general population and boy was I ready to go. I was in dire need of some real soap and commissary. It was funny because I still had money in my account from when I did that year at The Maryland Penitentiary, now known as Metropolitan Transition Center, in 2008-2009. The unit was flipping every day, guys would leave and new guys would come. They were locking niggas up so as the door to the unit opened up, I seen about 5-6 fresh maroon outfits hit the corner and I couldn't believe my eyes.

It was Lil Omari A.K.A Omari Thomas and right then and there I knew that was his name redacted in the indictment. The government redacts names and other information so people don't know. The reason his name was redacted was because they didn't lock him up yet. If I was able to see his name, I could have tipped him off, so they redacted it. I felt so bad as he walked in because he had a Lil girl and he was a great father. The government claimed he worked for me, going by the name Lil Brill, but it was a misunderstanding.

Omari was like family to Kelly and I knew him from being in the neighborhood, days later he got home confinement. I called Kelly one day and she said Furl got shot. I called Furl to see how my nigga was doing, he said that somebody came to his house and hit him through the front door. I thought "damn they wasn't playing with Furl ass"! Furl was telling me that morning

I got locked up, he was out there and saw police and took his ass back in the house because he thought they were watching them. "I wasn't even thinking to call you to tell you because you don't be around the way" he said. I was just happy my nigga was ok.

Furl is my heart, he taught me a lot of shit and always came through when I needed him. After three long weeks and the last one to leave, I was moved to D-unit. I couldn't wait to get to population to see what was really going on at the infamous C.D.F. I didn't know none of the guys there and Twan and Munch were on different units. Wasn't nothing going on that I was into so I played in the law room. As days went on I did run into the nigga Wop from Chapel Hill Projects that was in east Baltimore before they were taken down.

I know him from hanging with Oski who is from Latrobe Projects in east Baltimore. I fucked wit Wop, he was crazy as shit, but cool. I just had to ask him about that time he called saying he got pulled over coming back from New York. During the time Freddie Gray got killed, me and Oski went up to New York for some days until the riot shit cooled down. Wop end up coming up there and hanging out, so when Wop was coming back home he got pulled over on 95 soon as he got in Maryland. So as Wop called telling me the story, I asked "So what's the problem?" He said "Man, since when do the State Troopers let you go without a license?" I thought yeah he got a point but thought nothing of it.

So after a while we went on back to Baltimore to face the madness. When we got back, Oski said to drop him off at a hotel in Towson, Maryland and I headed on home. Days later I ran into Oski and he was acting funny, so he ended up telling me that when I dropped him off that night Baltimore County police blitzed him like 15 deep. Now Oski can be one crazy mothafucka at times so I didn't put it past him but I didn't 100% believe him. So we had a little falling out about that whole situation.

Sometime maybe a week or so later I met up with him to talk and he was with Kelly and her friend Aja, who is Oski's baby mother. We talked the issue out and I could tell he wasn't in crazy mode anymore but he stood on his police story and I explained I had nothing to do with that. Now that I think about it, that was D.E.A Task Force Office McDougall behind everything I bet you. When he arrested me he made a comment about how I like going up to New York. So when I ran into Wop he said "Man they searched the shit out of us than let us go, something wasn't right."

Anyway what fucked me up was out of the 80 guys on the unit, only a handful went in the law room to work on their case. Everybody knew how serious it was to be fighting a federal case and I guess they didn't take the shit seriously. C.D.F was fucked up, mice running freely and the unit smelled like shit and piss, and the cells were 90 degrees plus in the summertime. I guess the max wasn't so bad compared to other pre-trial spots. You were able to have a TV, Xbox and CD players. Of course I thought that was the case to keep you from really seeing the shit they were doing. The government plays chess for real, and if blind, you won't see the next move.

Another month had passed and all I did was think about Kelly and Tone, how I left them. My first lawyer, Teresa Whalen, came down there and I thought she had some news. She didn't want shit but to tell me she can't be my lawyer because of a conflicting interest. She didn't say what the interest was, but all that meant was she or somebody from her office were representing somebody that has something to do with my case. I went back to the unit and just thought, that's all a wise man can do. Most of the fools around me were fools, and I could tell the last thing they did was think. It wasn't even a full two months when something I was trying to figure out hit me like a ton of bricks.

During the year 2016 I would notice I was unhappy, the feeling came on and off and I didn't know what it was. As a drug dealer and degenerate gambler I was up and down financially, so I thought it was not having the money I was used to having fucking with me mentally. I would hustle diligently to get my money up, but I soon noticed that I would still feel unhappy. I found myself asking "What the fuck is the problem"? I never could figure it out, and would have to tell myself to snap out of it. I would bribe myself by buying things I didn't need, or going places I didn't have the money for to duck the feelings.

However, it would follow me around like a lost dog. Then I started to notice everything I touched turned into muss. I owed this guy, started robbing Peter to pay Paul, business slowed up, phones stopped ringing and I remember sitting on my porch just lost. I didn't know how to ask for help or knew where to find it, I just felt like a lost dog. When my house got raided in

October 2016 that's when I really started to try to figure out why I felt funny and unhappy, without a doubt I ran right into the same dead end. My birthday came around October 30th and I hung out with Flip, Fresh and Nico (my two guys from Old York). I didn't have the money I wanted but I had a good time and felt funny at the same time. I made enough to keep the bills paid but that was about it.

The feeling I felt the second month at C.D.F was damn near supernatural like. You know how something is on the tip of your tongue then it pops in your head? It felt like that but times ten. The shit I felt had to be from some-body or something with power out of this world. I can't really explain it, but right then and there I know why I was unhappy. I also felt relieved from life's worries and didn't have a care in the world. I knew I had gun and drug charges pending in Baltimore City Courts and had conspiracy to sell heroin charges pending in Federal Court but it didn't feel like I did.

What was so hard for me to realize that I was tired of that life? The drugs, the girls, the partying, the gambling, the lying and having to watch my back everywhere I went. What was so hard about realizing that? When I told the story to Brother Menes, he is the wise fella who wrote the foreword, he said it was an epiphany I had. Which means a sudden striking understanding of something. It should say a supernatural understanding that gives you an outer body feeling because I felt something. Right after I started to read the Bible looking for answers and viewed things through a different lens. The more I read the better my understanding of life became. I later found out why it was so hard for me to figure out why I was so unhappy. I'm not a Christian or Muslim, my belief is hard to explain. What I can tell you is that I believe the true religion is Islam and I'm a believer in both the bible and Qur'an.

Romans 7:14-20 – *"We know that the law is spiritual but I am unspiritual, sold as a slave in sin. I do not understand what I do. For what I want to do I do not do, but what I hate I do. And if I do what I do not want to do, I agree that the law is good. As it is, it is no longer myself who does it, but it is sin living in me. For I know that good itself does not dwell in me, that is, in my sinful nature. For I have the desire to do what is good, but I cannot carry it out. For I do not do the good I want to do, but the evil I do not want to do — this I keep on doing.*

Now if I do what I do not want to do, it is no longer I who does it, but it is sin living in me that does it."

Romans 8:5- *"Those who live according to the flesh have their minds set on what the flesh desires; but those who live in accordance with the spirit have their minds set on what the spirit desires."*

2 Corinthians 4:4 -*"The God of this age has blinded the minds of unbelievers, so that they cannot see the light of the gospel that displays the glory of Christ who is the image of God"*

1 John 2:15-17 -*"Love not the world, neither the things that are in the world. If any man loves the world, the love of the father is not in him. For all that is in the world, the lust of the flesh, and the lust of the eyes, and the pride of life, is not of the father, but is of the world."*

James 4:1-5 -*"What causes fights and quarrels among you? Don't they come from your desires that battle within you? You desire but do not have, so you kill, you covet but you cannot get what you want, so you quarrel and fight. You do not have it because you do not ask God. When you ask, you do not receive, because you ask with wrong motives, that you may spend what you get on your pleasures." God has set a seal on their heart and on their hearing, and on their eyes is a veil; Great is the penalty they (incur).*

Al Isra: 45-46 -*"And when you (Muhammad) recite the Qur'an, we put between you and those who believe not in the hereafter, an invisible veil (or screen their hearts, so they hear or understand it not). And we have put coverings over their hearts lest, they should understand it and in their ears deafness. And when you make mention of your lord alone (none has the right to be worshipped but Allah) they turn on their backs, fleeing in extreme dislike."*

The reason why I couldn't figure out why I was unhappy was because as an unbeliever I was blind (and or had a veil) and a slave to sin. I had my mind set on what the flesh desires (what is called worldly desires), money, cars, clothes, sex, drugs, and I sold drugs to get those things. Once my spirit got tired of doing those things, it spiritually made me unhappy. But the sin in me kept on doing what I didn't want to do. I didn't see it because I was blind, meaning my mind blocked me from seeing what was making me unhappy. When I had the epiphany/supernatural feeling, I believed it was Allah taking the blind fold off my mind so I could see.

Allah will blind unbelievers so they won't see what it is they doing or feeling until Allah is ready. The bible speaks about everyday life and has brought me a long way mentally. Everything that is going on has been going on since forever. Ecclesiastes 1:9 *"What has been will be there, it's nothing new under the sun."* I'm not sure if you will understand how I came to this conclusion being the reason why I couldn't figure out why I was unhappy, but if you take your time it should come to you. The reason I say Allah is because I believe Islam is the true religion and so people can know I'm speaking about God.

Some People believe when a person says Allah that person is Muslim, I am not Muslim. However, I believe there is none worshipable but Allah and that Muhammad is his servant and messenger. Allah is God in Arabic, and for some reason people think Allah is some other God. There is only one God. I say Allah because some people believe that Jesus (Peace Be Upon Him) is God. So depending on who I'm talking to, if I say God, they think I'm talking about Jesus (Peace Be Upon Him). Anyway, as time went on my new lawyer Joseph Murtha came down to see me and it blew my mind because he said everything Nelly said he would say. Murtha didn't say anything bad, it just goes to show all them lawyers are running the same game.

I can't trust C.J.A attorneys (The Criminal Justice Act appoints lawyers for people who can't afford them). I feel like there is a conspiracy to keep people in prison that everybody's involved in. Murtha was my lawyer for two months and once he saw how sincere I was about my case and what the law was, he told me he only took my case because he was told it was an open and shut case that was soon to be resolved. Who would mislead him to believe something like that? Why would somebody even say that? Like this isn't a very serious matter. More guys need to learn more about the law and put less trust in lawyers that throw our asses to the wolves.

Of course time went on, time waits for no man, and if I wasn't in the law room I was talking to Kelly or watching TV. I did learn how to play chess and that's the most extreme game I ever played. So one day I was playing chess, this was January 2017 and I seen and heard a guy at the door ask, "Is Brill over here?" The guy was talking to Slick A from east Baltimore (he's a local rapper.) As I looked up I saw Slick A turning around to my attention, then called me over to the door. "What's up Brill, I heard you were over here. You need anything? Lil Meat told me who you were." I told the guy I was good and I would holla at him during rec. I went to ask Slick A who that was and he looked at me as if I was crazy for asking and said "That's Fat Relly!" I didn't know fat Relly but I damn sure heard of him. I think anybody in Baltimore who knows what's going on in them streets heard of Fat Relly. He is from Chapel Hill Projects that was in East Baltimore.

The beef between Fat Relly and JR will forever be talked about in Baltimore. I remember the Mayor came on the news asking the feds for help because the murders behind that beef were just out of hand. I was on the first pod and Relly was on the fourth pod. He gave them Correctional Officers hell, he would not stay out the hallway, and getting him to lock down was another job itself. Lil Meat A.K.A bright eyes, was another name that ringed bells though East Baltimore streets. I wasn't from East Baltimore but I mingled with the killers and drug dealers so I always heard a thing or two about the who's who in the East Baltimore streets. And word was niggas was scared to death of Lil Meat.

So it was now March 1st, just days before my love's birthday. I was in my cell doing the Jane Fonda and I heard all the guys yelling, so I knew something happened. I came out to see what the fuck all the noise was about "Yo what happened?" as I yelled. "Boy what the fuck, you ain't see the news? They locked Jenkins and Hersl bitch asses up" said a guy from West Baltimore. I thought damn, all that shit they were into caught up with their ass. I called Kelly moments later just to see what my love was doing. I'm sure she was at work making women beautiful, she was the best at her trade and always took that shit seriously. "What's up baby, what are you doing?" her reply was "Did you see the news?" "No, but I heard they locked Jenkins and Hersl up".

Everybody knows who Jenkins was, he is way more known than Hersl. As I explained, Jenkins was a member of O.C.D (Organized Crime Division) which is just like G.T.T.F (Gun Trace Task Force) when it comes to their granted access to Baltimore City as a whole. Whereas Hersl worked in Eastern District for the most part, which means Hersl was confined to East Baltimore only. Of course Kelly knew who Jenkins was, because her boyfriend was a known drug dealer and had many run-ins with Jenkins. "Fuck that they locked up Momodu too" (Momodu Gondo is a Baltimore City Detective that I personally knew from my neighborhood. He was best friends with Lou, who was and still is a dear friend of mine)

I said "Damn that's crazy" "Guess who else they indicted?" she asked. I said "Who" waiting for her to say Gladstone. But the answer she said I wasn't ready for "Lou" she said. "WHAT?" I replied in disbelief. "They added Lou and Momodu to y'all indictment, calling it The Shropshire Drug Trafficking Organization" she said. I was fucking confused as shit. First they say I conspired with Twan and Munch. Four months later they charge Lou and Momodu and say it's all one indictment, this is ridiculous. "Everybody's been texting me all day about the shit, that's how I found out. Somebody texted me the indictment" Kelly says. I was so confused because I don't see how it was even possible.

It took me a week to get a copy of the indictment and once I read it, I thought these people got a lot of shit with them. But as I have learned, they can indict a ham sandwich and if they don't have the facts, they will make them up. Lou ass was on the run, and it wasn't until July 2017 when they caught him. It was two indictments that came out on February 23, 2017 which they didn't make known until March 1st. One was of Jenkins, Hersl and several other Baltimore City detectives that were all members of the department's G.T.T.F unit, charging them with Racketeering (from stealing drug to overtime, and lying to jurors and judges) and the third superseding indictment, which charged Gondo, an G.T.T.F member, with the rest of us. I heard later that it was Justin Fenton, a Baltimore Sun journalist and author of the book "WE OWN THIS CITY" that posted the indictments on his twitter account, causing the news to spread like Covid-19 through the city.

Since I've been in, Fenton reached out to me for my side of the story for his book "WE OWN THIS CITY" and I did not think twice to give it. As I explained to Fenton, if I don't give him my side, he would only have one side to a two sided story, which is without a doubt why I planned on testifying at my trial, so the jury could have both sides. Yes, I know a journalist is going to put what they want in their story but I wanted Fenton to have my side and not just the government's side so he can choose what to put. The way I felt was, I couldn't let a story run if it's false. You have to speak up for yourself because people tend to believe what they read.

About a week went by and they were bringing guys in left and right. Two new guys had come in on our pod and the fat one everybody knew. It wasn't long before I heard his name and I couldn't say I didn't hear it when I was on the street. Baltimore is only so big and if you don't know a person, you know somebody that did. So I guess from people on the unit calling my name, he heard it and pulled me up. "Yo you know Five" he said, "Yea I know him" I replied "Did y'all use to do business before?" "Yeah he would buy 10-25 grams here in there." "Yeah, that's him, he asked me if I knew you and showed me a copy of your indictment on his phone, said you be with Georgie".

I wasn't surprised because when the indictment came out I heard the word spread like wildfire. I heard niggas was talking crazy about me like insanity pleas. The big fella's name was Dorsey and it was a privilege to meet him and Relly. Dorsey was from East Baltimore as well, not sure what part though. He was just as confused as I was about my case when I first came in. Dorsey was concerned that Five may have set him up because the day before he got locked up, he sold him some dope. As time went on big fella was mad as shit because he got a copy of an old indictment from 2014 that had Five's name on it as a defendant. Dorsey showed me the indictment and I was blown away. How the fuck is your name on a federal indictment from 2014 and your ass ain't in prison?

Dorsey said he started hearing all kinds of shit about Five and was pissed because nobody said anything to him about it when he was home. I was just as confused as he was and asked "Why is Lil Meat and them fucking with him?" Dorsey was lost for words. Now I'm not saying Five did anything because I don't know. All I'm saying is I saw his name in an indictment from 2014 and I'm wondering why he is not in prison. Without a doubt if I find out this man is fucked up, I'm putting him out there.

The government wanted Dorsey so bad the dude he came on the pod with, who was his cell buddy, was a federal informant. His name was Derrick James or Durk or Dirt James, from one of the counties in Maryland, closer to D.C. The nigga James, ended up testifying at Digger and Jeezy's trial. That man didn't know them or Dorsey and still went to testify at their trial and was willing to testify on Dorsey. That's called jumping on a nigga case. Digger and Jeezy are from Greenmount in East Baltimore. So always watch what you say out your mouth to people you don't know, shit in their case, they didn't even say nothing and a nigga still jumped on their case. Also, they put listening devices in the law room at C.D.F, so just don't talk about anything.

I remember the heat stopped working, so they took some people to the bookings and some to J.C.I (Jessup Correctional Institution). My pod and another pod were the ones to go to J.C.I. They put us on the blue bird (prison bus) and it was about a 30-minute ride. Everybody enjoyed the ride, shit anything beats sitting at the jail all day. So we got there at like 3 in the morning and as soon as we got inside, the inmates at J.C.I were on their door looking. It wasn't long before you started to hear guys that came on the blue bird being called by the guys at J.C.I. "Yo Brill what's up?" It was Fats who I knew from hanging up Park Heights (Northwest Baltimore) with my man Rico.

"Fats Boi Fuck is up?," I said. He yelled back "Snoop down the hall" and before I could yell back the C.O. took me in the room to take the cuffs off. Snoop A.K.A Chris was like family. That was who drove me to the hospital when I got shot the first time. He was locked up fighting an attempted murder case and I haven't seen him in damn near two years. We were only at J.C.I for like 30 hours and word spread quickly that we were there. Niggas was coming out of everywhere to holla at Relly and Dorsey. I heard somebody yell to Relly "Ball on the other side, he holla at you real loud" (Ball is a local rapper from Baltimore). Snoop came to holla at me the next morning and got somebody to bring me some food. He told me my cousin Moonie (from West Port, south Baltimore) was on one side, and my man Bo was on the other side.

We talked for a little minute and I was even able to talk to Bo through my cell window. Everybody heard we were there and I heard Bo calling me when he was in the yard. Bo was serving a 25-year sentence for gun and drug charges. Him and Snoop now are home. Moonie sent me a kite (note or letter) that one of the C.O's brought me. It was good to see Snoop, that's my heart. Our families grow up together and it fucks me up to see pictures of our sons hanging together. All I think about is how me and Snoop was young hanging together.

Snoop sent up the paperwork on Emmanuel Washington a.k.a Pimp or Man. He's an old head nigga from around my way that came to testify at Snoop trial. As I read the paperwork I couldn't believe how niggas be telling. Pimp and Black Aaron a.k.a. Aaron Anderson got arrested together with some dope and guns, Aaron ended up testifying at my trial. Niggas is telling at an all-time high and niggas and bitches still fucking with them. Snoop beat the charges and had me laughing like shit because he said "Man you should have been let me kill that bitch a long time ago." I cried laughing because he was right. Me and pimp had an issue years ago and Snoop was on his ass, but after he was nowhere to be found I said let it go. I was getting too much cash at the time, plus I overthink shit. I felt that if Pimp scared ass got smoked I would have been the first nigga to get grabbed.

Y'all seen The First 48 before. The first question they ask the family is did he have any problems with anyone. See it all the time. If they know you getting money and you start to get niggas killed, they will get your ass off the streets. It's almost like they let you get the money, but once bodies start dropping it's all over.

One last story before I close this chapter out. It was early September 2016 and I was leaving Kelly shop "Studiofix" on my way to get Tone. It had to be around 8pm, I turned on 32nd street and a marked police car pulled me over for nothing. I was driving my 2016 Honda and I'm trying to tell you that a Honda with tinted windows in Baltimore is a police magnet. The cop was a rookie, black younger officer and he was scared to death. The young punk pulled me out of the car and kept reaching for his gun every time I moved. I wasn't trying to get shot and I damn sure didn't know why he had me out of my car. I lifted up my shirt and pulled my pants down so he could know I didn't have no gun and yelled "Stop reaching for your fucking gun."

While all of this was going on his sergeant was coming down the street, an evil white one. He hopped out and said "lock his ass up for indecent exposure" and I couldn't believe it. I cursed his young ass out all the way down the bookings because he shouldn't even had pulled me over scared as his ass was. So as I was sitting on the benches waiting to be called for processing. This white guy brought in this younger black guy. I heard the black guy telling the guy next to him he had a federal warrant. So the white guy who brought him in must have been some kind of federal agent or task force officer. I started checking the white guy out just to see what all I could notice about him then I looked away. I felt somebody looking at me so I looked and it was the white guy.

We eye balled each other for a quick second then I looked away then he said "What's up Brill" I heard what he said clearly but wanted to make sure. "What you say?" I replied playing dumb. "I said what's up?" "What did you call me?" He replied, "Brill! that's your name right?" Deep down I was fucked up in the head, scared to death for real, but I said "Hell no that aint my name." He said "Oh, my bad" with a hell of a look on his face. Me and the black guy caught eye contact and he just shook his head. I thought about that shit my whole stay at the bookings that night. What's so crazy is I ended up bumping into the black guy at Chesapeake Detention Facility months later.

When he saw me, we were both waiting to be seen by the dentist and said "You look familiar." I laughed and said "Man I was the guy that was down the bookings when they brought you in and that police said what's up to me." The guy couldn't believe it. I asked him where he was from and he responded "McCabe." I asked "You on Big Head Charlie and them indictment?" and he confirmed. I asked what unit he was on he said "C." I said "My co-defendant Munch down there." He said "That's my cell buddy." I thought damn it's a small city. So right before I was about to leave C.D.F, Dorsey was telling me that there were trying to charge him with racketeering. I told him to stay in the law room and learn all he can about the law because lawyers ain't shit.

I left C.D.F in March of 2018 and went to F.C.I Beckley in West Virginia. I was on lock up and my mother used to send me stuff from the Baltimore Sun Newspaper. I opened my mail and just shook my head. On the front page it talked about Dorsey pleading guilty to racketeering charges. Claiming he ordered B.G.F (Black Guerrilla Family) members to kill two guys. I was hurt because Dorsey was a good man and good men need to be on the street to take care of their family and keep shit in order, which is why shit is out of order today. Fat Relly ended up dying from health related issues and Lil Meat got killed at Latrobe Projects in East Baltimore the day after Relly died. Relly and Lil Meat both grew up together in Chapel Hill Projects.

BODYMORE, MURDERLAND

Fort McHenry is the birthplace of the United States own national anthem, The Star Spangled Banner, which sits at the mouth of Baltimore Inner Harbor. The harbor is the area tourist know of which offers many different shops, upscale crab places and attractions like the Civil War era warship the USS Constellation and the National Aquarium that showcases thousands of marine creatures. I remember going to the harbor as a kid for Fourth of July. That was some dangerous shit. Just imagine hundreds of bad ass kids all turned up because it's the 4th of July.

Before them wild ass Europeans came to Baltimore, the land belonged to the Susquehannock Native Americans. We all know the Europeans tricked and killed people for their land. However, it was British colonists that established the Port of Baltimore in 1706 and they made their money from the tobacco trade. They established the lovely town of Baltimore in 1729. The Battle of Baltimore was a Crux engagement in 1812. The Barrage of Fort McHenry is when Francis Scott Key wrote the poem that became the American national anthem in 1931. Baltimore Maryland, the old line state, free state may be nothing to you but it's everything to me. It's crazy because shit been going down in Baltimore since the Pratt Street riot in 1861 which was some of the earliest violence associated with the American Civil War.

As of 2018 the population in Baltimore was 602,495, but abatemented to 593,490 in 2019. The city that reads is located just 40 miles from our nation's capital, Washington D.C. making it a Principal City in the Washington Baltimore Combined Statistical Area (CSA), the fourth largest CSA in our nation. I know for a fact Baltimore has a lot to offer the natives who are passionate and motivated. People like Oprah Winfrey started in Baltimore, reporting the news for Fox 45 in the 80s. Oprah used to get that curly bush cut at "House Of Naturals" on Schroder & Fayette back in the 80s. But once people can get pass the shit that happens 10 minutes from the inner harbor, Baltimore's reputation wouldn't be so bad. And with a cognomen like BODYMORE MURDERLAND, it won't be easy.

Since I could remember guys woke up and had murder for breakfast. Damn near every day you hear about someone getting smoked like a backwood. And as sad as it is, it's been that way of life for the people of Baltimore. You either hear about the high ass murder rate, the fucked-up thing that happened to Freddie Gray, the 2015 riot or shit about us having the best seafood. We do have a long history as having an important Seaport. I do know after Freddie Gray was killed in 2015 shit got wild in BODYMORE. Yeah I said killed what you think happened? Gray was a 25-year-old black man that died after being arrested by Baltimore police.

The medical examiner ruled his death a homicide. Did you not get the memo? The shit the police are doing has been out of hand and the shit needs to stop. The shit that has me disheveled is the black on black violence. I understand the shit police and some white people do. Understanding something is to perceive and comprehend the nature and significance of knowledge. People tend to ruminate when someone says they understand something that they are agreeing with. Understanding and agreeing are two different things. What I understand is that the police and some white people were raised and taught to hate people of color. You don't just wake up and hate someone, hate is taught.

Did you forget the people that oppress us are the ancestors of the same people that Raped, Killed, Branded and hung our people? So I don't know why people are so disheveled when it comes to the shit black people go through. I'm a street nigga, so I understand and agree with the laws of the street. Now that I think about it I'm Disheveled about the shit black people do to each other that leads to them killing each other. Like why do something that you know somebody will kill you over? I hate to keep having to put it all on what these people put our people through, but all roads lead back to that. It's all their fault that some of our race are behind, back forwards, and ignorant. But instead of making it right they continue to be the oppressor and treat us unequal. Sadly, killing and crime has been in Baltimore culture since forever, as long as I could remember.

I always heard about somebody getting killed, shot, stabbed, beat by the knockers or you heard the streets talkin."Them Niggas Beefing About This", The Feds Grabbed Yo", or "Yo Dumb Ass Got A No Brainer" (No Bail). Now don't get me wrong, evil comes in many different shapes, sizes and colors. I knew some evil black people and I hate to even say this, but some niggas deserve to get rolled up and smoked like a Backwood. Overall the things we do to each other needs to stop, which will stop each other from having to kill the other person. I don't know where the name Bodymore Murderland came from but I can't say it wasn't no truth to that joke. I came to prison and became a lot of things but I always felt black on black violence needs to stop.

I've been accused of my share of violence but I stopped violence from happening as well. One thing for sure: you're either on one side or the other side of that gun when you're playing in them Baltimore streets. I assure you that it ain't no fun when the rabbit got the gun. In fact, I saved a lot of people from getting gunned down like the dog they were. Take my former best friend Boo, as one example. Me, Furl and Boo were Best Friends coming up. Somewhere down the line me and Boo's relationship grew apart. That was still my man but I was into other things so I guess Boo felt like I didn't love him. So in 2012 (I believe it was) I was out front of an apartment I used for a number of reasons talking to Lou, and Nick had just pulled off. The apartment was at Fairways of Towson just about 12 minutes from my neighborhood. That's actually where me and Kelly's first apartment was in 2005. So I seen two guys walking down the street.

There were dozens of apartment buildings so I didn't really pay them any mind but I was wondering where they were going. My back was to them as I leaned in the car talking to Lou, 2 o'clock in the afternoon. Before Lou said he was about to park and come in, I asked, "Where them Niggas go at?" Lou said, "he didn't see anybody", so I just thought they went into one of the buildings. As I stepped in the building I saw the two guys talking to the foreigners that worked at Valentino's who live downstairs from my apartment. I thought what the fuck they talkin about. Valentino's is a 24-hour restaurant that is in Northeast Baltimore. Soon as I walked up the first set of stairs one of the guys was on the phone talkin about the girl giving them the wrong address. The two guys started going towards the exit so I walked up the next set of stairs and looked out the window to see which way they were going. I heard the door open so I went back down the steps thinking it was Lou to ask him where they went but it was them.

All I seen was the Dope boys Uzi, the nigga with the braids was holding. I don't recall what he said but I already knew what time it was. I went right in my pocket and gave them the money. I had just sold a nigga 50 grams for $4,000 and got some pack money from two of my little men. So I had between 6 to $7,000 on me. All the money was Block money, so it was all 5's and $10 bills so it looked like a lot more. The money was all stuffed in my pocket so as I pulled it out some of it fell. I don't know what it is but I can stay calm in any situation. Like when I got shot those times I stayed calm and they say a lot of people die because they start to panic. Plus, I am thinking motherfucka I was about to try the nigga with the uzi, he was too close to me. Then he asked where the watch was and grabbed my wrist to check for it. Nick had just bought a Bus Down, and the Mothafucka was Hitting. So I knew what watch he was talking about.

He then asked what apartment was it in? I told him I don't know. Clearly he thought I was Nick and didn't know it was me. The other one was still picking the money up and letting them niggas take me in the apartment wasn't going to happen. Whatever they were going to do had to happen in the hallway. I thought let me try this nigga. Lou was on his way in and as slow as he moved, his ass should have been walked in. So I thought I could tussle with one and Lou should be coming in to help. In the apartment I had 700 grams of heroin and $20,000. That was a cool little lick for them, but I wasn't going in no apartment, that's dead.

After the dude got all the money off the floor, he said come on man let's go and they jumped down the steps running right into Lou, of course they robbed him and ran out the building. I wasn't even mad about the robbery, that shit was peanuts. I was mad because I seen them niggas but didn't know where they went. It was no way I would have went in the building had I seen them go in. Anyway, one day I got a call some 2 years later, it was my man

Furl. "Yo, you got robbed like a year ago?" Furl was short and wild as shit. He acted like Martin Lawrence, but reminded you of O-Dog from Menace to Society. Furl didn't play about me and was mad as Shit. I didn't play that talking on the phone shit, so we met. I told him what happened and he asked, "Why you didn't tell me?" Nobody knew but Lou and Nick.

I explained to Furl that if I told people, the story would have got twisted around and I wouldn't ever find out who did it. I'm trying to tell you I was a thinking mothafucka. So, a nigga was over the jail talking to his cell buddy about how he got his man nephew to rob me. Just so happen the cell buddy didn't know me but knew Furl. The cell buddy came right out and called Furl, asking did he still fuck with me. Further telling Furl that I got robbed by so and so and the nigga who set it all up was Boo. I put the word out that Boo can't be around the way. Niggas wanted to kill Boo ass. I loved Boo, still love Boo so I couldn't green light him. However, the penalty for the shit Boo did was death. The niggas that did the robbery, I ain't mad at them. They owed me no loyalty. I robbed a few niggas in my day so I knew how it went. I started out playing with the pistol. So I see why Baltimore is always in the top 3 cities for the most homicides in a year. Niggas be doing dumb shit and will make you kill them.

In 2015, the year Freddie got killed, there were 344 Killings. A 63% increase from 2014. I'm not sure if the city ruled Freddie Gray death as a homicide, but I would guess they didn't. So 345 killings in 2015. Following Freddie's April death, the month of May pulled 42 murders. The last time the city seen that was in the hot summer month of August in 1990. June pulled in 29 and July jumped to 45 killings which made July the deadliest month since 1972. What's so crazy is Baltimore had 300,000 less people then it did in 1972. Shit always been crazy in Baltimore and a lot of people think the surge in violence came from the death of Freddie. I'm not one of the many people who believe that theory. Whatever happened after Freddie Gray's tragic death was going to happen regardless.

Every year in Baltimore when shit gets crazy, there's always some official, whether State or Federal, saying the violence was drug and gang related. So when Freddie died that was something for them to say that was the reason shit was happening at an alarming rate. My man Nick said I'm always saving niggas, he never understood the science behind my madness. If I listen to him, I would have been in prison for murder for hire charges and not for drug charges. He always said, "Better them than me," and didn't give a fuck. Speaking of Nick, we used to pick the kids up from school every day. I had to get Tone from school every day except for Mondays. So one day I went to pick up the kid's and I went to get some Chinese food. Nick was driving the rental Durango I had. Lou was in the passenger seat and me and Tone were in the back.

Earlier that day they had met the nigga White Boy, at the gas station. They got back in talking to each other about somebody they had to meet at 5:30 at Chinquapin Park on the basketball court. I always played dumb, scared and slow. That was my "mind game". So it was 2014 about 5 p.m. Nick was calling Ivan to get the joint (Gun), but he got no answer. Ivan was famous for not answering his phone. We were now in front of my Grandmother's house. "I'm about to run Tone in, I'll be right back," I told Nick and Lou. But Lou turned around and said, "Naw yo, we be back to get you". Lou looked me in my eyes and I felt something funny. So I said ok. I guess he thought I was trying to tag along, but I really wanted to drop them off. I knew what they were going to do. So I didn't want my rental in the area.

Me and Tone walked in and my Mother was in the dining room. Tone sat at the table and I went into the kitchen to get sum bowls for the food. By this time like 7 to 9 minutes had passed and the ride to the park was nothing but 2 minutes' tops. As I reached into the cabinet I heard BLOCKA, BLOCKA, BLOCKA, and thought, "Damn they had to wear something out" then heard like 10-15 more shots. Tone said, "Daddy where Lou and Nick go?" My mother looking at me, the shots sounded like they were out back. I knew they came from the Park. Then my iPhone rang. It was Nick, "Yo" I answered. "I'm hit yo come get me" Nick said. I yelled in the phone "y'all got the fucking rental". Then the phone hung up. I couldn't do anything but call an ambulance, so I told them somebody was shot at Chinquapin park on the basketball court. Tone and my mother looking at me like what the fuck and before I could get to the living room my mother yelled, "Don't you leave the fucking house!"

I went on the porch and minutes later my childhood friend JR came running down the alley saying, "Yo Lou up here hit! "and ran back up the alley. A few people who was out there ran up there. White Boy and some other people came out of nowhere. "Yo, what the fuck happened up there?" I yelled at White Boy. I didn't know what to do. I didn't have a gun at my grandmother's, no car and my mother was on my ass. Minutes later a black BMW truck hit the corner like Batman, heavy tint on it, windshield and all. As the truck flew up my block it took me too long to realize it was Kelly. I was fucking out of it, my mind was somewhere else and plus I thought her ass was at work about 15 minutes away. Later I found out that Lou got hit once by one of two shooters going back to get Nick, who was the target. Kelly was doing Lou's baby mother's hair when his baby mom got the call. So they both flew up there, picked Lou up and took him to the hospital. Lou was trying to make it to my grandmother's house but fell out a block over.

There's a bridge that connects to the park that will lead you to my side. Them Shooters wore Nick's ass out and he got hit like 10 times. I guess God was on his side. Nick said niggas was out there just looking. I wasn't surprised because them niggas was scared to death of Nick around here. If it wasn't for Mott's pulling up, his ass may have died out there. Nick got locked up some months later and didn't come home until July 2018 and he's now locked up today fighting gun and drug charges. Kelly said she didn't know what was going on, all she knew was we had just picked Tone up from school.

In BODYMORE, anybody can get it and if you looking like money, a Two-eleven can turn into a One eight seven. I'm not sure what happened to Washington DC officer Tony Mason, but he was gunned down on November 4th, 2017 in West Baltimore. It's a fact there's no picks when that gun gets raised. I remember when former Detective Momodu Gondo got his ass popped. This was in 2006 and at that time I knew Gondo, but we weren't cool as we became in 2016. Everybody knew he was a cop, and we all knew him before he became a cop. I would guess the Rabbit behind the gun didn't know Gondo was a cop. As Gondo was getting out of his blue 2003 Lexus LS430 with matching rims to go to his mother's house, he was shot. I see why whoever tried to rob him, he looked like a walking lick. I know when he got shot the whole hood was on fire. A Baltimore police officer shot in front of his house. You know they wanted answers.

When Jenkins became Gondo's boss years later, former Assistant State's Attorney Anna Mantegna told Jenkins to watch out for Gondo and his partner Jemell Rayam. Who we call Big Head, because she heard they were dirty cops. Mantegna was fired as Baltimore assistant state attorney for allegedly leaking info about the FBI investigation into the Gun Trace Task Force. I found everything the Government says hard to believe, because they lie so much. Mantegna further explained to Jenkins that Gondo became more dubious after he got shot. I would guess they thought Gondo was into some funny shit after he got shot but everybody around my way knew it was a robbery gone bad. It's crazy because the poor lady Mantegna said she was not the one to leak the news, about the F.B.I investigation into the G.T.T.F, to Jenkins.

The government's theory is that because Mantegna talked to Jenkins, who she was friends with, that it had to be her. The government has not presented any other evidence, other than she talked to Jenkins, to show that it was her. Leo Wise, the head prosecutor in my case and the G.T.T.F case said, "The best way to keep a secret is to keep a secret". Mantegna made a good point, she said how would she have known about the investigation to even tell Jenkins. I believe her, I also believe that it was a lying ass Detective by the name Ryan Guinn who leaked the news to Jenkins. Guinn was questioned by the F.B.I, most likely by Agent Erika Jensen, who was heading the investigation into the G.T.T.F and who interviewed Mantegna to see if she did leak the news of the investigation. The F.B.I questioned Guinn for information on Gondo, following up on what he said about Gondo in the past. Guinn went to Jenkins for more info on Gondo and told Jenkins that the F.B.I wanted to know. Guinn being so stupid and thirsty to tell the F.B.I shit, he went to ask the master mind of the police corruption (Jenkins) and told him the F.B.I was snooping around. Jenkins being the great detective he was, it was nothing for him to put two and two together and common sense would tell you that's how he knew.

Mantegna took the fall causing her to lose her job. This happens to people all the time. The government starts putting shit together without knowing 100% of what's really going on and the shit fucks people's lives up. Once the smoke cleared and everybody went to prison, internal affairs charged Guinn with tipping Jenkins off. In my eyes, Mantegna deserves her job back, but after getting fucked around by the government, who is famous for manipulating circumstances, she shouldn't even want her job back.

Anyway, I never understood how they used to come to the fact that Baltimore was the deadliest city when Chicago had way more killing going on. I found out that they go off the population of the city, then divide it by the homicides that City had that year. According to the FBI, the 342 homicides of 2017 was 56 per every 100,000 people that lived in Baltimore. The data is from the 2017 edition of the FBI's annual crime in the United States report, which relies on statistics reported by local law enforcement agencies. Baltimore had the worst homicide rate among the nation's 50 largest cities in 2017 and the second highest violent crime rate overall, according to the data from the FBI. I was of course at CDF the 2017 year and we were locking down at 9:30 to 9:45 every night, just in time for me to catch my news, that I watched every night that came on at 10 p.m. I have to catch the news at least once a day. It's a must I know what's happening in Baltimore. I was like that when I was home.

It was September 3rd 2017 and soon as the news came on they were live at the scene of a shooting. The reporter was saying there's been a shooting here at Canton, an area just outside of East Baltimore. It was a small ass block, and you can see the man's hat laying in the middle of the street, the reporter says. It was dark and rainy that Labor Day weekend and you could see the crime tape in the background as the reporter spoke. I sat watching the news thinking like damn who the fuck down Canton getting their ass wore out. When a person hears Canton they think of expensive homes and a few dozen places to get food and drinks, a big party scene. So to hear somebody got shot in those nice white people's neighborhood, I know that had them ready to skip town. Those white people try to get the bars in the area shut down about the noise, so just imagine how they reacted when somebody got shot.

They carried on when the news broke about who it was. That next morning, I called Kelly as I did every day, 50 times a day. The news she had for me, I'd never thought I would hear. "Georgie got killed last night," she said and that was truly paralyzing to hear. I asked where he was, not even thinking about the Canton thing I saw on the news. She said "Canton," I couldn't believe it for real though. I explained to her I was watching the news last night and saw that they were at the scene. "He had just called me like an hour before to see what I was doing," she said. Me and Kelly had just bought our house in August 2015 so we had a lot of get-togethers and cookouts and we hosted Thanksgiving that year and 2016, which Georgie, his wife and youngest daughter had stopped by.

I remember the Mannequin Challenge was out, so we all did the challenge and I loaded it up on my Instagram page (@TMC_YO). It was a Labor Day weekend, so knowing Georgie he was out and about looking for something to get into. I'm sure if I was home we would have had something at the house and Georgie knew that, which is why he called Kelly. If you ever were around me and heard me say something was paralyzing, it was because Georgie used to say it and it rubbed off on everybody. It's like since I've been locked up I see things differently, and if I was using my higher self when I was home I would have seen things going south. I call Georgie "The Mayor of Baltimore." It wasn't a person that hadn't heard of him. You heard the phrase, "That's the Big Homie" right? Well he was the Biggest Homie. And the respect people had for him went through the roof. It's always a pusillanimous that takes a Good Man from us. We damn near did it all, from fucking up local clubs in Baltimore, to Vegas Mayweather/Pacquiao Shit. It was nothing but a pleasure to be in the man's presence and anybody will tell you that.

To Antoine "Georgie" Rich, Got Damn Slim Man. You know this shit hurts, I know you in another life balling. The yacht we were on was sinking when we were out there, and we were either too blind, drunk or high to notice. It was nothing but love over here and you will be truly missed. REST In Peace, Slim!

It was now October 30, 2017 and we were in our 11th day of trial. When I walked in the courtroom, I looked up in the stands and seen Kelly with a shirt that said "Happy Birthday" and my family held homemade signs that read "Happy Birthday, Tony!" I was turning 32 years old and despite being in the middle of a battle that was designed for me to lose, I felt good seeing my family showing love. *The United States of America vs. Antonio Shropshire,* I sat there thinking how the fuck I get myself into a situation like this. I quickly snapped out of it because we were at the end of the trial and I didn't want to miss a beat.

We thought the jury was going to start deliberating that day, but they wasn't going to start until the 31st. I thought getting a "not guilty" on your birthday would be the shit but that thought turned into one hell of a day for a verdict. It was a jury of 11 white people and 1 black person, mostly women. I wasn't sure what deliberation meant so I looked it up in the dictionary and it said the meaning was (1) determined after careful thought; (2) done or said intentionally; (3) un-hurried, slow. I thought damn, I never knew the correct meaning and they damn sure didn't determine my fate after "careful thought".

When we all got back in the transport van, Twan said "Lil Tay got killed earlier." "How you know?" He said "I read somebody's lips on the way out the courtroom" I felt confused! Does Twan know what he talking about? What the fuck was going on in my life? It wasn't just about "Georgie" and "Lil Tay" but about everything that was going on. We all were in different units so when I walked on the unit, I heard a lot of different voices yelling "Yo what happened today" or "Yo they was talking about y'all on the news." I kept walking though the unit, headed straight to my pod. When I got on the pod, a white boy, well I don't know his race but he claims to be a gypsy that spoke **10** different languages, handed me the twix birthday cake I asked him to make for me.

I wasn't in a celebrating mood and my head was pounding from Kelly who confirmed the news about Lil Tay. I asked what happened and she said "He was out Cedonia and somebody shot him around 2 o'clock today." It's now April 6th, 2020 and when I think about everything I've been through, it leads me back to the Epiphany I had back in December 2016. Lil Tay was the cousin of Damoe, and I will never forget he was one of the ones to raise me. When I first met Lil Tay it was at Damoe house and Tay was a kid, so I was one of the many guys who literally watched Tay grow from a boy to a man. I spent years out Cedonia and when I stopped hanging out there, I never lost contact with Tay or any of the good men out there. Me and Tay spent endless time together whether it was just us riding, smoking and joking, or at the club together. I remember back in 2002 when Druid Hill Park used to be jumping on Sunday's in the summer.

Me and Damoe used to have Tay with us trying to get him to drink. Tay was young as shit and would never hit the drink. Damoe used to come to the trial with Mike, Furl's brother, who I call my little brother. Twan was just telling Damoe to tell Tay to come down to the trial. Until this day the guys out Cedonia are a part of my extended family and played a major part in who I am today, especially Damoe. Every year when my birthday comes around, how could I not think about Tay? Shit I think about him way more often than that. Every time he saw me he would grab one of my stomach rolls and say "Brill look at your fat ass". Somebody killed the man 2 o'clock in the afternoon on the same block I remember hustling on as a kid.

To my brother Dontay "Lil Tay" Parker, I love you Lil brother and you will forever be missed. I will celebrate your life every time I go to celebrate another year above ground.

It's so crazy because shit be happening and after a while we think nothing of it and just move past it as if it never happened. It's not a night that goes by that I don't think about everything that has happened since I've been locked up. I'm so fucked up about how shit played out. As I learned it's all part of God's plan and I used to think some shit just wouldn't happen. I bet when COVID-19 hit, your ass didn't think you'll be out of work now did you? Things are beyond crazy and I think now is the time you get some kind of understanding with Allah, the lord of the worlds.

It was December 7, 2017 and I called Kelly. I'm so sure I drove that lady crazy with all the shit I put her through. She pressed five to accept the call and said "Travis got killed earlier. "All I could do was shake my head. My grandmother came to see me when I first got to CDF and she was an OG to it all. She went through this federal shit with my Uncle Rodney and her brother was a gangster for real. He used to keep the 38 in the Bible, so it wasn't nothing new under the sun for her. She was so happy to see me and started telling me about how she used to see trucks pull up and stop in front of her house. She said "Them white men used to look over at me when I used to be on the porch and I used to call you to see where you were, you remember? I would call you and you will say you over west Baltimore and I will say not to come around here." Then she said "God put you here for a reason." Had to be realist shit I heard at the time.

I asked Kelly where Travis was and she said "Around the Alameda Shopping center". Right then and there, what my grandmother said went ringing through my head. Travis getting killed hurt the worse out of everybody I lost since I've been gone. He was younger than me and lived a block over from my grandmother's house and we grew up together. He wasn't my cousin but we called each other cousins, but it was more like blood brothers. Travis' uncle and my Uncle Rodney grew up together. I think they were co-defendants in their federal case. Our families were like family. If I wasn't over west Baltimore, then I was in Da North with Travis. I very well could have been out there with him that night. I was really lost for words when it came to Travis. I had talked to a friend of mine around the time and she was saying how sorry she was to hear about Travis and was asking how I was doing.

Travis was my heart and I'm sure it stops at some point. She was telling me that the last time she saw me, I was with Travis and I was high as shit. I'm sure I was high off weed mixed with either lean or perks. I told her I don't remember. She said, "I bet you don't," then said it was right before I got locked up and it's a video of me and him on my Instagram page from that night. It's a damn shame I don't remember and I was told the video is there and I can't wait to see it. For all I know that may be the last time I saw Travis. He was the super go hard type and backing down wasn't an option.

I don't know what happened that day but I feel responsible. I feel responsible for anybody in my neighborhood that something happened to. I was dealing with a lot of shit going on in that neighborhood. Today, me and the guys I came up with helped pave the way so when shit happened to my loved ones around there, I feel at fault. I always felt like it was my place to see to it that everybody that was around me was OK. Travis' grandmother ended up dying a few weeks later and I'm sure it was from a broken heart.

"To my heart, Travis Carter, I will be home one day and I will make sure your son is ok. You know I love you and I wish things wasn't this way."

I remember going to see the nurse some weeks later and I was in the hallway talking to my man Barney and a female correctional officer came to me and said, "I'm glad you're here." I looked at her confused and she continued, "Not like that, but I always see your Instagram post on the explore page and everybody you were around is getting killed." I couldn't do anything but agree with her. Then she said "You seem like a good dude, just thought I'd share that with you." 2017 was a motherfucka for me and I hope one day I can forget it all.

Being from Baltimore, Maryland or should I say Bodymore Murderland, it's a whole different type of motherfucka. That city is the creator of a fucked up day, week, month, year or rest of your life. In the city of crabs (as I heard many times before) there will always be at least one person that will pull you back down if you try to climb out of that bucket. If you can survive Baltimore, you can survive anywhere. Makes me wonder what happened to the 300,000 more people Baltimore had in 1972. A lot of killing comes from retaliation from some shit the person got killed, or did or just from being disrespectful. I'm sure you heard it was over a basketball game where somebody stepped on somebody's shoe etc. It wasn't the incident; it was what was said or done after the incident happened.

We don't live in the times where people fight and it's over what somebody says or puts their hands on you. Their ass is getting smoked, period! It's a fucked up world we live in and things shouldn't be that way, but they are. Nobody wants to be on the wrong side of the gun, so it's a get you before you get me game. In 2016 it was 318 murders, 2018 at 309 in 2019 brought in 348, so this is an every year thing. The Bodymore Police Department started analyzing information about 2019 murder victims and suspects. The information revealed that people with criminal history were killing people with a criminal history. My son could have told them that 81.4% of the suspects had prior records, 60.5% had previous drug arrests, 44.2% had been arrested for gun crimes and 12.8% were prior homicide suspects. Shit goes down in my town.

All I can say is please be-more-careful next time. 2020 brought in 335 murders, 13 fewer than the previous year. But 2020 set a record for the most women killed in a year, with 48 future Queens being taken away, truly sad. The year of 2021 doesn't seem to be creasing fire. As of May 1, 2021, there has been 138 murders, up to 8 from the same time in 2020. From the looks of things, there will be another troubling year of 300 plus murders for the great city of Bodymore, I mean Baltimore.

According to the Government

Members of the conspiracy known to law enforcement as the Shropshire Drug Trafficking Organization, distributed Narcotics in Northern Baltimore and elsewhere. Members of the conspiracy primarily distributed heroin around or near the Alameda Shopping Center in Baltimore, Maryland. Members of the conspiracy distributed heroin to customers which resulted in multiple overdoses; including overdose deaths. Members of the conspiracy utilized residences within Baltimore, Maryland to process, cut, repackage, and prepare heroin for distribution to customers. Members of the conspiracy routinely carried firearms in furtherance of the conspiracy conducted counter-surveillance of law enforcement in an attempt to prevent law enforcement from detecting the illegal activities carried out by the Shropshire Drug Trafficking Organization.

Members of the conspiracy removed, caused to be removed, or assisted others in removing law enforcement GPS tracking devices from vehicles so that, members of law enforcement could not track the movements of the organization. Which then could disclose locations of sources of supply ("stash") locations where narcotics were stored, locations of firearms, and other criminal activities involving members of the conspiracy. Members frequently changed cell phones, used to arrange narcotic sales, so that law enforcement would be unable to intercept illicit communications involving members of the conspiracy. It was further part of the conspiracy that, Baltimore Police Department- Detective Momodu Gondo, provided sensitive law enforcement information to other members of the Shropshire Drug Trafficking Organization.

In order to prevent law enforcement from disrupting or dismantling the organizations Narcotics trafficking operations and further to protect Gondo's co-conspirators. Investigators say that Antonio "Brill" Shropshire, led a drug crew that emerged as the largest suppliers of Heroin to suburban Baltimore and Harford counties. Captain Lee Dunbar, who investigates overdoses for the Harford County Sheriff's office said, "More than 60 people overdosed and 15 died from heroin supplied by Shropshire's crew". A confidant source told Baltimore County Police Detectives Grant and Kilpatrick that "Brill, commonly gives his phones to other individuals to facilitate his drug organization when he isn't around and is the largest Heroin dealer around. He has been selling Heroin for over 10 years".

The list of allegations are endless and if you ask me, this is all one big misunderstanding. According to the government, I have been under investigation from 2013 up until my arrest in November 2016. Before I go any further, let's get something straight, I sold Heroin, NOT conspired to sell Heroin (which is a big difference in my situation). Under Federal Law 21 U.S.C and 846, requires proof beyond a reasonable doubt of three elements: (1) An agreement between two or more persons to engage in conduct that violates a federal drug law; (2) The defendant's knowledge of the conspiracy; (3) The defendant's knowing and voluntary participated in the conspiracy. Proof of a conspiratorial agreement need not be by direct evidence and rather may be proven inferentially and by circumstantial evidence.

In December 2015, my co-defendant Antoine Washington A.K.A "Twan" was arrested and charged with Possession with Intent to Distribute and Distribution of Heroin Resulting in Death. In May 2016, his brother Alexander Campbell A.K.A "Munch" was arrested and charged with Washington. The government charged both of them with "conspiracy to distribute" a kilogram or more of Heroin. In November 2016, Omari Thomas A.K.A "Lil Brill" and I were charged in a Second Superseding Indictment with Washington and Campbell. In February 2017, Glen Wells A.K.A. "Lou" and Detective Momodu Gondo A.K.A "G-Money" were charged in a Third Superseding Indictment with the rest of us. So, these guys are my charged co-defendants and we are all charged with conspiracy to distribute Heroin from 2010-2017 (the time of the last person arrested).

This is what the government calls "The Shropshire Organization". This is the government's theory. I am going to tell you the truth. One thing about the government, if they don't have the facts, they will make them up and when it came down to my case- that's exactly what Assistant Attorney Leo Wise and Derek Hines did.

As the first story ran in the Baltimore Sun Paper: "Federal Trial to Open against Alleged Heroin Ring Protected by Baltimore Police Detective". I learned more and more about the case. I started to put it all together, while picking it apart at the same time. According to multiple sources, this all started over people overdosing in Baltimore and Harford Counties. According to Captain Lee Dunbar, who investigates overdoses for Harford County Sheriff's Office, more than 60 people overdosed and 15 died from Heroin supplied by "Shropshire's Crew". Let me tell you the truth. Nobody overdosed on Heroin I sold. This is all one big coincidence and instead of clearing things up or catching the people behind the overdoses, they put it on me and my purported crew.

I remember a lot of people use to ask for the yellow Heroin (fentanyl) and the guys working for me use to say; "Everybody wanting this yellow dope". I did some investigating and found out it was coming out of my neighborhood. So what would happen was, people would call one of the many phones I had asking for this yellow dope. After somebody would tell them we didn't have it, they would either call and find it or get a call from the people with it, and would overdose. After that, somebody would call 911 about their overdose. Baltimore or Harford County would take and download the victim's phone to get their call history, contacts, text messages, etc. So because my name, amongst others, were ringing bells, they suspected that I was responsible. They would check the victim's call history and see the name "Brill", a name they had been hearing since they started the investigation and tried to put the pieces together.

What made it worse was people used to lie and say they worked for me so people could buy dope from them. The police thought people worked for me who really didn't. I know for a fact nobody overdosed off dope I sold because I cut every gram I received. I also never sold Fentanyl, didn't want the problems it came with. But in the end I still had problems. Harford county is right off 95, North of Baltimore City. As another story ran in the Baltimore Sun, "Police say the Drug Crew Led by Antonio "Brill" Shropshire emerged as the Largest Supplier of Heroin to Suburban Baltimore and Harford Counties." Due to the fact that Northeast Baltimore is the first exit off 95 coming from Harford County, it was the first stop for drug users. It's a fact that, D.E.A task force officer McDougall, ran through Northeast Baltimore arresting most of all northeast's Heroin dealers that sold to Harford Counties drug users. I know 15 guys that are either in Federal Prison or have pending Federal charges that stem from McDougall's investigations.

As the indictment came out, that added Wells and Gondo, I couldn't understand it. Those were huge allegations and I was dying to know how they were going to prove it. Gondo never once provided sensitive law enforcement information to me or ever prevented law enforcement from locking me up. I knew Gondo from Wells, as I explained, I knew from Nick and hanging on their block. I don't remember how we got cool. I do remember people saying, "You fucking with the Police"? I guess they didn't look at it like I did. I was always into something, whether I was in the North, over West, or in "Pigtown" (South Baltimore). I had something going on. I knew Gondo worked multiple sides of town, so I didn't want Gondo to think I didn't fuck with him because he was a cop. Furthermore, I didn't consider meeting Gondo at 3 D.C. clubs and being at the same dinner party, "hanging out". I never heard anything or seen "Gondo" doing anything but being the detective he was. He even had the cop breath and all.

One time, years ago (2012-2013), I was at the Havana Club which was over top of the Ruth Chris Steakhouse in downtown Baltimore. Nick G and I bumped into Gondo at the bar and his breath was smelling just how cops breath smells. I had enough cops in my face to know the smell, trust me. When he left, I turned to Nick G and said, "You smell yo breath? He got that cop breath"! Nick G fell out laughing and ever since then we called Gondo "Cop Breath". The shit is still funny till this day. When I heard all that Gondo was accused of doing, I wasn't surprised. But, I really had no idea. If I knew he was into that, it really would have been a "Shropshire Organization" and I wouldn't be so mad about what the Government put together.

Once the news broke, Wise really put on as show as if Gondo really played a part in what I was doing. As I explained, there was a period of time that "Twan" and "Munch" worked for me (2007-2009), but it all ended when I came home in July of 2009. I have no knowledge of Wells and Gondo's relationship because when we were together we didn't talk about "Cop Breath". As I explained, the three indictments came out as separate. First, Twan and Munch, then Omari and I, and lastly Lou and Gondo. If this was one big conspiracy going for 6-7 years, why were we charged the way we were? There are over 3500 wiretap calls and I'm not on one talking to anybody about drugs. There was a lot of surveillance during the 3-year investigation. Including pole cameras and physical surveillance. They used GPS, traps, and traces, pen registers, and caller identification features. I will explain what all of them do if I didn't already.

Long story short, there is no physical evidence that I had conspired with these men. The government's case was built off a jail call between Twan and Munch, where Twan said: "When I get home, I'm getting the team back. You, Brill, and Lou". This took place in December 2015, when Twan was the only one locked up. The government kept replaying that call. During the trial, that's the only thing they had to go off. I have no idea what Twan was talking about. Twan and I barely talked when he was home. The only thing the Government had to go off when it came to me and Gondo, was the wiretap call when I called him about the GPS I found on March 31, 2016. Gondo's testimony during the trial wasn't about this big conspiracy where he protected members of the purported "Shropshire organization."

Gondo testified about a home invasion that "allegedly" he, Lou, and Detective Rayam did. Gondo said he provided Lou with law enforcement information and that he "allegedly" told him that Lou and I sold drugs. Gondo also said that Lou didn't get into great detail about it. He believes I sold drugs because his "police training" led him to believe so. What kind of shit was that? Gondo testified that he never seen me sell drugs so, that would make clear that he had no knowledge if I sold drugs or not. His police training is not having knowledge of an agreement to sell drugs as required by 21 U.S.C 846. There was no evidence that Lou and I ever sold drugs together. I sat at this trial in disbelief. I can't understand how these people are able to do the shit they doing. If I was fucking with Gondo, Lou, Twan, and Munch I would just say it.

During the whole trial I sat there saying "What the fuck that got to do with me?" in my best "Big Worm" from Friday voice. The Government had nothing to hoot and holla about, so the jail call and the GPS call was their go to. If you found a GPS on your car, what would you do? I'm going to assume I should call the police right? Well that's what I did. I didn't call 911 but, I thought about it. Then I thought, why call 911 when you know the police. People do it all the time. Something may happen and they call their cousin or uncle who's a police officer to get advice. I didn't call Gondo knowing he was involved in shit he wasn't supposed to be involved in. I called him because he was a cop. Yeah, I was a drug dealer and knew to check for GPS but, that's beside the point. I've heard about guys putting GPS on people's cars so they could find out where you live then rob the shit out of you. I didn't call 911 because they would have been all in my business. I knew I was a known drug dealer to them.

What pissed me off the most was the government put out there that it was the GPS call that led them to Gondo, which then led them to the Gun Trace Task Force. The "G.T.T.F", was an elite gun recovery unit for the Baltimore City Police Department that Gondo and 6 or 7 other federally indicted officers were members of. I assure you two things: First, I have no reason to lie. Second, that's not how the F.B.I got on to Gondo or the G.T.T.F. Once the story broke about my case and Gondo's "alleged" role, journalists started to reach out to me about my relationship with Gondo. There was Jessica Lussenhop from the "BBC News", Baynard Woods- a Criminal Justice reporter, Justin Fenton and Tim Prudente both from the "Baltimore Sun". They all had questions. I explained to all of them "Cop Breath" and I relationship was parties, drinks, and girls. I'm not sure if the journalist believed me or not but I'm sure they didn't.

After the government's uncorroborated theories got out there, it's hard to convince someone otherwise. Now follow me, because I'm going to prove to you that the F.B.I was already on Gondo before I called him about the GPS. The government's indictment claimed Gondo was protecting the "alleged Shropshire Organization" that came out in late February, early March of 2017. I'm not sure how many articles there were but Tim Prudente wrote 5-7 articles right before the trial started and during the trial. Justin Fenton wrote in the "Baltimore Sun" on February 13, 2019 issue (which was right after Gondo's sentencing) that, "It was Gondo's contacts with a North Baltimore drug crew that led investigators to the corrupt police unit.

Harford County Police investigated a rash of drug overdose cases. They listened in on a drug dealer's phone (which was me) when they learned he was speaking to Gondo". You have to keep in mind who was on this elite unit. You had Wayne Jenkins, Daniel Hersl, Maurice Ward, Evodio Hendrit, Jemell Rayam, and Momodu Gondo, all who are known by internal affairs. It was like one big set up having all of them in one unit in the first place. In October of 2015 (according to what Jessica Lussenhop was told by lead case Agent David McDougall and also what Gondo testified to) Gondo placed a GPS on "Aaron Anderson's" car. Aaron Anderson A.K.A "Black Aaron" was from "The Alameda" as well. His rat ass wasn't from my block or from my co-defendants block, but from another block in the area. "Black Aaron" testified at my trial that "somebody" broke into his house. That he knew all of us from the neighborhood and that he sold Heroin to "Twan" a handful of times.

I remember seeing "Black Aaron" and he told me that somebody broke into his house and what they took. He said if I hear something to let him know. I didn't have any problems with Aaron. I actually tried to keep him out of prison. Once, there was this one white guy named John Riffey A.K.A "JR" that I knew worked with the police and I knew Aaron and Twan used to sell "JR" Heroin. So I, being the nice guy I am, told Aaron and Twan not to fuck with "JR" because he put me on with the undercover police. Now, I didn't fuck with Twan because of his past actions and Aaron and I never were friends but, one of them tells "JR" what I said. I couldn't believe it.

Anyway, I told Aaron "Sure, if I hear something, I'll let you know". Of course, I would have done no such thing. I could have cared less what happened to him. So, come to find out, Aaron was under investigation by the same people that had me under investigation and they locked him up 2 weeks after someone broke into his apartment. Also, Aaron been was a rat and was working with a Baltimore City Detective. When McDougall arrested Anderson, one of McDougall's colleagues went to recover a GPS that he (McDougall) placed on Anderson's car. He found another GPS other than the one he had been sent to recover. According to Lussenhop's story, McDougall found that to be funny because to his knowledge, Anderson wasn't being investigated by any other agency because it didn't say so in the database. McDougall checked, as if it's going to say somebody is under investigation every time. McDougall subpoenaed the company that manufactured the "Mystery GPS". It came back to be owned by John Clewell. McDougall found out that Clewell was a Baltimore City Detective who was working with the "G.T.T.F."

According to the story, McDougall then formed a rough theory about what happened at Anderson's house. McDougall's theory was that a Baltimore officer used the tracker, waited until Anderson's vehicle was far away from his home, then used the opportunity to rob his apartment. According to the story, it was the kicked in door, the methodically tossed apartment, and the GPS that belonged to an officer and the fact it didn't say Anderson was under investigation, that led McDougall to believe it was police officers who robbed Anderson's apartment. I talked with Ms.Lussenhop through email and she told me she came to my sentencing. She did, in fact, talk with McDougall who told her this bullshit. Please tell me that McDougall's alleged theory wasn't a load of bullshit.

When I read the story, I damn near hit the floor reading it. Why would McDougall lying, Jimmy Neutron looking ass, out of nowhere, think that Baltimore City officers were the ones who robbed "Black Aaron"? McDougall "allegedly" called the F.B.I in December of 2015. The F.B.I came to Baltimore City Detective Ryan Guinn, who had previously worked with Gondo and his partner Jemell Rayam. Guinn was also with detectives Wayne Jenkins and the late Sean Suiter when they framed a guy named Umar Burley.

Guinn told the F.B.I he saw me and Gondo at Mo's (a famous seafood restaurant in downtown Baltimore) and Gondo told me Guinn was cool. Which made him feel uncomfortable and he recognized me and he was pretty sure I recognized him.

Everybody knows Mo's is a food spot that all the Dope Boys and wanna-be dope boys hang out at every day of the week. So first, why would Guinn be there? Second, why would I go there with Gondo? And third, Gondo did not party or hang out in Baltimore, so it's no way Gondo would have gone to Mo's with me. Guinn's story just don't add up. This is small shit and if I was at Mo's with Gondo and we saw Guinn, somebody I don't know, I would just say it but I was never at Mo's with Gondo. This man Guinn is a got damn lie and if anybody knows this coward, tell him I said, "KEEP MY MOTHERFUCKING NAME OUT HIS MOUTH"! The only restaurant I was at, that Gondo was at, is STK in Washington, D.C. and we didn't come together. It was a guy from the neighborhood's dinner party.

This took place in 2016. It's a lot of fishy shit going on and they got me caught up in the middle of it. So on March 14, 2016, Leo Wise filed for a warrant to place a "Pen Register" and caller identification feature on Gondo's phone. All this stuff happened before the March 31, 2016 GPS call to Gondo. So why is the Government telling people it was the GPS call that led them to Gondo, who led them to the "G.T.T.F"?

It was brought to my attention that they put it all on me to cover Clewell and Guinn so, they don't get "Blacked Balled" by other officers for telling on Gondo. At some point, Clewell had to get pulled up by the F.B.I about the tracker and I'm sure he told them he gave it to Gondo. Let me explain this again. In October of 2015, McDougall called the F.B.I about the G.P.S he found on Black Aaron's car, that belonged to Clewell, a member of the G.T.T.F. Somewhere down the line, McDougall teamed up with Wise, and on March 14, 2016, Wise filed a warrant to place a pen register on Gondo's phone. On March 31, 2016, I called Gondo about the G.P.S I found on my car, they know this because my phone was tapped. So can somebody please tell me, how the fuck was it the March 31, 2016 G.P.S call, I made to Gondo, that led the government to him? Them people was already up Gondo's ass, and they trying to put it on me. This is clear evidence, that the government and law enforcement will lie and mislead anybody to believe the shit they want you to believe. Its people who has been following the G.T.T.F and my case since day one, and they all believe that the G.P.S call is how they got onto Gondo, which is how they got on to the G.T.T.F. Now you got the six hour limited series show "We Own This City", which is being filmed in Baltimore, and is to be aired on HBO. The show is based on the book "We Own This City." Clearing this up won't change anything with my case but, don't mislead the people to believe it was the GPS call when it wasn't. According to Gondo, it was Twan who bought the idea to rob Anderson to Lou. Then Lou brought the idea to Gondo. I don't know what happened because I wasn't there. Lou and I didn't talk about our business when we were together so, when I heard Gondo say that, I was just as surprised as everyone else. It was the Government's job to prove I was involved in this conspiracy, the home invasion, and the overdose of "J.L" back in December 2011. If there is any truth to what Gondo said about the home invasion, why didn't he just get the GPS off Anderson's car? The GPS wasn't found until October 19, 2015 and the robbery happened on the 5th, so Gondo had a lot of time to get the GPS, and had he got the GPS they would not have found it and maybe, just maybe the F.B.I wouldn't have got involved.

The evidence the jury heard was from 13 drug addicts that testified to buying drugs from Twan, Munch, Omari, and I. There was one witness Leon Koger A.K.A "JB", who is from East Baltimore but was hanging around McCabe (which is in Northeast Baltimore). JB got indicted with a lot of other guys including: Charles "Big Head Charlie" Galliker and JB told everything he knew about his friends, then got the bright idea to lie to the Government that he was there when I bought drugs from "Big Head Charlie". Now, it wasn't until after Georgie got killed (which was 2 months before the trial) that JB told the Government he was there when I bought drugs from Georgie. This, man JB, is a mothafucka and I hope he goes straight to hell fire.

Out of the 13 drug addicts, all of them said they bought drugs from me; 6 said they bought from Twan; 5 of them bought from Munch; and 9 of them bought from Omari "allegedly". The Government presented no evidence that I sold anybody drugs but two of the witnesses. The jury heard them say they bought drugs and found us guilty. Nobody said we worked together. Just that they bought drugs from us. In fact, Benjamin Waldman testified that Twan and Munch both made it clear in 2010, they didn't work with me. Let me ask you a question. If somebody testifies that they bought cheeseburgers from McDonalds on Monday, Tuesday, and Friday and then bought burgers from Burger King on Wednesday and Sunday and both McDonalds and Burger King right across the street from each other, would that mean they conspired to sell that witness burgers? I would hope you said, of course not.

Well then why am I guilty of conspiracy then? As I explained, I'm not saying I didn't sell drugs. I'm saying I didn't conspire to sell drugs with these men. It was the government's theory that we all sold heroin together near

"The Alameda" and Gondo protected us. The government proved multiple conspiracies and when they did that, under Federal Law, they failed to prove the changed conspiracy. The government proved four different conspiracies and not the one they charged. I had multiple people selling heroin for me from 2010-2016 and none of my co-defendants were any of them. The whole shit was confusing to the jury. Had they been able to put aside the fact I sold heroin, they would have seen I didn't conspire with these men.

The Fourth Circuit Court of Appeals says, "A court need only instruct (the jury) on multiple conspiracies if such an instruction is supported by the facts (of the case)" see United States V. Mills 995 F. 2d 480, 485 (4th Cir 1993). The court instructs the jury regarding their duty, should they find that two or more conspiracies have been proved and must find the defendants not guilty of these conspiracies. It's rare that the trial judge would give defendants multiple conspiracy jury instructions, but guess what? The honorable Judge Blake gave us a "multiple conspiracy instruction!" The government didn't have me on conspiracy charges, but here I am. The case had a lot of loopholes and the government got a lot of shit with them. Our case was originally in front of Judge James Bredar but, somewhere down the line (two months before trial) my case, the "G.T.T.F" case, and "The Thomas Finnegan" case went to Judge Catherine Blake.

Now the reason for this, according to the court order, "The undersigned will assume the role of Chief Judge in District. The Chief Judge carries a reduced caseload in comparison to that of the active judges". On October 6, 2017 the current Chief Judge, the honorable Catherine C. Blake, will resume regular active service with a full caseload. After consultation and to assist in the appropriate adjustments of these caseloads, the clerk is directed to transfer these matters from Judge Bredar to Judge Blake, effective immediately. What I didn't understand was how "somebody's" caseload was getting reduced if Blake got three of Bredar's cases, and Bredar got three of Blake's cases? I know this because four trials started on October 16, 2017.

The vast majority of federal criminal cases are resolved through guilty pleas. In fiscal year 2018, nearly 90% of federal criminal defendants nationwide pled guilty. Within Maryland's Fourth Circuit, the percentage is even greater (96.4%). If more guys fight their federal cases, the federal system would collapse. Have you ever heard Trump talk about when the Democrats were in office, they didn't have that many Federal Judges? Trump always talks about how he got more Judges sitting in. It's not that many Judges and if more guys were to buck at the system, I believe the Government would act like they got some sense. Anyway, I knew the case got switched because the 3 guys and I were all in the same unit. They all had Blake and I had Bredar. Then the switch happened and they got Bredar. What I found to be funny was that I read, with my own two eyes, a court document (from Bredar) saying he didn't trust anything Daniel Hersl says.

This document was one of Bredar's opinions on an unrelated case. Two of the Government's key witnesses were two of Hersl's co-defendants, former Detectives Gondo and Rayam. Defense attorney Marshall Henslee, who represented "Lou", objected to Gondo's and Rayam's testimony. Arguing amongst other things that Gondo and Rayam are not credible. My hypothesis is, the Government knew Bredar may not have been on board with Gondo and Rayam testifying, so they switched Judges. Everybody knew Gondo and Rayam lied to juries, prosecutors, and judges. So do you think Bredar would have allowed them to testify? Or do you think he would have agreed with Henslee's motion to exclude Gondo and Rayam's testimony because they were not credible? There was a lot of funny shit going on so, I made it my business to express as much as I could at sentencing; without ruffling the Judge's feathers.

Judge Blake: "Mr. Shropshire, if there is anything you would like to say, you certainly have the right to do that (you don't have to). I wouldn't hold it against you, if you didn't. But if you want to speak, you have the right to speak."

Shropshire: "I have a few things I would like to address. First, Mr. Alfred did a great job with what he had. I had four different attorneys through this process and Mr. Alfred came in, about two months before the trial, so it isn't really much that he knew about the trial or the discovery (I would say more so). I was able to review the discovery through Judy, the Paralegal. She came down a number of times. Lawyers didn't come see me. I understand they have very extensive workloads which is why they sent Judy. Anyways, I've reviewed this discovery from top to bottom. As you can see, I'm still here today reviewing this discovery. There are a lot of things that have been said that simply are not true. I have a few things, which I have written down, that I would like to discuss."

"Before I begin, Your Honor, I want to tell you that I have the utmost respect for you. I don't want you to think or take what I have to say as a sign of disrespect because it is not directed towards you. There are some things that need to be said that I'm not sure you are aware of. The fact that I have to go to jail for 10 plus years because of what somebody is saying, is injustice. It was the government's job to find out what was going on and they failed. There is no evidence that I sold or bought a kilo of heroin. The government is going off what someone told them. That is called "going off allegations". There is no reason that I should be spending 10+ years of my life in jail because of "he said, she said".

"Mr. Leon Koger is an opportunist. He is a liar, drug addict, gang member, and a murderer. When Mr. Koger heard I was charged, he saw a window of opportunity to get less time by lying on me. Mr. Koger was "allegedly" a part of a charged conspiracy with Mr. Galliker and a number of others. In Mr. Koger's grand jury testimony, he stated that Mr. Charles Galliker sold me drugs for seven to eight years, and said nothing about Antoine Rich A.K.A "Georgie". But at trial, Mr. Koger testified to a completely different story. Since Mr. Rich was shot and killed on September 2, 2017, which I'm sure Mr. Koger heard about, he saw another window of opportunity to tell more lies. During the trial, Mr. Koger testified, that over the summer of 2016, I bought drugs from him, Mr. Galliker, and Mr. Rich."

"I was under investigation since 2015 and the government presented no evidence that would suggest that I purchased any drugs from these men. Not to mention, Mr. Koger and Mr. Galliker were under investigation during the same time. So between the two government investigations going on, why is there NO EVIDENCE to suggest Mr. Koger (who's an opportunist, liar, drug addict, gang member, and murderer) is telling the truth? There is no evidence to corroborate the testimony of Mr. Koger. Science tells us now that the view of human memory is fundamentally flawed. The mind, not only, distorts and embellishes memories but a variety of external factors can affect how memories are retrieved and described."

"For example, Corporal McDougall testified during trial that I was arrested with $8,000 and Mr. Wise had to correct him because I was arrested with $5,000. It's a number of reasons that I can think of as to why Corporal McDougall testified falsely under oath but, I'm going to give him the benefit of doubt and assume, like science tells us, that the human mind fundamentally distorts and embellishes memories. The grand jury testimony of the government's witnesses were all inconsistent with what they testified to during my trial. My theory is, if you're telling the truth, it should only be one story to tell. Memory errors can be particularly problematic in judicial settings. There are several different types of memory errors, in which, people may inaccurately recall details of events that did not occur."

"During trial, 13 individuals testified that they are suffering from drug abuse, testified falsely, and are not trustworthy. One person identified Attorney Alfred Guillaume, as the person who sold her drugs. One person was honest enough to tell the court that he was "burnt out" and wasn't sure how many times he bought drugs. Mr. Taylor testified that he buys nothing less than 10 grams of Heroin but he was heard on the wiretap buying 2 grams of Heroin. It's crystal clear that he is a liar and embellishing about the amounts he purchased. Mr. Taylor also testified, he has the ability to remember numbers (again he was caught in his lies because he was on a wiretap saying he didn't remember Mr. Thomas number). Another witness said she didn't see the person who sold her drugs in the courtroom but, was able to identify a photo of me that Mr. Wise put on the screen, which was very leading and suspicious."

"As if I looked any different in person than the picture. Another witness stated, "All blacks look alike". One witness, Mr. Riffey, during his testimony stood up and said, "I can't do this," in which, Mr.

Wise told Mr. Riffey, "sit down, he's not finished". I believe that to be a form of pressuring Mr. Riffey to testify. During his testimony, Mr. Riffey testified that he lied to his probation officer, gave someone else urine, and has been doing so for two years. I believe he lies to his probation officer to stay out of jail and what makes court any different? Drugs are one of the external factors that can affect how memories are retrieved and described. There has been research showing heroin causing brain damage in a few different ways. It causes the structure of the reward system in the brain to no longer function normally."

I remember that commercial with the frying pan and the egg that says "This Is Your Brain on Drugs". So I don't see how 13 individuals, which at some point were pressured to testify and are suffering from brain damage from years of drug abuse, would know and testify truthfully how many times they may or may not have bought drugs over a 7-year period. I asked myself what I wore for Thanksgiving dinner seven days before I was arrested for this case back in 2016 and I honestly don't remember. Corporate McDougall doesn't do drugs, or so I would assume, and he had a hard time remembering what he wrote in his reports during trial and embellished about how much money I had during my arrest."

"My life is on the line and there is no room for error. Just as easy as it was for Corporal McDougall's mind to forget and embellish, it has to be even easier for drug addicts who have been threatened to testify and who are suffering from drug abuse to forget and embellish about drug transactions. The fact that all the government witnesses are drug addicts and their testimony has to be reviewed with caution (and their testimonies were inconsistent) without physical evidence to corroborate their testimony, lacks sufficient evidence of reliability. Several other Circuits have applied these commissions' sufficient indicia of reliability when it comes to drug addict testimonies in reference to drug quantity, especially if the testimony is inconsistent. (See United States VS. Mielie 989 3rd Circuit 1993; United States VS. Robinson 904 6th Circuit 1990; United States VS. Belier 20 7th Circuit; and United States VS. Simmons 964 8th Circuit 1992)."

"All vacating cases because of inconsistent drug addict testimonies about drug quantity. Also, Mr. Wise and Mr. Hines are liars. During trial, Mr. Hines told (Your Honor) that I had Mr. Anderson's watch and Mr. Wise wanted nothing to do with that. Mr. Wise is trying to enhance drug amounts based on a "hunch and speculation", not on specific evidence of Narcotic transactions. Under the United States sentencing guidelines, which instruct that where there is no drug seizure or the amount seized does not reflect the scale of the offence, the court shall approximate the quantity of the controlled substance. The only definite amount of Heroin established by the Government was 71 grams, which I am responsible for." "I am, also, responsible for my actions in counts 3 and 7. But with all due respect, Your Honor, I am not guilty of count 1."

Honestly, had I had my trial preparation material, that I had been gathering since my arrest and that I invariably requested for and experienced lawyer, I would have been found not guilty on the conspiracy count. I really picked this case apart and needed my material for the trial.

According to "We own this city" written by Justin Fenton, between October 15, 2015 – January 1, 2016 me and Gondo exchanged 99 telephone calls. Fenton got this information from search warrants/affidavits that were submitted on Gondo. As I explained, law enforcement misleads damn near every judge in their search warrant applications. So whoever wrote the search warrant on Gondo, which is funny because I'm mentioned in nearly all of them and never got a copy of any of them, lied to the judge, which misled that judge to believe we exchanged 99 calls. I'm very familiar with the evidence in my case and what I did and did not do. There were 19 pen register warrants signed in my case, which could suggest I talked with Gondo 99 times.

First of all, the numbers the government knew about pertaining to me, were either (1) phones used to talk to customers (2) Kelly and others, such as my barber or (3) my iPhone which at the October 2015 – January/2016 time was phone number 443-787-9071. I was paying my cousin to answer that phone, which I will explain more later. In other words, none of these phones would have been used to call Gondo on. One of the numbers the government had was the number of a guy who was running around pretending to work for me. Second, I went to trial and Fenton has spent countless hours reviewing the transcripts of my trial. So this question is for anyone who believes that I exchanged 99 calls with Gondo as mentioned in the warrants, why wasn't the evidence present at trial? The government has to prove beyond a reasonable doubt that I conspired with Gondo and if they had proof we exchanged that many calls, wouldn't you think they would have presented that evidence?

Not only does that evidence not exist, Gondo himself testified he never saw me selling drugs and it was his police training that led him to believe I sold drugs. So like I've been asking, when did I conspire with him?

Go to pacer.gov see for yourself. Everything that was said at my trial can be viewed on pacer, case # CCB-16-51 or 16-51. Gondo testimony can be found on docket 403, pages 83-153. According to "We own this city" Leo Wise said during an interview on February 21, 2018 that he knew Gondo was not funneling drugs he stole through the alleged drug crew. There was simply no evidence I was working with my co-defendants. Also According to Fenton's book, F.B.I Agent Jensen's idea was to let the wiretap on my phone do the work. The wiretap on my phone was from March-2016 – May 2016. Ask anybody that knows, that's a short time for a federal wiretap for the type of case the government claims was going on.

If this big conspiracy was going on, involving a Baltimore city detective (Gondo) who was allegedly protecting drug dealers, and if the wiretap, signed by Judge Richard D. Bennett was supposed to do the work, why didn't the wiretap run for more than 60 days? I tell you why, because the judge wanted to see evidence of the allegations and their lying asses could not present any, which in turn, the judge did not grant their request to extend the wiretap. The taped phone was still on, so why wouldn't the wiretap still be going. The reason why they didn't get any evidence was because the shit they alleged was not going on. "We own this city" is based on, in part, law enforcement reports. "LAW ENFORCEMENT HAS ENCOUNTER UNUSUALLY HIGH OCCURRENCE OF SETBACKS IN THESE ENDEAVORS" also written in reports, "INVESTIGATORS BELIEVE THAT SHROPSHIRE CONDUCTS HIMSELF IN A WAY THAT SUGGESTS HE RECEIVES INFORMATION FROM SOMEONE WHO HAS KNOWLEDGE OF LAW ENFORCEMENT TECHNIQUES".

I assure you a few things, I never told the government Gondo protected drug dealers from my neighborhood or that Gladstone stole $50,000 from Wells as stated in "We own this city". I talked about Gladstone stealing money in this book, but never said who he stole it from, so why would I tell the government that. I also never told the government what me and Gondo talked about outside of a Home Depot as stated in Fenton's book. I'm not surprised the government put words in my mouth and misled Fenton to believe that was true. They misled federal judges for a living, so who is Justin Fenton?

No law enforcement taught me ANYTHING, or provided me with any law enforcement information or helped me in any way, besides what I said Jenkins did. They just so use to niggas being so dumb, that when there's someone (me) that had enough sense to search the world wide web and study and learn different things about law enforcement, they think that person (me) got help. I'm on these people's ass about my freedom, so don't be surprised if you see me one-day walking down the street whistling the Andy Griffin theme.

WE LIVING WITH CORRUPTION

In 1983, 14-year-old Witt Docket walked to school in his Baltimore neighborhood. Somebody shot and killed him for his Georgetown jacket and it wasn't Alfred Chestnut, Ransom Watkins, or Andrew Stewart. Between the hidden evidence, corrupt prosecutors, being black, and a non-deliberating jury, the three men didn't have a chance. One of the men did in fact have the same Georgetown jacket as Witt Docket, but this jacket had no blood, no bullet holes and came with a receipt. Yes! The mother of the convicted man had the receipt for the jacket she bought her son. I guess the jury fell asleep when the receipt was presented into evidence. For years the court sealed documents, but public records requests revealed the Baltimore city prosecutors hid evidence. The hidden evidence pointed to another teen that was shot and killed about 20 years ago. The Judge had released the three innocent men and apologized on behalf of the 1983 criminal Justice system.

Baltimore City has been dealing with corruption for a very long time and it's very much still going on today. From city hall to police officers down to correctional officers and the city had seen its share. The justice department learned and said that all levels of the Baltimore police department had not implemented fundamental principles of community policing. It's funny how officials and different departments claim what they do is for the community but don't listen to the people in them. Like did it take the D.O.J to be going through some reports to realize that's what was going on in African American communities. What the fuck they thought was going on; since forever. In 1964, Baltimore police officers illegally searched and terrorized African Americans residents' homes looking for "The Veney Brothers" who allegedly wounded one officer and killed another. Sounds like what officers did in the "Bennett Place" neighborhood of west Baltimore when they were trying to find a suspect in whatever happened to Detective Sean Suiter.

Suiter was 43 and was shot in the head with his service weapon on November 15, 2017 while investigating a triple homicide in the Bennett place neighborhood. The Baltimore City Police Department has the biggest gang in Baltimore and when something happens to a fellow gang member they go crazy. If they fought just as hard for the community they swear to protect, maybe they wouldn't be so bad. Back in the day officers did things without court ordered search warrants, like "Pomerleau" for example, who did illegal surveillance and phone taps of black politicians, ministers, reporters and civil rights leaders. Once Pomerleau activities were exposed, it came out that he illegally tape recorded Mayor William Donald Schaefer in City Hall.

When Pomerleau died in 1992 he was said to be the most corrupt cop of all. I think some members of the Gun trace task force and some other officers got Pomerleau beat. Everybody of age heard of King and Murray. They were two corrupt cops involved in a lot of stolen drugs, robberies, shit like that. It's like Baltimore is the type of place that turns the good to bad. It's almost like the shit rubs off on the good. Well, it's out with the old and in with the new way officers do things. There's no more, well that's a broad statement, and I have the tendency of speaking broadly. It's not so often that officers do things without a warrant, but the most popular thing officers are doing more than ever is lying to state and federal judges to get signed warrants.

For example, like Louisville Metro Police Department detective Joshua Jaynes who wrote the sworn statement affidavit for the warrant to search Breonna Taylor's apartment. Taylor was shot and killed back in March of 2020, by officers of the Louisville Police Department during a "no knock" warrant. The police officer, Jaynes, lied to the issuing Louisville Judge, claiming he verified through a U.S. postal inspector that a friend of Taylor's Jamarcus Glover had received packages at Taylor's address. According to postal inspector Tony Gooden that was a lie. Search warrants are based in part on sworn affidavits, and little info like packages coming to Taylor's apartment could have made the Judge say yes to the warrant or no. In my case, during a May 2017 motion hearing, the government wanted to use evidence that was seized during an October 2016 search of my house by Baltimore police.

I had to argue with my piece of shit ass lawyer to speak up about the lie former Baltimore city detective Robert Hankard told Baltimore city judge Berry Williams in a sworn affidavit, Hankard claimed he saw my Honda parked in front of my house in the third week of September of 2016 on multiple occasions. Little did Hankard's lying ass know, my Honda was in an accident in the second week of September and was in the body shop until late October. Once this was proved to be a fact to federal Judge Bredar, the government changed their tone and agreed to not use this evidence from the October house raid. What about Harford county sheriff's office own Corporal David McDougall? Who lied to federal Judge Bennett in March of 2016 to get a wiretap warrant on my phone. McDougall claimed in his affidavit to the judge that I was responsible for 8 drug overdoses between August 22nd through October 10th of 2015.

McDougall said the victims called me on 410-371-4603 and bought drugs from me and overdosed. One of the bullshit lawyers I had asked the government for proof of this and the government never turned it over. If it wasn't for me again, like the old saying says "if you want something done right, do it yourself." I found out that the phone number ending in 4603 was in fact deactivated on August 4, 2015, so how can I be responsible? People put too much trust into the government, state officials and the police. I'm not saying all are bad, because it's a lot of good, honest, and fair ones in the world. I do know one thing they all have in common, they're all human. And if it's one thing we all know, humans lie consciously and unconsciously.

Between the death of Freddie Gray, the riots, the alarming rate of killing and the Gun trace task force, which the Baltimore police department has not offered a public accounting of the scandal, the city has a funny color light over it. Among the detectives that were all convicted of federal racketeering charges was the alleged ringleader Sergeant Wayne Jenkins, who was sentenced to twenty-five years. Jenkins admitted to many crimes including lying about drugs that other officers planted on an innocent man, and conspiring to sell one million dollars' worth of drugs with a Baltimore county bondsman. Jenkin's crazy ass was so paralyzing that he had a bag of tools and mask to carry out robberies and BB guns to plant in case of an accidental shooting, according to different reports.

Evodio Hendrit and Maurice Ward both received 7 years for their role, Sgt.Thomas Allers received 15 years, Momodu Gondo received 10 years and his lifelong partner Jemell Rayam received 12 years. Daniel Hersl and Marcus Taylor both said fuck admitting to it, you going have to prove it beyond a reason doubt. Both men went to trial and received 18 years. Sounds a lot like the crew of Baltimore officers that got federally indicted back in 1972. I always hear older people say "don't nothing change but the time" so when shit got real the long time partners both started telling on each other. Gondo said Rayam shot a man then covered it up, Rayam said Gondo told him that he killed somebody before. Gondo also threw the last Sean Suiter under the bus.

Gondo said Suiter used to steal money in 2009 when they worked together. Rayam also was involved in illegal activity with Eric Snell who was a Philadelphia police officer who received 9 years for his crimes. According to the government Rayam and Snell were close since 2005 and met at the Baltimore police academy. I would also guess Rayam put a female Baltimore police sergeant on blast about being pissed about not getting her share of the money from Snell. The female Sgt. wasn't named but according to reports she was with the department for six years and has since resigned. It's a lot of shit going on in Baltimore that's for sure. I have had a lot of run -ins with Baltimore city police officers whether they be beat cops (foot patrol), narcotics detectives or homicide detectives. I assure you that narcotic detectives are the worst of them all. In my best "Law and Order" voice these are my stories:

It wasn't nothing but eight months later, when I was able to put Jenkins' "if you get in trouble call me" to the test. I had a white pick-up truck as a rental because Lou had one of those drunk nights and drove my 2015 Honda Accord up on the sidewalk and fucked something up. It wasn't too late, maybe like 8pm, and I was waiting on two calls, one female caller was in East Baltimore and the other female was in West Baltimore. I pulled onto Northern Parkway & Falls Road and pulled up to some apartments called Belvedere Towers. The apartments are next to 83 Jones Falls Expressway, which can take you either south towards East Baltimore/Downtown or North which will take you to 695 beltway, the Northern part of Baltimore counties, or into York, Pa. So I pulled to "Belvedere Towers" and whoever called first would be the one I was hanging out with. I sat in the apartment parking lot for like 30 minutes chasing the gram and shawty off of 83 south called first.

Right there is a Shell and Exxon gas station and I pulled up to the Shell. While the gas was pumping, I jumped in the pick-up part of the truck and started throwing trash away then pulled off. As I started to pull onto 83 South, I saw flashing lights so once on the Jones Falls Expressway I pulled over. A slim tall black knocker with a bullet proof vest that read police on it came to the driver window. I wasn't dirty so I didn't care what was going on nor did I know. What did freak me the fuck out was the white guy's tactical vest said A.T.F on it. The black detective said "Where you off to?" I replied, "On my way downtown to meet a friend, how can I help you boys?" "We seen you at the apartments for some time, then you pulled off to the gas station and was fooling around in the back of your truck.' I knew those apartments were a hot spot, I used to have an apartment there some years back but damn. "Yeah, I was waiting for a phone call to know which way to go on 83, then got some gas and cleaned the back out from a moving job I had earlier today."

As soon as I said that, the white guy hopped in the back part of the truck and started looking around. "You know these apartments are a hot spot for drug transactions right?" Ain't no question I knew that, and so did Jenkins, who in Spring/2015 interrupted a sale of a large amount of marijuana in the parking lot. According to documents, Jenkins took a bag containing 20 pounds from the seller and a bag containing $20000 from the buyer and didn't charge either person with a crime and gave his partners $5000 each. I responded, "No I didn't know that, I was just waiting on a call." The A.T.F guy jumped out the back and said "What's this?" I looked at it and forgot that was there. In Baltimore we call it a "three in one" which is 3 bars of mannite and 28 grams of quinine used to cut heroin.

"I'm not sure what that is, the guy I moved for earlier called and said not to throw it away". They didn't buy it! They both opened the doors, put the cuffs on me, put me in the unmarked police car and the A.T.F guy drove my truck. We went to the Baltimore Police Academy nicknamed "The Barn" which was on Park Heights and Northern Parkway, not too far from "Belvedere Towers". Once inside, the two introduced themselves. The black guy said his name was Detective Sanders and the white one said he was an A.T.F agent, I don't recall what he said his name was. But they both played their role, asking me about drugs, guns, murders, and more guns. I told them I didn't know anything about drugs, guns, and murders and asked why I was here. The A.T.F guy said "We came to test this white power substance we found inside your truck and if this test kit comes back blue its cocaine."

I knew what it was and it damn sure wasn't no cocaine so I played cool, until he came back with the test and the damn kit was blue. I thought all shit here come the bullshit, so I told them what it was and explained there must be some mistake. They kept asking about drugs, guns, and murders. It would have been nothing for them to arrest me and charge me with distribution of cocaine. It happens more often than you think, officers being dickheads saying it's this and it's really not. By the time it gets all figured out, you spend two days down the bookings, spend bail money if you get one and have to pay a lawyer. I wasn't trying to piss these guys off and give them a reason to do that, so I started to think, and telling about some shit was out of the question. So I pulled the Jenkins card and I said "Do you know Jenkins?" Sanders said "Wayan Jenkins?" I said "Yeah". "I know him why?" "Can I call him to straighten this thing out?" He said "Do you have his number?" I responded, "Yeah, it's on my phone."

Saunders took the handcuffs off and handed me my iPhone and told me to "Put it on speaker." "Yo Jenkins," I said. "Who is this?" Jenkins asked. "This Brill." Jenkins said "What's up Brill?" "Man, I'm here with Detective Sanders and they trying to say a 3 in 1 is cocaine. Can you help me out?" Jenkins said "Where is he at? Put him on the phone." "I'm here," Sander replied. "What Sanders is this?" "It's Tony Sanders," then he took the phone and walked in the other room. Sanders came back, looked at me funny and asked "You work with Jenkins often?" I had no choice but to say "Yes." He gave me my iPhone and the rest of my stuff minus the 3 in 1 and I walked out the Barn like damn the Jenkins card worked. They didn't have a real charge to begin with, but when you're dealing with these people shit could have gone either way.

They could have seen I wasn't going to crack and let me go, or they could have been like since he doesn't want to tell anything, lock his ass up and let the courts get to the bottom of it. On the ride home I threw every phone out the window and cut the iPhone off until I was able to get the sim card out of the phone. I knew I would have to deal with Jenkins shit when we ran into each other someday, and I damn sure wasn't going to make it easy for him.

On October 11, 2016 I stepped in the driveway and saw this baby blue Hyundai Sonata with tinted windows come whipping up in the driveway. I felt my heart drop down to my stomach because I knew it was the same Sonata I had been seeing for the last few weeks that I knew was the police. I was rarely in Northeast Baltimore but when I was in "da north," I saw this same blue Sonata. It wasn't unusual to see police in rental cars with tinted windows around my way. So when I saw the Sonata repeatedly, I thought nothing of it. One time I was going up Loch Raven Blvd and I saw the Sonata in the left lane behind the car on the side of me.

While at the red light I saw the passenger of the Sonata point to my car. I saw his white hand point through the windshield which had no tint. I thought nothing of it because Hondas draw a lot of law enforcement attention. One time I was on my way downtown and I was on Harford Rd and 25th street, this had to be around 12am and that same Sonata pulled me over. They pulled me out of the car and searched it and found nothing and let me go. I didn't know who it was in that sonata, so if I wasn't going to see my family I stayed the fuck out of northeast Baltimore. Also anytime Jenkins made his rounds I got a phone call from somebody saying they saw him around, I damn sure wasn't trying to run into him.

I had 2-3 guys working the Northeast area so there really wasn't any need to be around. "Search warrant, search warrant" is what I heard when I saw the doors fly open on the Sonata. I really couldn't believe it and the 25 grams I had in my pocket must've slipped my mind. There were two plain clothes Baltimore City detectives. The younger black one name was Toro-Munford and the Asian looking one was in charge, his name was Robert Hankard. After searching me, Toro-Munford yelled "He 1030" which was a code to let Hankard know I was under arrest for the 25 grams of heroin he found. After a failed attempt to locate the keys to the house, Hankard asked "Where the keys to the house?" I told him "I don't live here." After a quick look over the 5 bedroom, single family home, he realized it was a code to get into the house.

"What's the code to the front door," he said. "I don't live here" I said. "Come on man, we see you come and go all the time" he said.

I looked at him as if I was deaf, dumb, and blind. "Come on, your girl isn't going to like if we fuck her front door up" he said. I thought this man must not know who he talking to, and just stared at him like he was speaking in his foreign language. He went to the car and grabbed a ram and hit the door until it popped open and took me inside. The alarm beeped, waiting for a code to be entered and after a failed attempt to get the alarm code from me, the real alarm sounded. About a minute later, you heard dispatch radio to nearby units in the area, over the detective's radio. Then one of the detectives radioed to dispatch that it was them serving a search warrant. By the time the alarm stopped, four other detectives walked in the house. Soon after Kelly pulled up asking what was going on and was placed in a part of custom Dior handcuffs, explaining that they have a search warrant.

Hankard and the others flipped the house while one guy watched us. It wasn't long before they found a gun and asked whose it was. Nobody said anything and they pulled Kelly upstairs and asked her who's gun it was. She said, "I don't know nothing about a gun." Hankard came back down and said "You going to let your girl go to jail with you?" I didn't say nothing but thought "Hell yeah, she's going to have to go today." I saw too much, knew too much, and had a lot on the line. One thing for sure you can't convict two people for one gun, it has to be somebody's. Another thing there's something called the second amendment, you know, the right to bear arms:

"A well-regulated militia, being necessary to the security of a free state, the right of the people to keep and bear arms shall not be infringed."

So it's not illegal to have a gun in your house. It's illegal to have stolen guns and to be a convicted felon in possession of a gun. I'm not saying you can ride around with a gun, I'm saying if you're not a convicted felon, you can have as many guns in your house as you want. So the way I looked at it was that's Kelly house and gun, not mine, and she has her constitutional rights. Yea she would have gone down to the bookings, but so what. I would have bailed us both out and we would have both beat that shit. I saw guys beat gun charges and they both were felons in a car with one gun. The government or state has to prove whose gun it is.

Anyway, as far as the search warrant they claimed to have, it was fucked up according to my attorney Robert Cole. This one older detective stepped in and told Hankard, "If you lock her up, you're going to complicate the case more than it already is." And that was what I already knew. So he took the cuffs off and told her to either wait outside or leave. So as they flipped the house some more the older man looked at me smiling. It wasn't long before he said "Hey Brill." I try to never let them see me sweat, it's truly hard not to though; these people are trained to do different things. A lot of them have college degrees and I always tried to learn as much as I could about law enforcement. When you are in the streets you have to know how to move, so you have to know their moves to know how you should move.

I smiled and said "Hey sir, how are you today?" He said, "You're a hard man to catch up with, and every time I try to get you, you get away." I got a good look at him and started to run him through my database in my head. I tried to learn the faces and names of these officers and keep an ear or 10 to the streets to know who got locked up and by who. I ask questions like where were they (the person who got arrested) at? What were they doing? Who was it that got them? This detective who was standing at the island in my kitchen going through every card and piece of paper in my wallet didn't look familiar. He was too happy to be in my house and said I always got away from him. So I said you must be the world famous Gladstone. The smile on his face was priceless and he asked me how did I know. I have heard many different stories about detective Gladstone, I know two guys personally that he took $50,000 from and didn't submit a coin. It is a fact if Gladstone is involved, he's looking to take your money, and send you to federal prison.

"It was a lucky guess," I said and it really was. I told him "I heard so much about you, it's an honor to finally meet you." He said "I heard so much about you as well." He was done going through my wallet and came in the living room and sat on the couch across from me and we talked as if we were friends for years. He was talking shit and asked "How's my buddy Georgie doing? I heard you two are close friends." I couldn't do nothing but laugh because he acted like he had all the sense. "He's doing fine; I'll tell him you asked about him." A detective came upstairs with a hydraulic compressor and Gladstone asked, "Where the bricks at Brill?" The whole time I was thinking of a way to get out of this and I thought about asking Gladstone will money make this all go away. I knew him and Jenkins worked together for years so I inquired if I could call Jenkins. "Hell no you can't call Jenkins, come on Brill, you know I taught him everything he knows".

Before I could ask him about money, he said "There's no way out of this Brill, unless you got somebody who can go in your place." "Well I don't have anybody to do that." "Come on Brill, call one of your friends and tell them to come with a brick and we will let you go," he said. That wasn't going to happen in 9 lifetimes, so I didn't say anymore. Gladstone explained that it was Hankard's case and he was just here for the ride, then explained I was going to federal prison. I asked, "For what, y'all don't have nothing." "Brill, do you know how many different agencies want you?" I didn't know what he meant but I later found out. I had no idea Baltimore City, Baltimore County, Harford County and the D.E.A was up my ass. I asked him if he was the one who put the GPS on my car. He smiled and said "No, but I know who it was." I asked who it was and he replied "Why would I tell you?"

I thought he was full of shit, then Hankard came down stairs sweating like a Hebrew slave and didn't find shit but the gun and $2000 punk ass dollars. I can tell they all were highly disappointed. Hankard tried to get me to say something but it wasn't going to happen. Telling will leave you and your family with a lifetime of hardship and will follow you wherever you go. Hankard asked me 5 times "Where's your Honda at?" I never answered. Later I found out that he had a warrant to search the Honda, to put a G.P.S on the Honda and a warrant to use the stingray (see chapters Do's and Don'ts). Gladstone and Hankard later got indicted in 2019. Sometime in 2014 Gladstone received a call from Jenkins, he was out of his mind telling Gladstone how he ran someone over with his car in northeast Baltimore and needed help.

Gladstone got the bright idea to call Hankard to get a BB gun and went to plant it at the scene of where Jenkins hit the guy with his car. Gladstone pleaded guilty to planting that BB gun in February 2019 and I was told Gladstone snitched on Hankard, not sure how true that is. Hankard was charged with false declaration before a grand jury in January 2020. I knew all about Gladstone but never heard of Hankard before, but I knew when they both sat in my living room they were up to no good. I believe the only reason why they didn't hit Gladstone where it hurt, was because they saw how past cases were getting over turned when the G.T.T.F got indicted. One thing about these people, they learn quickly. Gladstone was the one who got the big dawgs off the street, his track record goes way back, and he was a task force officer with the D.E.A, which means the D.E.A works with him and many others task force officers. A lot of state officers are task force officers with the F.B.I, U.S. Marshals or the D.E.A.

Had they charged Gladstone with stealing, planting drugs, etc. the state and federal cases which he was the arresting officer on would have opened the floodgates. Guys he arrested would be filing motions left and right, I'm sure guys already are now. His charge will make it harder for them to argue their case and the people who indicted Gladstone knew that. Gladstone and Hankard knew I was under investigation and only came there thinking I had money there. I did have more money there but they didn't find it. I wouldn't be Brill if I didn't move like the Brill from Enemy of the State, now would I? I went to the bookings and was charged with distribution of heroin and felon in possession of a firearm. I was given a $100,000 bail and the case dismissed. 37 days later which was November 30, 2016, I got arrested for this case. During my stay at C.D.F I was able to talk to Jenkins who was there as well. I'm not sure of the date but it was before the trial started (October 16, 2017).

Me and my co-defendants were on different units and I was on D-unit. The cell I was in faced the rec yard and I could see the first cage. The first cage I could see was the cage that C.D.F used for the guys that's on lock up, which is the B-unit. Lou and Twan, my co-defendants, were on lock up for beating some nigga up. They both knew I was on D-unit and they both knew that cage faced D-unit. So when my co-defendants used to call me I would talk to them through the window. One day I was talking to Lou and we heard Jenkins calling both of us. I'm not sure what unit he was on but he was under my unit. We both thought it was funny talking to Jenkins in jail. We asked him what was up with him and he ask was we going to trial and how we were doing. I asked him if he was going to trial and he said "hell no I got kids, I'm trying to make it home one day". He said he was about to take 30 years and I told him he would be crazy to take 30 years. Lou started asking him who told on him the last time Jenkins locked him up, but Jenkins wouldn't say.

It was just after the 4 o'clock count and the cells were opening to let us out. It was late November or early December of 2017. At C.D.F. you could have TV's, CD players, and an Xbox in your cell. I don't know what I was watching, I think it was TMZ which came on at 3pm and went off at 4pm at the time. If they did not let us out at 4pm I would watch Fox 45 News until they open the cells. I heard my man Barney who was watching the news yelling "Yo Brill, they are talking about you on the news". By the time I turned it on, it was gone. I asked what they were saying. He said "They were talking about the police that got killed, saying you sent him on a high speed chase and he locked you up before". I thought damn I knew it was him, I was just telling Kelly when the shit first happened with "Sean Suiter" that he looked familiar. It was the scar on his face that was familiar. I knew that was the same guy who I was beefing with the day me and Twan got chased.

I'm wrecking my brain trying to think when this was, I'm sitting in a prison cell writing this so I don't have access to Google to know the dates, so please forgive me if my dates are off, I would say this was between 2010-2011. One day I was fucking with Twan on the block and he bugged the shit out of me to take him to meet one of his sales (customer) who turned out to be a cop. We got in my car and pulled four blocks north and I parked. I was driving a 2005 black Honda Accord coupe with tinted windows. Twan called the sale asking where they were at, but I saw this red F-150 coming up the block that looked like it was trying to block us in so I pulled out of the parking spot and the F-150 blocked us. The only way out was to hop the curb and drive on people's lawn, so that's what I did.

I drove down the block driving on 10 people's lawn and unmarked cars were coming from everywhere. We were on a two-way street that was already small as shit to begin with. I blew out two tires somewhere along the line and all the unmarked cars were now behind me and I had them beat by at least a block. We threw what we had out the window and I drove like a mile away, made a few rights and a few lefts then I stopped. Twan got out and ran but got caught, I didn't have time. They pulled up too quickly. Had I been on all fours tires, their asses would have been smoked. I've been in many police chases and law enforcement don't have a chance if I'm behind the wheel. They hopped out mad as shit with guns drawn. It was late detective Sean Suiter who was the toughest cop out there. He was a little guy with a lot to say.

I was all kinds of ass holes and was asked do I know how many people I could have killed driving like that. Me and him argued the whole time I was out there. Three facts about me (1) I'm a driving motherfucka, (2) I don't care who you are, you start talking crazy we going to see what you all about and (3) It wouldn't matter where I was at in northeast, if I was stopped by the police or getting arrested somebody would see me and call Kelly. So it wasn't long before she pulled up asking what's going on. Suiter was saying he was going to do this and that to me when we got back to the station, so I told Kelly take pictures of me and to call the lawyer. So when Barney said something about me getting chased, I knew it was him. Suiter was scheduled to testify before a federal grand jury the following day of his death in connection with the Baltimore police department's gun trace task force corruption investigation.

I ended up catching the new clip and what I got from it was that it wasn't a coincidence that Suiter worked with the officers that were charged with stealing and he didn't. What they did think was a coincidence was that he arrested me and I allegedly conspired with Gondo to sell drugs, somebody Suiter worked with. Suiter's death had people in Baltimore wondering what happened. Some say other police set him up because people who kill themselves don't do it in an alley in west Baltimore. Some say he killed himself. Former G.T.T.F detective Hersl writes the Maryland state commissioner from his prison cell about his speculations about Suiter's death.

According to Hersl, Suiter testifying against fellow officers would put him in an extremely dangerous situation. Hersl tells Maryland state authorities "I am aware that both Suiter and Gondo were acquaintances with two individuals that resigned in the neighborhood of Bennett place," (where Suiter was shot). Hersl said that Gondo knew two people who lived in the Bennett place neighborhood. Now I don't know what happened or not) so why would he have to kill a witness when he is a witness? If you ask me Suiter ass was scared to death to get locked up for the shit all their asses were doing. It's a fact he worked with Jenkins, Gondo and Gladstone and they all stole money amongst other shit. So I would put money on it that Suiter did as well. Once Gondo said Suiter's name to the F.B.I, Suiter couldn't take the hot and got the fuck out the kitchen, if you know what I mean.

Do's and Don'ts

When it came to selling drugs I took the hustle seriously, and always thought of all kinds of ways to play the game safe. Anybody that knows me from selling drugs knows that I was meticulous. I remember there was this one guy who I met through the haze (weed) man, and he used to buy 200 grams of dope every week. It got to the point that I used to go to Towson mall and call him from one of their phones in the AT&T store. I had an apartment right across the street so it was nothing to run in and use their phones. I would tell him where to go and what time I would be there. I used to do all kinds of wild shit, like once I wrote down all the numbers I knew I would need (I had no phone) and used everybody else's phone and either pay phones, of course they were hard to find but I found them. So, when you are in this line of work you have to pay it safe. I was knowledgeable about a lot, but not federal drug conspiracy law and the shit they do when there's an investigation going on. If you're going to do something, do it right. My father used to say "I don't like doing shit twice" so he made sure it was done right the first time. In this case, doing it right the first time will save you from spending years in prison. This chapter is about doing it right, selling drugs that is. The way federal law is or I should say the judicial system as a whole, nobody needs to be selling drugs, in fact, nobody should be selling drugs because it destroys the person that uses and sells that drug. So If you are selling drugs you really need to stop! Selling drugs is outdated any way and if you cannot stop breaking the law, (I would recommend no one break any laws) do white collar crimes instead. These people are crushing black people for selling drugs, you damn near get the same time for drugs than you do for murder. Lord forbid you have two prior felonies and catch a fed beef, you will be a career criminal or they could file 851 enhancements. White collar crimes are the way to go if you just can't help yourself. Fucking with dope you asking to be put in the fish grease, I'm talking extra crunchy. My advice from federal prison is to stop selling drugs and start a business today! If that's not an option than follow these rules and when they caught up with you, it won't be so bad. Because there isn't no ducking the D.E.A, F.B.I, A.T.F, or the Marshalls, once they are on your ass it's a wrap sir. I learned some of what they do and I know what I was doing worked because after seeing the discovery (the evidence against me) which was well over 2000 plus pages, I didn't see a lot of what I was into. What I learned about evidence is that just because it's there on paper, don't mean it's admissible at your trial. There's something called "Federal Rules of Evidence" (Fed.R.Evid) which means that the evidence against you has rules to it. A lot of the shit I seen in the discovery didn't come into the trial because it didn't meet the rules. If you ever in a federal situation you have to learn federal law and the Fed.R.Evid. DON'T TRUST YOUR LAWYER! I don't care how much you paid your attorney, don't trust him/her as far as you can spit. There will be a law library with a computer in there, that's where you need to spend your time. The lawyers will only tell you half of the truth because they know you don't know nothing. I have seen so many guys get tricked by their lawyer. If the lawyer says something, check the computer to see if it's true. You have to learn the law, or they're going to try to sell you a 1995 Honda for $9700. The evidence presented against me during the trial was as follows:

14 Witnesses, 13 of which were drug addicts, 1 of which was a drug dealer. The 13 testified that they bought drugs from me and others and the 1 said he was there when I bought drugs.
2 Jail calls between "Washington & Campbell"
5 wiretap calls of "Thomas"
1 wiretap call (G.P.S.) between Me & "Gondo"
1 wiretap call between Me & a friend of mine's cousin
1 wiretap call between "Wells' & "Gondo"
1 video/audio of me selling drugs to an undercover state trooper (count 3)

188 grams of cocaine, 15 grams of Heroin that I had in the car during my
    arrest (count 7)
6 controlled buys from 2 of the 14 witness

Testimony from lead case agent (McDougall) about seeing me talking to
Washington & Campbell once at the Barber shop and that I was arrested with
a phone that had the same number as the one Thomas used.

I stated what had to be proved to prove conspiracy (count 1) somewhere
in this book. The 14 witness's testimony didn't prove I conspired because
all they said was I sold and bought drugs. No one said I sold drugs with
Washington, Wells or Campbell. The video of me selling the police drugs, the
drugs I was arrested with, McDougall's testimony, the six controlled buys, and
the G.P.S call don't prove I conspired to sell drugs with anybody. Fed.R.Evid
801(d)(2)(E) is a hearsay rule against co-conspirators' out-of-court statements.
E.G, let's say Jack's phone is tapped and he calls John and says "me and Brill
just sold Paul 500 grams." The government can use that wiretap call to prove
Brill conspired with Jack to sell Paul 500 grams, but there's rules to this out-
of-court statement made by Jack. The government has to prove that (1) A
conspiracy did in fact exist (2) The Declarant (Jack) and the defendant (Brill)
were members of that conspiracy (3) The statement (made by Jack) was made
in the course of, and in furtherance of the conspiracy. The government has
to prove that Brill & Jack were conspiring together at the time Jack made the
statement to John and they can't use the wiretap call of Jack and John to prove
it. So because the government didn't have evidence of me calling, hanging
out, selling drugs to, or getting money or drugs from Washington, Campbell,
Wells, Gondo, or Thomas. They tried to prove I conspired with them by their
out-of-court statements about me, which makes their statements inadmissible
because they present no evidence I was dealing with them. If the government
didn't take my stuff 3 days before the trial started I would have objected to
their out-of-court statements. (On October 8, 2017 (8 days before the trial
was to start) my lawyer came to see me to show me the Jencks material, which
is all the statements made against you and who made them. The government
is only entitled to give you the Jencks material if you are going to trial. If you
don't go to trial you will never see (in black & white) who said what about you

to the grand jury, the government or the officers investigating the case. So the paralegal who was helping us prepare for trial gave me a document that had the names of all the people that made statements against me and what they said about me. She wasn't supposed to give me the document because I'm not supposed to have a copy of the people's names due to alleged safety concerns. So because I was doing my own investigation and preparing for trial I wanted to get dirt on the witnesses so I could show the jury that these people are not trustworthy, it's called impeaching the witness. So I gave Kelly the names of the witnesses and asked her to look them up on Maryland case search, which is a judicial site that offers information on peoples pending charges and prior convictions. With that, and the information I already knew about them same witnesses, I started to prepare impeachment questions and information to go over with my lawyer. I also took a lot of notes and prepared a list of reminders (such as, to object to all out-of-court statements). If you were fighting for your life would you put your trust in somebody else to help you and sit around and do nothing? Of course you would take their assistance but I would hope you would want to do all you can do to see to it that you don't get a life sentence in federal prison. Kujichagulia! (which means self-determination) So because I have seen that these court appointed lawyers are not to be trusted, I took matters into my own hands and started to study federal law and prepare my own defense, which the Sixth Amendment says I have a right to do. Of course I pressed my lawyer to tell the court I needed my trial preparation materials back but my request went on deaf ears. The government did give me less than half of my stuff back during the trial, however, they didn't give me any of my handwritten notes or other things back until 3-4 months after I was found guilty. The government told the court that they gave everything they took back. I was told by Lt. Harcum (the correctional officer who took the stuff) that my materials were given to the U.S Marshals service. My lawyer made requests to C.D.F, The U.S Attorney office and The U.S Marshal's office, and put it all on the record. They all said they didn't have my materials. I filed a complaint with C.D.F about those materials and they were told by U.S Marshal David Ashton that the U.S Marshal's service had my materials. The Government's action ran a foul to my Sixth Amendments rights and I should be granted a new trial. As of today, I have a 2255 motion (that I prepared Pro-se) pending with the court on this very issue along with my law-yers' failure to object to Washington and Wells' out-of-court statements about me.) My lawyer wasn't experienced enough to object to the out-of-court state-ments, but I knew to. So, because I did not have my trial preparation materials, I did not have my reminders/notes. That's why defendants should study the law if they have pending charges and put less trust into their lawyer. The out-of-court statements the government used are as follows:

Washington: "when I come home I'm getting the team back me, you, Brill and Lou"

Washington: "where the fuck Brill at"

The out-of-court statements made by Thomas I did not argue to the court because some of the witnesses said we work together. 5 wiretap calls of "Thomas" talking to some customers

"Nah this Lil Brill"

"I just got the phone back from B"

"This Brill phone"

"B don't want me selling it"

"This Brill phone but I got it"

1 wiretap call between "Wells" and "Gondo" is one of the calls I argued to the court. The call played is too long to state. I will sum it up. "Wells" was telling Gondo that he was out with me and Kelly and she was watching him to make sure he was watching me because she knows he's the enforcer and/or he is the enforcer. Wells said he wasn't fucking with me when he comes home (from doing 6 months for a D.U.I) because I was fucking up and he shouldn't come home in be in front of me. This call of Wells is nothing more than his opinion of what he thinks Kelly was doing, and what he feels I wasn't doing and should have been doing, not a fact at all. Part of the reason there is an out-of-court statement rule is so the jury can know if what the declarant is saying is a fact or not. The government didn't have evidence I conspired with my co-defendants between 2011-2016 because I really wasn't. I got found

guilty of conspiracy because the jury heard I sold drugs, the jury didn't care what the conspiracy law was. What I'm trying to explain is that between 2011-2016 I had 7 different guys working for me and none of them are in prison or were mentioned in the government's discovery. The government claims they have been investigating me since 2014 and they had no idea what I was doing or who I was getting drugs from. They had 3500 plus wiretap calls of either me or Thomas, and not one of them were off me talking to my co-defendants, there were two pole cameras, one at my house which is how Jimmy knew I walked through the alley and one at the barber shop I went to once a week. In 2015 there was a G.P.S on my car for 5 months, from July-November. There was a pen register/trap in trace on 8 of my prepaid phones May/2015-March/2016, and there was one on Kelly's phone in Jan/2016. A pen register/trap and trace is a surveillance device that captures the phone numbers dialed on that phone, trap and trace devices capture the numbers that calls that phone number and/or called from the phone number. They don't reveal the contents of the communication. Being thought we live in an increasingly connected world, having a log of the numbers that you call and who calls you provides a very complete picture, a profile-of your associates, habits, contacts, interests and activities. Pen registers and trace devices are very helpful to law enforcement. Even though a 1986 federal law requires a court order for use of the devices, the standard used for approval is little to nothing. This investigation shit is real, and once they are on you, you can cancel Christmas. Out of all the investigating they did on me, they didn't raid any of the apartments I had or where I lived. The only people who raided were the corrupt Baltimore City Officers (most likely looking for money) who both were indicted for their crimes.

Out of the many agencies investigating me, the only federal investigating was the one D.E.A Task Force Officer McDougall was doing. Out of all the shit I was doing, they never caught me doing it because I moved a particular way. I was slipping like shit when they had the G.P.S on my car for 5 months, but what does that say about their investigation? How you have a G.P.S on my car for 5 months and find out nothing? This case against me is bull shit and I'm really not supposed to be in prison for conspiracy. The whole shit start as a joint investigation between Harford county & Baltimore County Police into drug overdoses. People would come to Baltimore City from Harford County and Baltimore County to buy drugs then go home and overdose. The drug addicts that bought from me were either from Baltimore City, Baltimore County, Harford counties, or West Virginia. Once the investigation starts, they going to use confidential sources, pull your credit, visual/physical surveillance, G.P.S'S, check your trash, search warrants, pen registers/trap in trace, toll records, review old/new jail calls, stingrays, phone pings, and a lot more. These people got a lot of shit with them when it comes to an investigation and they spend a lot of money doing it. I knew about the stingray and pings when I was on the street, so I used at least 5 phones. There's a lot of talk about stingrays, which is an investigative technique use by state and federal law enforcement. Of course obtaining information is their goal, and the stingray is their go to tool of choice. Stingray mimics a cell phone tower and many reports say that the device can pick your location, contacts, call history, browse history, text messages and can listen to your calls. According to law enforcement, the stingray is nothing but a pen register device, but many reports say otherwise. The stingray is such a big deal that law enforcement is told not to testify about how it's used. It's reported that it can get your number out of thin air. My advice is if you want to last in the drug game, don't use a phone, own a phone or be around a phone when doing business. (I also would highly suggest STOP selling drugs.) If you can learn when, where, and how to use the phone you might just be able to last in the drug game. One thing for sure, once you're under investigation so is your friends, family, girlfriend, baby mother, kids (if they are old enough) and even your dog. Everybody has what is called known associates, which can be someone you were arrested with 10 years ago, a legal business partner, girlfriend, and/or anybody you are tied to somehow. When I was home I Google my name and beside finding out somebody with my name (different middle name) was wanted for murder in another state, there were sites to see my criminal history. So I paid the $15 and I saw a list of names and addresses, but guess whose name was at the top of the list for known associates? Kelly's! Anyway. Back in 2009 while I was doing the year I was sentenced to, the prison I was housed at had cell phones. So I would Google different things and read different cases. I came up with the idea to use one on one phones when I got home. I would buy brand new prepaid phones and give the other one to whomever I wanted to call or call me, mostly people who worked for me. I talked about getting Kelly a one on one, but that was only because I broke the law, not her, and because she had the same number 20 plus years. I knew about pings, and stingrays so I knew if law enforcement was to ever get on me they would start with Kelly knowing I wouldn't be too far behind. The purpose of one on one phones is so law enforcement can't get your number, which will lead to your phone getting tapped. It's so easy to get your number if you're under investigation. Either an informant will cough it up or you will make a big mistake. One of the many mistakes is by not knowing how to use your phone. Let's say they can't get a number on you, but know your baby mother's number/girlfriend or an associate's number. They would put a pen register/trap in trace on their phone to see who calls them, hoping you call. Using a pen register they can't hear the call but can see the numbers calling or being called. Of course you will talk to your girlfriend 50 times a day, so they will say, "this has to be him calling all damn day". It wouldn't be anything to call the number and ask for you or just to see who answers. Also the pen register can cross reference numbers. E.G. Kelly's phone and my phone both had a pen register on it and the only number we both used to call from our phones was my father's number. So that's how they can get your number using pen register devices. With using one on one phones you don't have to worry about this and I'll explain why. You buy two brand new phones, you take one and give whoever one and only call each other from that phone, how can they get the number? Besides the stingray (allegedly) and or the other person giving them the number? Without the number they can't use the pen registers, stingray, or tap your phone. Everybody that worked for me I gave them a one on one phone, I even put my plugs down with the one on one game. I put restrictions on all the phones, so they could only call me and 911 and only I could call them. As long as the two people only talk to each other on that phone they can't get the number. The restrictions were a safe guard so the user wouldn't call anybody from that phone. The guys I was dealing with were so hard headed and I couldn't afford them calling the weed man or their baby mother from that phone. You don't want them to call somebody who's under investigation, people who sell drugs hang with other people who sell drugs. Everybody I was hanging with had their only investigation going on when I was home and are either in prison or somebody killed them (BIG FACTS). I may be in prison, but I know this works because out of 3500 wiretap calls, I'm not on one talking about drugs. They had no clue who I was getting drugs from or who really was working for me. I also switched the phones every 30 days. This is the most effective if done before the investigation comes because if you get real money, busting down bricks it's just a matter of time before the investigation comes. If it was somebody I did business with or I talked to everyday I got them a one on one phone. If somebody wanted to talk to you badly enough, they would call from the phone you gave them to call you from right? I'm sure you heard guys say "this my family phone" right? Or "I only call my family from this phone" and they carry the phone everywhere they go, right? Those people know you don't talk business on that phone that's in your name, your business name etc. So they make it their business to track the shit out of you on that phone. You can't take your so-called "family phone" with you when you are going to drop 10,000 pills of dope off to Lil Joe Joe and them to open up shop in the morning. The same goes for when you going to see the plug, or going to the stash house. If it's not a one on one phone don't take it everywhere you go. Once they get on you all they want is a phone number on you, they don't care if it's just for a week. You think they don't know who your aunt is? Or your cousin who you got the BGE (Baltimore Gas and Electric) in their name for you? How easy is it to get a person's number? It has to be even easier to get somebody's number that's not breaking any law. They work the street until they get your number, why you think detective Jenkins asked me for the guy blue-black number? Drug dealers don't understand how this shit goes with just having somebody's phone number. Once they get your number it's going to be a lay-up to get a warrant to ping your phone. Once that phone is pinged they sit back and watch the ping. They want to know your daily movement, they say "ok so at 3am the target is here every night, he must live there" Then say "everyday he goes here for 2 hours that must be the stash house." Next step they put a team to watch your house and the stash house to see who comes and goes and to see if you or whoever is carrying any bags when leaving that place. They get all of this just from pinging a phone number. But if you had a one on one phone, didn't take phones to the stash house and checked for G. P.S they wouldn't know where it is. The same when you are going to meet the plug or handling serious business. I never met the plug with any of my phones but the one on one I was calling him on. That explains why they never caught me on 95 with heroin, knew who the plug was or knew where the stash house was. I never took a phone in the stash house that wasn't a one on one phone. I remember I got Amy a one on one phone because I used to pull up with no phone to call her on. Because I believe you shouldn't have a copy of a key on your person to the place that has guns or drugs in it, I either used keyless access or hide the key. So to get in the front door of Amy's apartment building you needed a key. So she used to hide the key and when she was getting her pussy licked by one of her little niggas, she would move the key, so I use to be mad as shit because I would be sitting outside with hundreds of grams of coke or heroin, after driving sometimes hours with it, just to not be able to get in. It's also best to park around the corner and walk to the spot, you see your surroundings a lot more that way. There was a gas station right around the corner from Amy's and I used to pay the gas station man to park there. You must check for the G.P.S once a week and right before you are about to do something big. I know it's hard if you are a major player, but carrying bags will get the sparks knocked out your ass. Them people think everything is drugs or money, if it's in a bag. So tape it to your body or something because walking out with a bag is suicide. Any phone that isn't a one on one phone, take the battery out before you pull up somewhere important. Not all my phones were one on one's, I had to have at least one phone to make calls on, and I had an iPhone. I only used the iPhone for emails, internet, social media, out of towners, and for people that weren't friends or family. I didn't never take my iPhone into any stash house. I may be in federal prison but I know if I wasn't doing these things they would have found my stash spots, who the plug was, and caught me with at least 1000 grams. My plug wasn't always on but even when I was getting dope from Baltimore guys I called them from a brand-new phone and never called nobody else from that phone. Always do that, because other guys maybe under investigation. You calling them from a phone you use to call other people is a sure way to have them people all into what you doing. I remember having to go to 10 different stores to buy my phones. Wal-Mart, Target, and some Family Dollar stores will only sell you 2 prepaid phones per person. It's against some kind of federal law to sell a person more than 2 prepaid phones at a time. I'm telling you this shit will work, I did it and they had no clue what was going on and there's no way they can stop it. The way they were able to get the 11 of the 14 witnesses was through the wiretap. They called them and told them they were heard on a wiretap and told them they could be arrested for buying drugs. Scared the shit out them white people knowing damn well they wasn't going to charge them with buying drugs that they didn't arrest them with. Them not really knowing no better, they came to court and testified I sold them drugs. What you do with your trash is very important. (Don't throw away the hard plastic the prepaid phones come in just anywhere.) If the police get the numbers that came on the plastic, they can get that phone number once activated. The whole purpose of the one on one is to keep the police from getting the number. If you getting money, you should know what to do with your trash. This is for my up and coming Bricklayers. Under U.S. Supreme Court case California v. Greenwood law enforcement may search trash left at the curb side without a search warrant. No matter what you sell, get a market bag and put all your trash and that bag and take it with you, throw it away somewhere else. I use to wash everything before it goes in the bag. I used to buy two phones and some Lysol wraps from Family Dollar. You don't want them people to see them brick wrappers, they get a hard on when they know you catching bricks. Always clean your area, the blender, the compressor, table, everything. It's part of their investigation to go back and listen to your old jail calls, you and anybody that you deal with. I never spend more than 7 months and jail, but my friends did. I got sentenced to 14 days in Baltimore county for driving on suspended license back in October/2012 and they put what I said in one of the jail calls in the wiretap application in March/2016. Anybody that called Kelly from a Maryland jail/prison they listened to the calls. It all comes in your discovery, everything they did. I listened to calls of her and her childhood friend, somebody I don't even know, or had anything to do with. A lot of my friends called her to get in touch with me, so I heard them calls as well. I guess they can put a number in some kind of system and anybody that called that number from jail will come up. I use to have a phone just for guys in jail. You don't want them to call your phone and it's not right to not talk to the good men in jail, so I got a phone just for them. I said this before and it needs to be clear, you have to check for a G.P.S once a week. Take your car to the neighborhood shop, pull it on the car lift, get a flashlight and look under the car for a box big or small. It won't be hard to find if you look. The one I found had "air bag sensor" written on it, but it had somewhere that you could plug a USB charger in it. You should also invest in counter surveillance, bug sweepers, etc. If you catch bricks you should without a doubt buy different devices. I paid $300 for a wireless device detector that picks up G.P. S's, hidden cameras, or anything wireless. I saw this one device that picked up cameras and it had a screen on it that would show you what the nearby camera sees. There are endless things out there, even devices that will tell you if your phone is tapped. There's this company name "Kryptall" that claims to guarantee you privacy. They have phones that can't be intercepted, traced, or recorded and work anywhere in the world. Under 18 USC & 2510 Interceptions of wire, oral, or electronic communications, is a last resort by law enforcement. Last resort means the police has to first conduct surveillance, G.P.S, trash pulls, search warrants, pen registers, etc. on a target before they can ask for a wiretap. Before asking a judge, law enforcement has to ask the Department of Justice, criminal division for permission to ask a judge. They have to submit an application to somebody deputized by the U.S. Attorney General. They will get an approval letter then they have to submit another application & affidavit from the lead case agent showing probable cause to a judge. They have to explain to a judge a lot and need a phone number as well as know who will be using that phone. The warrants are always no more than 30 days. After that they will have to submit another application/ affidavit and the issuing judge could ask what they have learned. What's so funny was that they only had wiretaps on our phones for 60 days. I believe that when they went to ask for more time, the judge asked them what they learned. And because they didn't learn anything, I believe the judge said no. Because the wiretaps were in March 2016 and the phones were still on after the wiretap ended. So why not keep the wiretap going? I didn't get arrested until November/2016, the investigation was still going on because they did a controlled buy from me in September/2016. You should get new phones every two weeks. Don't make their job easy, make them work to the point they get tired of submitting warrants to the judge. The wiretap (title III) applications are 200+ pages, switching phones will give them hell. A one on one phone will make it damn near impossible to get the number. Please don't go get a new phone and call everybody you used to call from the old phone on that new phone. A new phone should be used to call people who got a new phone as well. If your phone was tapped and you get a new phone and call everybody you were calling from the trapped phone they will get your new number. When a phone is tapped they start to monitor some of the people the tapped phone called. It's way around the last resort thing, they do this all the time e.g. tell the judge that the target is buying or selling drugs from the phone number 443-207-2489 and we need to get a wiretap on that number to further our investigation. We did surveillance and it's too dangerous to send a confidential source, trash pulls would be pointless and if we search that will tip the targets off. I read cases and this is what they say and the judge signs the warrant for the wiretap. So let's say you are the target and your phone is tapped, the people you call or the people you are doing business with get their phone tapped. So, when you get a new number and call some people on their old number, which may be tapped now, or at least have a pen register on it from when they were talking to you, they get right back to you. It's a lot to go through but 25 years in prison is a lot of time to do wouldn't you say? I'm telling you, I've been through all this shit, I reviewed over 2000-3000 pages of discovery, read 100's of other people's pages on the computer, I know what I'm talking about. I used to buy a lot of phones and used one phone to talk to multiple one on one phones. As long as you put restrictions on their phones and you only call them and they only call you, you don't have to have a phone for every person who has a one on one phone. As soon as you make a mistake and call somebody who don't have a one-on-one phone from your phone one on one, they all are compromised. If they are on your ass, they can easily get on to that phone which will put them on the other one on one phone. These people sit around and get paid to wait for you to make a mistake. I used to read different stories about federal investigations when I was home to learn what they do. I was reading online that when your phone is tapped it will make different noises and your text messages would come thru more than once. I had this one iPhone that I broke 10 different times and would just keep getting it fixed. The sim card slot wouldn't even open. All my phones were pre-paid, so I would just keep changing the number on this iPhone. I didn't take it with me everywhere because I knew I had it forever. I used to give it to my cousin to use and got her a one on one. I used to give everybody that number and paid her to text me the people's names and numbers who called. This iPhone used to make noises and cut on and off by itself. I thought about it being tapped but didn't know or care because I didn't use it like that. So one day a friend of mine texted "wya" but the message came thru twice. So, I called and asked "how many times did you text me" and they said "once", I said "text me again" and the message came thru twice again. When I got locked up I learned that iPhone was tapped. So if you hear noises, clicks, the phone cuts off then back on, text messages come thru more than once get rid of that phone and don't call nobody from the new phone until they get a new one. Changing the sim card or number will not stop the wiretap etc. They put the phone's ID number in the wiretap application, so I'm sure they can tap the phone itself. I don't know how they got that iPhone number, but I would guess from me calling everybody from it. Fucking with them phones is no joke, just ask Felicien Kabuga and his children. Kabuga was said to be one of Africa's richest moguls and allegedly helped unleash the Rwandan genocide of 1994. Kabuga vanished and was able to avoid charges for more than two decades. It wasn't until detectives from The United Nations said it's time for Kabuga to have his day in court and started searching for him again. Kabuga was a very powerful man and had lots of help in evading law enforcement, but it was old cell phone location records that led to his arrest. Once they was back on Kabuga's ass in March of 2020, they looked into where his daughter used her phone when she was in France. As I explained, whenever someone use their cell phone, the signal locks unto the nearest cell tower which in turn leaves a log that can be reviewed in real time or recent history (with a warrant of course) if they have the number of that phone. Long story short, they found out the general area of the calls and then learned that a family member of Kabuga had an apartment in that same area. They did a little leg work and after looking for this man for 20 years they found out where he was at. Weeks after his arrest they interviewed his family and they said that they knew talking on the phone was dangerous and had dropped their guard in recent years but had to communicate with each other about their father's health. Further stating "of course we knew that it was risky. It was something that we thought about, but what can one do?" Well had they had one on one phones to communicate on and was staying at an apartment that was in somebody name who had no relation to them The United Nation would still be looking for Kabuga, who's said to be a key culprit in the genocide of nearly a million people. It's a growing world out there and if you think you're going to last in the criminal world, you need to start learning about the tools being used against you. With devices like the "Triggerfish", that's used to obtain the IMSI and ESN numbers (the phones id numbers) associated with specific cell phone numbers, which I believe is nothing more than a "Stingray". In other words, I believe they can get your number out of thin air. The devices are used to get your number so they can then get a warrant to subpoena your real time and historical cell phone location records and even wiretap warrants. Again, I would suggest not breaking any more laws, but if you are, don't have a phone with you and if you just have to have a phone, make it a one-on-one phone. Let's say you got an apartment for a stash spot and you get cool with somebody who works in the leasing office. They are famous for giving you a business card right? I never had apartments in my name but I have been to the office a lot, trying to get cool with somebody there. Don't put the card they give you in your wallet or in your car. Throw the card away, because that's a clue. If they don't know about the apartment they will find the card if they lock you up or if they just so happen to have you some where pulled over just to fuck with you, so they will start thinking why do you have that card. Then they will go to the leasing office, show them your picture and ask them if you have an apartment there. Of course they ain't trying to lose their job so they are going to tell everything. The same for my guys that use storage units, don't have the card to the place you use in your car or wallet. Try to use keyless access to places that drugs and guns are stored at. It's really easy to argue you don't live there, if you don't have access to that place, or hide the key somewhere. It's going to be hard to tell a judge at the motion hearing or a jury that you don't have access when they got the key off your belt loop along with your Gucci keychains. I saw them take the whole lock out the door, with the key still in it, just to show you have access. Of course they have to also prove that you knew that stuff was there. Don't have mail or personal things at places where drugs/

guns are, and wipe down your fingerprints, they test everything to build an airtight case. For my guys that hustle off the phone, put locks on your pre-paid phones and erase your text messages after you read/send them. Also if the knockers (plain clothes officers) pull you over and start looking and fucking with your phones, get new ones. I saw this one officer get the number to a phone, then store his number in a contact that's already saved in the phone. So when you think John is calling to get 3 grams and a few 50's of crack, it's the knocker that pulled you over 3 days ago. You should know this but don't put the apartment, or the gas and electric in your name. If you got money, drugs, or guns there. Them people pull your credit to see what's in your name. It's nothing to call whatever company, give your name and social, and get an address. I used to park my car on the next block over from my house. Everything was in Kelly's name so I'm sure somebody would come pass trying to pop a G.P.S on my car. This shit is super easy for them to get a number on you and find out where you live if you live with your child's mother. What I'm trying to do is prepare you for what's next, G.P.S's, pinged phones, a lot of people giving info, then wiretaps. Check for G.P.S's on your car or your rental car weekly. One on one phones and not having phones you talk to everybody on with you when you are at the spot, going to see the plug or going to make a big sale, will save you from future problems. Also don't tell your girlfriend/babymother where the spot at. When females get in their feelings they don't think. I never used to tell Kelly where my spot was because I knew I would do something that would make her mad. So this one time I told her where it was. I don't remember why I told her but we got the beefing and she was out front blocking my car in. I was so mad because I knew I should have never told her where it was. I had to drive on the sidewalk to get out of the parking spot. Just imagine if she would have tried fighting me and somebody called the police and said I was beating my girlfriend up and they told them what apartment/house it was and they went inside and found drugs and guns. Shit like that happens all the time, and now you fighting a fucking drug/gun case because your girl couldn't keep her emotions in check. So don't make that mistake because it could happen to you. I always was a fast driver for a number of reasons and if I was first in line at the red light I ran it, of course not if I had drugs or guns with me. It's hard to follow somebody that speeds everywhere and runs damn near every red light. I was reading the discovery and I see a report that said they couldn't follow me because I always was speeding and ran all the lights. I ensure you that if I said it and this book I did it, I have no reason to lie. If you know somebody that knows me, ask them to tell you. There's so much more I was doing that I can't say in this book. I can't put everything out there because I see they wasn't on to it. I talk so freely because under federal law 18. U.S.C. 3282 they only have 5 years to charge you federally with that crime. Of course it gets a little tricky when they charge you with conspiracy. I would strongly recommend again, if you are selling drugs to STOP! If you won't stop, get in touch with me and if I can tell you are official, I will tell you what I can't put in the book, my breaking law days are over. The only reason why I'm writing to tell people this stuff is because I want people to stay out of prison. Plus, I understand why people sell drugs and after what them evil people put our ancestors thru, they left a lot of us with no choice. They gave our ancestors nothing after 400 years of hell, and that had a domino effect on us today. Our people are fucked up because of the games they played. I'm not breaking any more law because I lost everything doing it, but I will try my best to stop you all from selling drugs. I know a lot of our people won't stop, so I have to give the knowledge to our people so they can provide for their family. It may not make sense to you, and if it doesn't it wasn't for you to understand.

Pretty Boi Gangster

A s I stood in the computer line, I asked an amigo name Joker, from Texas did he have any books for sell. "Naw Brill I don't have any" but while joker was talking he moved his head in the direction of the guy standing behind him. Books are 20 mailing stamps, used or new and it's the money in federal prison. Each prison the price of a book is different, here at McDowell F.C.I (federal correctional institute) a book cost anywhere between $5-7 dollars. So the guy standing behind joker said "I give you 20 books for $140 Brill" This guy was from one of the Carolinas and we rarely ever talked at the time. So, I looked at him and thought "he must think I'm sweet, why would I pay $7.00 a book"? So, I just smiled and said, "Man I can't afford that, I'm just trying to spend $60.00." He said, "Oh ok" and turned back around. A few seconds went by and he turned back around and said "come on Brill, stop faking we know you got money, I already heard about you". Anybody that knows me, knows about my famous smile, so I smiled and said "you can't believe everything you hear" he said "big homie already told me about you" I said "who's big homie? He said "Ali" I laughed. Ali was from 20th & Kennedy in east Baltimore, but lives in North Carolina somewhere. When I first got here to McDowell, I was sitting at the Baltimore table with the old head Kim from west Baltimore and he called Ali over to the table (Ali was on Muslim time, meaning he sat and rolled with other Muslims and not other Baltimore guys.) "This the new Baltimore homie" Kim said. "Where you from" Ali said, "I'm from the Alameda" I told him "Oh yea you know Brill?" The last time somebody asked me did I know me I said no. "I am Brill" I replied, "I thought that was you, wasn't sure thought" he said. I had a confused look on my face because I didn't recognize him. Then he said "I'm Tray brother, Big Bunk" once he said I'm Tray brother I knew exactly who he was, and thought damn I haven't seen him in years. He said "You know the last time I seen you? You was in front of Motts house in a gold 750". I said "Damn that had to be in 2008". I'm sure he didn't recognize me; I was fresh off lock up weighing 205 and the last time he seen me I was 275 easy. Motts is my man, he from Ramblewood in northeast, I got tight with him from hanging on their block with Nick, and that's where I know Tray crazy ass from. Every time I think about Tray, I think about how he talked me and Nick into catching the gray hound down to Contour, North Carolina to rob some niggas. This had to be 2002-2003, and Tray had them Carolina dudes scared to death. The first night down there Tray had us kicking in doors and running through the projects getting chased by the police. I remember I had to stop the nigga World from killing one of the niggas for having no money. I knew where this was headed so I got the fuck outta there and was on the next bus back to Baltimore. I still thank Allah, because them people would have put our ass in the hottest fish grease known to man if they would have caught us doing that shit, I'll just be coming home. Anyway, the guy trying to sell me the books said "yea Ali know what he talking about, you smooth, stop being cheap" I smiled "when I first got here and I told Ali what unit I was on, he said you was up here and I should fuck with you" he said. I didn't say nothing just smiled, he said "you a Pretty Boi Gangster, I be watching you". I thought damn I heard people call me all kinds of names, Brillion, Uncle Brill, Brilliant, Big man, Big dawg, Paulie, Brillo, Brillet and even Gangster, but Pretty Boi Gangster was a first. As I met new females, I'm always asked to describe myself and since I'm writing this book, I thought I'll describe the old me for the people that thought they knew me and for the people that don't know me. I don't know about you, but it's never easy to describe yourself. I only can go off what people said that I felt sounded about right. As I explained, Brill was a character I created to think and move smart. I was good at playing dumb or slow, even weak. If something was to happen, I always wanted to act like I didn't know or like it wasn't a problem so I could be the one behind the scenes pressing the buttons, but it was my mouth that I never could control. That's why that nigga Chauncey started calling me Gangster, I talked a lot of shit and thought I was the baddest mothafucka on two feet. I would say I was never the back down type and didn't never play the tough guy role. In Baltimore you had to be either tough or smart, and if you were weak, you wouldn't last long, so I used the smart card. I thought my way to the top, and learned a lot from a dummy. Before I ever read 48 laws to power, I played "a sucker to catch a sucker" and seemed dumber than my mark (see law 21). It was all who Brill was, and playing tough either got you killed or a first class ticket to prison for everybody knowing you killed or had a nigga killed. I use to trip off the people that thought I was some soft nigga from northeast Baltimore. Somebody was on their side, because I was the total opposite. A lot of people thought they knew Brill, but I only showed them Tony. I never was the flashy type, but heard more than once I had a demeanor that said I had money. I always thought being flashy was like having a sign around your neck that said "arrest me", isn't that what Frank said on American Gangster? Taking pictures with money or guns was the craziest shit ever, only goofy niggas did that (my opinion). That's part of the reason why the government couldn't present any evidence of any kind of worth when it come to me. Anyway, it gets lonely being in prison without a female to talk nice to you, so I got on an inmate dating site. I had fun writing my bio, I describe myself as an individual-ist, characterized with charisma, astuteness and handsomeness, mixed with the ability to make you smile. If you ask me, that sounds about right. It's a fact I'm a person of independent thoughts and actions, has the power to attract followers, hardheaded as shit, and very very easy on the eyes. I'm a really nice guy, caring, loving, but when I'm upset, it's no good for you. I wasn't the slick-est dressing nigga, but I use to put that shit on, now that I lost 60 pounds, got a little figure, their ass is in trouble out there. I heard a lot of people didn't like me, said I always looked like I had a problem. I was the coolest, funniest guy you could meet, and would give you the $500 shirt off my back. I think it's my eloquence that's always visible that made people say they didn't like me. Baynard Woods, an investigative journalist describe me in his book "I got a monster" as being "smart but erratic and sometime careless." I didn't know what erratic mean but it's says "having no fixed course" or "characterized by lack of consistency." I didn't know how to feel about that, I'm the man with the plan, fail to plan and plan to fail. I would say I lacked consistency because I'm always calling audibles like Tom Brady and will look your ass off like

Drew Brees, so I could see that. Woods also said I was a "Bulky street dude with a thin bread and a big smile. I thought damn, I do have a big smile and how did he know about my famous smile. A female friend said I use to walk in the club like I owned the joint, I would say I was doubtless and confident. Some called it arrogant, I'll say I was just being Brill. When I tell you I was a party animal, I was the party man. Shit, I didn't miss a party, even the one's I wasn't invited to. The way I saw it was, I wasn't invited, but I'm glad I made it. It wasn't a party promoter that I didn't know, they may not have known my name, but they damn sure knew my face. I know I can't wait to come home and throw a welcome home party. I'm sure I'm going to go through some more shit for people to talk about, like how I gave this 25 years back, that everyone seems to think I'm going to have to do, so I'll make it a welcome home/book release party. I tell my man Cheeks all the time, "its operation shut the whole shit down" when I get there, and they all know it. Kelly knowing first hand, asked what will she have to prepare herself for when I get home. Basically saying she knows I'm going to cut up. I told her I will just be living life, because she damn sure is. I'm sure it's so easy for her to just go about her day not having to see or hear about me being out and about. I guess she had to ask herself, knowing damn well I'm somebody on the street. Well I can tell you now, there won't be any not hearing about the kid when I get there. You know how it is when a nigga come home, he's hot as fish grease.

I believe she will be sick seeing me out and about, knowing I was a good man to her, not to mention looking fine as wine. It will be a whole different affect when I'm on the street with that shit on, with a Bruce Leroy glow outta this world. One things for sure, I was Covid-19 sick just hearing about her being out with another nigga, I couldn't imagine seeing it, but I'm so glad I'm over it, because I have to admit, I was sick! I can see me now, telling a Goddess "let's go hang." I know me, Rolex, no chain, out and about laughing like shit, of course I still find everything funny. But cutting up would be an understatement, more like "operation shut the whole shit down."

Anyway, I remember the time I was at a party at The Pimlico Race Track, and some Southwest Baltimore niggas trashed me. According to this little bitch I was fucking with, my back was turned and one of them hit me with a Rose' bottle. She said once I hit the floor, the niggas I was with (my Ramblewood family) went to work. I don't remember shit, nor did I see it coming. She told me who the niggas were and we wanted answers. I remember talking to Lou at the ER that night, he was all over it. They claimed it was about their man getting killed by my cousin's brother allegedly. The way it was put to me was, their man and his homeboy threw a drink on my cousin's brother homeboy's mother. So from what I was told, who knows if it's any truth to any of it, the mother called her son, and the son and my cousin's brother came up there and smoked their man and his homeboy. What I had to do with any of it, who the fuck knows. According to them, they jumped me because that was my cousin, which didn't make any sense at all. I think it was that, and also the fact that I was fucking with one of their baby mother's, more so the baby's mother part. I kind of feel like she pointed me out to them niggas, because I remember talking to her at the party, then getting jumped a minute later. Then it was brought to my attention that this one girl, who was fucking with one of them, who knew that was my cousin, told them that he was. I was from Northeast, so how else would those niggas have known that was my cousin. I guess she still thinks I don't know it was her ass who told them. I wouldn't say there is any beef between us now, I'm really over the shit, it was years ago. Both of their men were killed, my cousin's brother and his man were killed, one of the niggas that jumped me was killed, so enough is enough at this point in my life. Anyway, I don't know how oh hell Kell would describe me, I'm sure as a liar and cheater. She used to say I was charming though, and one of the last times I talk to her she said I had an authority problem, a female friend I asked said the same thing. I wouldn't say that, I would say that I let it be known what I want and what I'm willing to deal with. So People including Kelly always took that as me telling them what to do. What happens is, they thought in their head I was the boss, so they always took it as me giving orders. Mix that with how I was trained at a young age, by Swo, to think and move like Carmine Persico, underboss of the Columbo crime family, I see why they think what they thought. I guess at the end of it all that's why my man called me Paulie, because I was the boss. The way you carry yourself has a lot of meaning. We send signals about who we are and how we want to be seen, by friends, enemies, and potential mates. I took how I wanted to be viewed seriously. I guess you can bottle me all up and say I was a Pretty Boi Gangster. I'm charming, good looking and capable of tricking you out your life all at the same time. Deep down inside though I'm a big family man, it wasn't nothing like going home to Kelly and Tone, and being a Gangster, /Gan-ster/: A member of a gang of criminals, took that away from me. I damn near will give anything to go back in time, I would had made the right instead of the left.

It's nothing pretty or gangster about waking up to the same 128 niggas every damn day. A total of 64 cells, 32 upstairs and 32 downstairs, the shit will drive you crazy. Makes you think about what you got yourself into, every day I think about it. Each unit has 6 phones, 4 computers, 190-degree water heater, ice machine, 9 TV's, and no microwave. This will be your home until the B.O.P done with your ass. I never did no real time before, so I wouldn't know the difference between state time and federal time. I just wish I did some time years ago, because I would have learned my lesson then. I love my freedom and Ruth Chris too much to spend my days in prison. The shit isn't for me and I see why Tommy was like "the only way the county or the state going to see my is in a bag." This some tough shit, I'm trying to tell you and if your ass go to prison you can forget about it! Forget about what? Everything! What they say "You can cancel Christmas? Well while you at it cancel Easter and the rest of thát shit to. Once your ass get behind these walls, your dead to the people on the street. The way I try to stay alive out there is by having little cuz (who I got to double salute for being here for me 200%) post pictures on my I.G page. The streets got to see you, outta sight, outta mind. Go to my I.G. page @Tmc_yo and check a real nigga out. Like some pictures and shit while you at it. Once you get behind these walls the people on the street will show you a whole different person. I understand now, I did not show the love to my guys in prison, like I wanted people to show me while I'm in prison. I had a lot of good men behind the wall, that I should have been doing a lot more for. Don't get it fucked up though I had a phone just for niggas in jail/prison to call and I did whatever they asked me to do, whatever! However, my sandbox friend Justin A.K.A Hood, who is serving at least 30 years, I wasn't there for him the way I want people to be there for me. Anytime Hood called and said he needed this or that I made sure he got that, but its other shit guys in prison need, like pictures, letters, mental support, and a friend. Running in the streets you don't have time or think about the little shit. I never did a bid before, had no idea what a nigga in prison needed, and now I know. So if you got a good man behind the wall, send him or her some pictures without them having to ask you, it would make their month. I met a good man (in my book) named Tewhan "Mass" Butler from New Jersey. He wrote "Americans Massacre: Surviving Mass incarceration" I bought the book to support the brother, got to support all the standup men, but mass says "to be remembered was to be alive. To be forgotten was emotional and psychological torture" and I thought man that's really how it feels. I use to be in my feelings when people take hours to reply to my messages or don't reply at all. Mothafucka treat me like I was in last place out there in the world. It took some unworthy hours and a lot of vindictive thoughts to realize this was what I signed up for. I had to go back in read my contract, in the fine print it said "when you go to prison, they will forget about you." Since I took everything else on the chin, I had to roll with this as well. I ain't mad at nobody, and even though I don't talk to a lot of niggas they still the Bros. This prison shit is crazy, don't let them people send your ass to any prison in West Virginia, those people are crazy. They got their own shit going on up in them mountains. My first spot was F.C.I Beckley, West Virginia, then I was sent to F.C.I McDowell, West Virginia. Can you say Gnizylarap? That's Paralyzing backwards. You ever heard of a program statement? That is supposed to be the rules that all B.O.P's are to supposed to follow, but West Virginia on some "what program statement?" Program statement my ass. Them people in West Virginia so paralyzing, they tried to get their own time. Yes! All that, time go back and forward, east coast west coast shit, they trying to be on some West Virginia shit. I knew this wasn't the bid I heard about, and the guys I were around at Beckley and McDowell said this was the worst spot they ever been to. One thing that's a fact is they hate all 007 numbers, which is the last three numbers of guys from Washington D.C. You always hear in the feds D.C niggas did this or the Baltimore niggas did that. Since Baltimore and D.C are one car in the B.O.P 037 & 007 gets the blues by the staff. Soon as I got to the Beckley, they were printing my ID card and shit, and one of the officers came in and said "037 you from Baltimore, you a trouble maker" I thought damn I just got here. Then S.I.S pulled me in the room asking was I B.G.F (BLACK GORILLA FAMILY) and "what's this Shropshire Organization shit about." S.I.S means special investigative services, and they investigate any and everything. The government got me looking some kind of way with all the bullshit they put in my P.S.R (Pre Sentence Report). Fuck trying, they did throw the book at me, my P.S.R says I was responsible for 17,942 grams of heroin, firearm possession, threats of violence, maintain premise for drug distribution, attempt to bribe law enforcement and that I was the manager/supervisor of 5 or more people. At the end of the day all this shit from the court house to the B.O.P is all psychological and the government are the best at them kind of games. I was told before we were found guilty "don't let that shit brake you" and I see how it could. The guys I see around here have lost their damn mind. I can't explain it, but some of the shit they say shows they been in prison to long and its fucking with their mind. You can tell the ones that never had their own or never lived with a woman before. It's like how you don't get in the shower or clean up behind yourself. I'm so tired of guys, I mean just imagine being around guys all day, all the lying, back biting, instigating, the shit its crazy. Don't let a bitch (a man that likes guys) come on the unit. You'll really see who on ass and who not. Don't let a bitch with ass shots come around, these niggas might start fighting. I don't have a problem with any gays, or what you do, but I think there's nothing nastier than guys fucking guys and going home and fucking women. If you're going to fuck niggas, go home and fuck more niggas, don't mix shit with women. Then you got guys off the duce/K2, you want to see some funny shit, watch somebody off K2. That shit has guys doing all kinds of shit from jumping off the top tier to thinking shit was coming out the TV. The shit has crack head affects, because guys be selling everything they have to get more. It should be called Dunce (a slow stupid person) and it turns everybody that don't smoke K2 into cynic kind of people (one who believes all persons are motivated by selfishness). People say that it has rat poison, floor striper, bug spray and it. After they smoke that shit, they turn into the walking dead. The shit that goes on in prison has reality TV beat hands down. I guess you can label me a conspiracy theorize, put me in the class of coast 2 coast's own George Nore. If you ask me, the founding fathers of this country were no fools, and just like any other corrupt politician, they did what they wanted to. I don't have all the facts and when I was home I could have cared less. However, I believe once slavery was over, a lot of bullshit laws were made. Take trespassing, I believe its laws like this, that were made to arrest black people. I believe white people back then were so upset about slaves being free they wanted another way to get what they wanted, or just to be evil. The only people who had property back then where whites, and I don't see white people trespassing on another white persons property, so why was the law made? Of course to keep people off your property but to keep who off your property? Just imagine how many lost, confused blacks there were roaming around after slavery? Somewhere down the line the scheme became mass incarceration, and the 13 amendment makes that clear:

> Section 1 "neither slavery nor involuntary servitude, except as a punishment for crime whereof the party shall have been duly convicted, shall exist within the Unites States, or any place subject to their jurisdiction. Section 2. Congress shall have power to enforce this article by appropriate legislation."

This country was built by our ancestors with their bare hands. This country was built on crime, lies and corruption, so what you think after slavery they turned a new leaf? Check our history, since forever there was a greater scheme to things, they just mastered the way of covering it up and making you think there's nothing going on. Ask anybody, mass incarceration is the new slavery. I was told not let having 25 years fuck with my head, that's what they want it to do. They say guys come in with a lot of time and be fucking up, getting high or drinking, trying to drink the time/problems away and by the time they snap out of it, it's too late. I see it all the time and the way the courts and these lawyers are doing guys, I see how guys give up. The prison politics are always at an all-time high, and it's always a guy taking the walk or run up top, some call it the walk of shame. Going up top is going to lock up, the hole, protective custody or the correct name, the S.H.U special housing unit. Its many reasons why guy go up top, some go to avoid paying a debt, scared to death or just Hot. When somebody say "Hot" in the feds, they mean the person is a Rat, a Snitch, and without a doubt you will go by choice or by force for any reason. If you're from Baltimore or Washington D.C., you will need your B.O.P passport to stay. I can't speak on other cars (a group of people that hangs, sits, etc. together that are from an area, state, or organization. The Bloods have their own car, Baltimore/D.C is one car, you have the Down South car, or the Ohio car etc.) but if you from Baltimore/D.C and you want to be on Baltimore/D.C time you will need your paperwork/passport. Your paperwork is your sentencing transcripts, and docket sheet, which will show you not Hot. If You got your paperwork you can go to any prison in the B.O.P, which is why some guys call it a passport. All that so and so said this and that, "where that paperwork at?" Is the only thing that matters, and you got 30-60 days to get it. No paperwork, your ass is going up top by choice or by force. No matter how much I hate being in prison, I can say I learned shit I would have never learned had I never came. I met a lot of good stand up men from all over the United States, shit all over the world. Here in prison is where all the good men are, all the dirt bags, low life's, you name it, you'll find it here. I tell you this, I never been around a set of the funniest people in my life, it's never a sad moment and the jokes never stop coming. Being around different guys from around the world is almost like being there. It's so many different styles, and slangs, people are just different. One thing for sure I needed this, I wouldn't say I needed a 25 piece, but a little nickel would have been just right. In shaa ' Allah I give this quarter back. I learned so much about myself and others and everybody say when you get behind the wall, you really see who love you, and that's a fact. Ain't nothing like meeting other thorough men like yourself. Yea I'm thorough, what's up? Lol. Naw though, I have met a lot of wired ass niggas to. For the most part I be chilling, if I ain't playing chess, working out or at the law room, I am on the unit looking for the bid. Some people's bid is the phone, watching TV, or reading books. My bid is looking for all the funny burned out niggas to laugh at. Searching for the bid, I learned that "the difference between wise men and fools is often found in their choices of tools", Mass wrote that in his book, explaining how he received a note from a guy when he first got to the penitentiary that said that. Some shit you already know, but it takes for somebody to say it to realize it. Ruminating is my bid for the most part, I think that's what I do best. It took for me to come to prison to realize how powerful the mind was. Every time I start thinking I think of shit I wasn't into out there or shit I didn't even know I liked, you find yourself once you get behind these walls. It's like we confine ourselves to the hood so much, that we only know the hood. Some of the shit you day dream about while locked in the bathroom they call a cell can really change your life, or your way of thinking. Any successful felon with an idea I bet it all started while they were locked in that bathroom day dreaming. You have people like Wallo 267, who did 20 years and come home with some passion and an idea and took off like a rocket. One of the owners of the kite magazine (the biggest magazine for prisoners around, which is where I learned of Wallo), did some fed time. I believe their ideas come from many bathroom day dreams. As I laid on my bunk, reading yachting October 2020, I thought how I use to go fishing with my grandfather and that one time my father took me crabbing. Then I thought about how I'm spending another birthday in prison, right away I imagined me on that Ocean Alexander 27E, I than even seen myself living on the yacht in the ocean. I visualized slick Tone on a $10,000 Yujet Surfer, which is an electric surf board. Just that fast I had ideas and seen a different life for me and my son. My grandfather had a boat and I can see where my passion to want to be on a yacht came from. The way I see it is I have the time people on the street don't have to better their self. I spent my time studying law and preparing my own appeal, and now feel like I can do what any lawyer can do. I then put my focus on writing this book (my first, so bare with me) and now I feel like James Patterson. I wish I had this positive mind set when I was home. So now the appeal is filed, and the book is done, I will be learning more about myself, trying to learn the ways to get rich, build our brand (TMC), getting my credit together so I can someday finance that 27E through Essex credit, and what it is I will be doing with the rest of my life. As John Wooden said "things work out best for those who make the best of how things work out" so I will use this time wisely, you can bet your last on that.

WE SUPPOSED TO BE IN LOVE

Bates # W01-0074 states the following: "Your affiant believes Kelly is involved in the heroin trafficking conspiracy that Shropshire organized and manages; therefore, other members of the organization are comfortable calling her when needed to discuss issues related to the DTO" (drug trafficking organization).

All my friends call her Hell Kell and after I explained our new relationship to my man Wop from the North side of Pittsburgh, he calls her Killer Kells. I call her Kelly and all my special occasion cards were always addressed to my wife. If asked, I would have given my right arm for oh Hell Kell, but after July 2019 I would only be willing to give my left arm, with her name tattooed on it. I never knew I could put my finger on it, but it was always something about her that I loved since a kid. I don't remember how we met but we grew up around the same neighborhood. It's now been 25 years since I knew Kelly. A group of us used to walk home from Chinquapin middle school together. Nobody really remembers me because I was in special education, then was kicked out and went to Winston middle school less than a half of a mile away.

I remember being in a relationship with her as a kid; we were both the same age, "85" babies. Our first relationship we were like 13-14 and it didn't last long, but we stayed great friends. I remember being up on the phone 3-4 in the morning with Kelly. One of Kelly's friends Trina was Furl's cousin, and Furl's house was the hang-out spot, so Kelly used to be there and I would put my charm on as she would say. It was something super special about her and I never stopped liking her. We were always communicating so that part was easy. I knew a lot of girls, but Kelly always carried it like a lady since I've known her. I never would see her or hear about her dealing with this guy or her fucking this guy or that guy, really was the hard to get type. As a young boy, I didn't have the best game, but even with the slickest game shawty wasn't coming off that pussy. I remember Furl used to always say to Kelly "Bitch get them cobwebs off your pussy."

Since Furl house was the spot, we used to have girls over in the basement and you know Trina, Kelly and their crew use to come over and run the bitches off. Kelly used to act like we were together in front of the girls and all I could do was laugh. I used to see her coming through the Alameda Shopping Center when I was young and thuggin. We wouldn't talk but never was too far behind each other. It wasn't until the 12th grade when we started talking on that relationship tip and in June 2003 we got back together. In 2005 we moved into our first apartment together and been living together up until my arrest in November 2016. We had a lot of fun, but argued even more, mostly about me cheating. Kelly told me she was about to break up with me but later found out she was pregnant which was about 3-4 into our relationship. I was young and dumb, didn't give a fuck and treated her bad the whole nine months.

One night I was talking shit, what I do best, and she maced the shit out of me. She had to be 8 months pregnant at the time. I remember calling 911 because being 270 pounds at the time, my fat ass couldn't breathe. Baltimore County police came and asked if I wanted to press charges. I wouldn't ever press charges but it's funny as shit just hearing them ask. One thing that hasn't changed since middle school up until this day is the arguments between us. We would be on the phone for hours as kids then an argument would break out, somebody would hang up and we wouldn't talk for months. We both had the slickest mouths, had to get the last word and seeing eye to eye wasn't an option, which is why we are in the shit we are into today. I would say I was there for her and our son, minus the late nights partying, selling drugs or with other women, gambling, or down central bookings.

If you ask me, I was a damn good man and father. Yeah I cheated but what nigga in the street ain't going to do that? It's like if you pick a street nigga this is what you sign up for. I know I was a better man than a lot of other guys. I'm handsome, smart, caring, respectful, loving, non- abusive, an everyday father, paid the bills and took the trash out. Anyway, the question is why the fuck did we argue so much? Most of the time I was cheating but what about the other times? We were too much alike when it came to our attitudes which made us hate each other when we argued. Without a doubt I must tilt my hat to Kelly. She has been there for me before I was getting any kind of money, me getting locked up dozens of times with no money for bail, me getting my balls blown off and put back together than getting shot two more times after that. How could I forget the shit she did for me?

In the 16 years we been together I never caught her cheating. If she wasn't at work, she was out with her friends, home or we were together. What allured me the most was how loyal she was. She wasn't the type to sit around and let you talk about somebody she fucked with and not say nothing. I mean she was the perfect wife and had I not been so dumb I would have married her. Of course women are way slicker than men and are going to take some shit to the grave with them, that's a fact. I have caught her talking to a guy here in there but I don't think it was nothing more than them talking. Kelly is the shit in my book when it comes to being a good friend, girlfriend, and wife. One day she will make some man happy.

We have been through some rough times, but also had great times. I mean we did it all except for federal time. The most time I ever did was 7 months, so this 25-year sentence, is a different kind of animal. Once I got arrested I knew she was just as hurt as I was. We lived together for 11 years. If I wasn't down the bookings or out of town I made it home every night. When I got arrested we were together for 13 years, that's some devastating shit. We were one, always were together, a real family, me, her, Tone and as Kevin gates said "We posed to be in love".

I remember Kelly saying Nish (my man Bo baby mother) was holding shit down for him. (Bo was serving a 25 years sentence at the time). I agreed because she was holding shit down for him. I had no knowledge if she was or not, but I said what is she out here doing? If she fucking with another nigga I can't agree with that. Kelly said "As long as she is holding shit down, everything else doesn't matter," (I now agree with that statement). This had to be 2014-2015 and we went back and forth about the topic, of course she felt how she did and I felt how I did. I said "If I ever go to jail I ain't with that" and we left it alone. When I got indicted I felt that became my reality. I heard stories about guys going to jail and their girl leaving them. I saw it with my own eyes as well. My main focus while at C.D.F was to prepare for trial, but my other focus was to prepare for when Kelly wanted to move on. How could I not think about Kelly being with another man?

I wanted to address how I felt, because I believe if we broke up then, it would save me from feeling the hurt later. I would say and ask all kinds of shit and she would say "You worried about the wrong shit, it's too early to talk about that." I would say "I don't want to be lied to and we don't need to be together." "We don't need to be together for some shit that didn't happen yet?," she asked. I remember even saying "If you fuck somebody there won't be no wedding." She laughed and said "Boy be quiet." I meant that shit though. I never did no time before, so I didn't know that was a sure way to run your girl off. Through all the bullshit I put that lady through, she never missed a visit, a phone call, made sure I had money, sent pictures, took care of Tone and paid the bills at the house during the time I was at C.D.F (November 2016- March 2018).

The trial started on October 16, 2017 and she made sure she brought my trial clothes to the court every two days and never missed a day of trial. Some days I would look back and she would be sleep. I would never be mad, she worked so hard and did so much. "She must love you," the U.S Marshall said. "Why do you say that?," I said. "Because she forgot to put socks in your bag and took the ones off her feet to give to you." So the lady been down for me the whole 16 years we been together. However, somewhere down the line something happened and the people that knew we were not together always asked what happened, "I CAME TO PRISON IS WHAT HAPPENED."

I went on lock-up on August 21, 2018 only after being in the B.O.P (Bureau of Prisons) for four months. I stayed in the psychological torture chamber until July 1, 2019 in which during that time I only talked to Kelly 3 times. Each call was 15 minutes and I wrote over 100 letters and I received 70 letters from her in which I counted. She expressed her feelings about me being locked up and for the first 3-4 months I felt the love. I got 3 letters a week maybe, then it was 2 a week, then 1 a week before I noticed it was 1 every other week. Then one every two weeks. I guess this was around the time she started falling out of love with me, or somebody else had her attention.

I would say how I felt or I would ask is there somebody else she was fucking like all kinds of shit. The only thing that caught her attention was when I said dumb shit to her. The sexual, loving, sweet letters I wrote I got no reply as if what I was saying was inconvincible. I stopped writing to her and only wrote when I got a letter from her.

Now mind you since I have been gone I send roses on Valentine's Day and a gift on her birthday. I stopped asking questions and stopped saying how I felt. So July 1, 2019 came and I was moved to a different prison and I got a dude from Baltimore to send Kelly a message saying "Hey baby it's your Northeast nigga not your new nigga. They moved me to McDowell and I will call you tomorrow. I said it as a joke and little did I know there was a new nigga. I called her the next day and she didn't sound thrilled to talk to me, and I noticed but I didn't say anything. So I used to text her through my text services and she would reply. I wouldn't text her just to see if she would text me first, but she didn't. I was only off locked up four days before I broke up with her and maybe like she says, I didn't give it time, but I know when somebody ain't fucking with me. We been together 16 years, fuck do she need time to warm up to talk to me for. We ain't talked but 3 times in 10 months, so it was clear she was dealing with someone else who had her attention.

I called her on the 4th of July and the conversation was dry, like she didn't have nothing to say. So I said "Fuck you don't got no rap." She replied "Why do you say that?" I said, "Because you don't be texting me and you ain't saying nothing." You have to look for the dumb ass mind games people play. "I'm looking at the messages I send you," she said. "I reply to everything you say." I replied back and got in her ass about how I've been gone and it's no reason why she doesn't have anything to say. She got quiet. You know one of them I'm dead wrong quiet, so I hung up. She immediately texted me back saying ask yourself what have you sent me since you've been off lock-up. It's been damn near a year. I can't imagine just picking up where we left off. Mind you I know Kelly, like I lived with this lady for 11 years and I know when she's full of shit.

I've been texting the shit out of this lady saying Good morning, Wyd, Good night and I text her about how sexy she looked in the pictures she sent. When I was on lock up, there were some pictures I didn't see because they were on my property. I even told her how I watched the television show Charmed (her favorite show) that first morning off lock up and damn near cried watching it because I missed her so much. So instead of her just saying "I can't imagine just picking up where we left off," when I asked, she played mind games. Message from Kelly saying "Things haven't felt right for me in a long time especially given the fact it's been so long and I don't understand how you don't see that. I'm always gonna be here for you despite what happens with us and we have a long road ahead of us if we are together or not. I don't know what is best for us at this moment but I also don't want this to be an ongoing conversation or argument either." How the fuck was I suppose to guess that! Right then in there at that moment I knew something was up.

So I broke up with her. I've been around people playing mind games all my life so I knew it was more to the story. There were more mind game messages but I'm going to skip them. So as days went on, the Baltimore guys here at F.C.I. McDowell started calling home to see what's up with me, you know, to see who I was etc. One of the guys who were called knew me, and wanted me to call him. I texted him and he hit back and said "yo I heard what happened with the case, do you need anything." I said what I said and he hit back "I know Kelly your girl, but she been seen out with this one nigga more than once". You know I hit Kelly ass for answers. "Who is this nigga you be out with?" She found something funny. I ain't heard her laugh in about a year. She said "Well I be out with a lot of people, (mind game) who told you that?" I said "It don't matter who told me, who is the nigga?" (watch the mind game). "If you not going to tell me who is saying shit about me then don't tell me what you heard".

I thought we were back in 10th grade again. I felt some kind of way because she laughed as if this shit was a joke, so I said "Don't worry about it, I'm taking all the pictures of you off my IG" and I hung up while she was still talking. Clearly people in the streets talking and seeing them together, and instead of her been telling me she got a friend or whatever and we don't need to be together because I don't know how to feel, she laughed a nigga off and played mind games like I was a fucking clown or something. I'm not going to have you on my IG, posting pictures with captions like "characterized by beauty" and you out with another nigga, what sense do that make?

Shawty ain't even have the respect to take the shit up D.C, or out Maryland somewhere. I could see if she made it clear we weren't together or at least made sure I knew.

So I started asking around and two other people told me something along the same lines. One person said they seen them together before and seen a picture of the nigga on the Explore page at one of her birthday events. So I guess after Kelly thought about it, she texted me explaining she does have a friend but the people are lying about seeing them together. When she said they were lying about seeing them together, I thought this lady must think I was born at 1:05 am on October 30, 2018. Kelly further explains that the guy has nothing to do with how she feels about us, he's just a friend, he's not trying to come between us and that he doesn't talk no shit to her and our situation is due to the fact I was on lock-up for 10 months. She has to be the smartest dumb person I know IF SHE THINKS THAT MAN AINT TRYING TO FUCK HER, COME BETWEEN US AND IF SHE THINKS IM BUYING THE SHIT SHE SELLING.

Now I don't know what's true nor do I care anymore, but don't piss on me and tell me it's raining. A message from Kelly July 8, 2019 at 12:21pm "I never thought in my life I would be in a situation where you're not here physically no matter if we are together or not. But for so long I think I was hurt by the things you did in our relationship. I just wasn't happy anymore and I'm not saying you didn't make me happy but after you got locked up I saw how much pain I had in me and I never knew it was there until I saw how I was acting and reacting to things. I don't blame you for anything nor do I regret anything. Something's are probably my fault from holding things in and just moving on from pain and hurt even treating it like its normal. I really don't know but I know I was in a dark place once you were gone for a while. I have so much on my shoulders and some days I don't even know how I'm gonna get things done, I just get it all done."

I explained to Kelly that a big part of our issues are lack of communication. We still have this very issue till this day and I have said I was sorry and I know I have caused all the pain I felt in that message. I can't give a reason for my past actions and all I can do is learn from my mistakes and try to better myself. First, I didn't know that's how she felt, she had time to tell me this and I wish she would have said this on the July 4th call when I asked her what was up. But she waited until I heard some shit about her, then laughed me off. Why didn't she just put her big girl thong on and tell me what's up! I tell you why because she wanted to do what she wanted and either didn't think it would get back to me or just didn't care. I wish I could give Kelly the benefit of the doubt that she didn't think it would get back to me, but I can't. She didn't give a fuck, if I heard about whatever she may have been doing.

I then was told Kelly was running her mouth in her shop about her new nigga, so I asked her about it, of course she said it was a lie. So I was told again she was talking about that nigga. "You still running your mouth about that nigga?" Killer Kells tells me out of all people, "Why not?", and all I could do was shake my head, and I was supposed to believe the nigga ain't got nothing to do with our situation. I was tripping about the nigga, but after the sucker attack I had was over, I realize it wasn't even about the nigga. Me and my man Flip were talking about what I had going on with Kelly and he made a good point. He said "Shawty you got Shaq feet, can't nobody fit your shoes," and he was right. Another fact, niggas going lie and women going to be women. The saying really goes, "Niggas gonna lie, and bitches going to fuck" but I'm going to keep it respectful. So women are going to do what they want to do. That made me realize that my issue isn't she has a new nigga or whatever she wants to call it, it's the way Kelly handled the situation.

Of course getting Kelly to say she was wrong wasn't going to happen. So, she dressed it up and hit me with "It ain't no rule book on how to do things." I thought oh Slick Kells, can talk an Eskimo out of his coat. I had to agree but I explained that don't make it right, nor do it change the fact you handled things poorly. The respect I had for Kelly was slowly dispersing but after that "Why not" comment it vanished. Right then and there I knew she lost her mind and there wasn't a need for me to hit her about nothing. Until this day we don't see eye to eye and I don't call her. The only time she asks me to call her is when she wants to ask or say something. She hits me every 2-6 days asking how I'm doing and if I need anything. I feel like she wants to spoil me but all I wanted was her loyalty. Between being locked up those 10 months, us not seeing eye to eye until this day, and then the visits getting shut down due to covid-19, I haven't seen Kelly since July 2018.

One day I called Kelly because she wanted to make something clear to me and I said "This feels like old times, us going back and forth". She said "I don't want it to feel like old times, it was toxic". I agreed. I then said "Don't let nobody come between what's your best interest" and she said "What's my best interest?" I said "Me of course", but I was fucking with her. More so playing a mind game but she said you ain't my best interest. I thought damn that was cold, it made me think what makes me not her best interest? Is it because of what I did when I was home? Since I've been in prison I haven't been doing anything I wasn't supposed to be doing, so what's the problem? It became clear her problem was what I was doing when I was home and she waited until I came to prison to feel a way about it. Maybe I'm looking at it through a foggy lens, like she said it is what it is.

According to her, if I never came to prison it was bound to happen and she wasn't happy when I was home. Of course she would say that now, and I damn sure couldn't tell that was the case when I was home. I see it all the time. Women tell themselves different shit to justify their actions. It's like they say to themselves "any excuse will do". In 2015 we bought our first home and we had Thanksgiving there that year and in 2016. It was a nice family thanksgiving at our house, which she says is now her house. One thing for sure when the wife isn't happy nobody's happy, we all heard the saying "happy wife happy life". So I didn't see any signs then or around that time that Kelly was unhappy. I say that because everybody know when the wife is not happy ain't no fucking going on and that wasn't the case.

We were on our way to Miami and everything was going good if you ask me. Long story short, we would have gone to Miami, I would have spent money I didn't have at the time and she would not have had shit to say, so miss me with the "it was bound to happen" shit. That lady didn't say or act like she was unhappy and if I was home none of the shit she was claiming would even have crossed her mind (my opinion). It's really simple. This is how the shit goes when guys go to prison, I'm sure it's all in the contract I signed when I signed up for this life. The same shit happened to my Uncle Rodney back in 88 when the feds grabbed him and I'm willing to bet his child's mother's excuse was no different than my child's mother's excuse. Now I wouldn't dare front like the shit didn't hurt because it did. I guess now I know the feeling and like Miley Cyrus says "Nothing breaks like a heart".

The funny thing is I knew it would come to this. I saw it like a psych. I told slick mouth Kells that and she said "Well you should have been prepared for it". Our son slick Tone is far from a fool and knew what was going on, so Kelly tells me not to talk to Tone about our issues. I agree, but the man had a lot of questions and as his father I'm going to explain how things work with females and relationships when the man goes to prison, so I explained to him go to school and stay out them streets. Kelly says "Don't try to turn our son against me" and "I don't want him looking at me funny". First of all, I wouldn't try to turn him against his mother, second I told Kelly "Well don't do shit that will have him looking at you funny". Tone adds she is going to get her act together when you come home. I'm sure Tone wants us to be together. All he knows is us being together, waking up to us every day and our love and still love the family life. However, I will be a red tootsie roll sucker to get back with that lady.

I can hear my lower self now, "How many licks did it take to get to the center?" Later the lady takes the picture of the walls and from around the house and tells Tone to put them in his room. What kind of shit was that? Did she think about how that would make Tone feel or did she think about how sport coat would feel seeing the pictures around the house? I don't know why she took them down so I asked, and her response was "Because I wanted to." Shawty try to treat a nigga like a sucker sometimes and getting a straight answer is always out of the question. I didn't even argue with her and its shit like this, that makes me not fuck with her today. I can't respect that and I damn sure can't respect nobody telling me because I wanted to. What the fuck I look like the help? Got me fucked up if anybody thinks I'm going to allow that. She made her bed and I'm going to see to it that she lays in it. She talked so much shit to me, I had to get a receipt.

On some real shit though I can't blame nobody but myself. All the known cheating and the unknown shit I was doing will push any woman to the edge. So I understand why she feels the way she does. Now, just because I understand doesn't mean I agree, they are two different things. I just feel like don't wait until I come to prison to get mad or have a change of heart because of the shit I did when I was home. It's all part of the game I played so I'm cool with everything now, it just took some getting used to. It's a fact that if a nigga waits too long to get his act together something from his past will come back to kill him. Overall Kelly is a good, thorough woman, and all I can do is be sorry for my past actions. We had a lot of fun, you know, New York, New Jersey, D.C, Philly, North Carolina, A.T.L, Vegas, Bahamas, Jamaica, Punta Cana, and the list goes on. Without a doubt we tore Baltimore the fuck down. It will be a loss on both sides and I wouldn't be who I am without her and she wouldn't be who she is without me (my opinion).

It's truly sad things had to end because we posed to be in love. I think we both got in our own way of making it work mixed with being in prison and her looking at me as the old Brill without first learning the new Brill. Well according to her I haven't changed, what would she know, it's been 30 months and counting since we had a 30-minute conversation and 85% of our email correspondence we either were arguing or disagreeing with each other. The shit is just all fucked up and Kelly looks at it as I'll get over it. People say "Once a few guys treat her bad, she will realize ain't nobody going to love her like you did and she will be back and you going to go running". That statement is based off how things been going since forever, and how your typical jail nigga acts. I'm not your typical jail nigga and I don't care if I had life in prison, I don't deal with shit I wouldn't deal with on the street. The shit I see women doing and saying to the typical jail nigga will blow your mind. I just can't allow it, let alone deal with it.

The few jail niggas I do talk to about what I have going on always say "Well you won't have nobody". Well so be it then, because dealing with somebody doing and saying what they want is out of the question. So I explain to people who think Kelly is going to come back and I'm going to go running, that their supposition of me is based off how the typical jail nigga acts and once you jump off this Yacht, there's no getting back on. Further explaining that Kelly has a better chance of getting eaten by a shark then getting back with me. As far as Kelly, once she has her mind made up it's made and in my years of dealing with her I have never seen her mind change. She claims if I come home next week nothing would change. All I know is when I do get there she needs to keep that same energy and I'll do the same.

Now let's get this shit crystal clear because I know how people think. I'm not saying Kelly wasn't here for me or she dogged me in any way. Kelly offered her support in the form of asking do I need anything. I turned down what Kelly was offering because of how I felt she handled things with me and our situation. The way I feel has nothing to do with any nigga (that I'm willing to bet ain't around today) because at the end of it all, I don't know what she was doing or not doing. It's about all the slick shit that's been said on both sides, the way she chose to handle the situation, what I'm willing to deal with and the fact we can't see eye to eye. I don't have no problem with that lady, ain't mad about nothing and I will always be there if she needs me. She tells me the same thing.

It's really simple, you can't say or do what you want to me and think I'm going to just roll with it. As a man, I was wrong for cheating all those years and I said sorry. However, as the man I am, I'm standing on how I feel. I can't do anything about how Kelly handled things so my only option is not to deal with it or her. The love we had will never be the same and prison will fuck up any relationship and friendship, and my situation is no different of course. It's more to the story, but when two friends don't see eye to eye and hurtful shit been said and done on both sides, you have to split ways, and sometimes that ends friendships. As Kelly says "It is a part of life".

One thing about the government that I can't stress enough is that when they don't have the facts, they will make some shit up. All my co-defendants are from the same neighborhood as me and Kelly. The government was so far up my ass that anybody who called Kelly from a jail or prison phone in the state of Maryland, they reviewed there calls. So since it could be a United States v Brady violation, they give me a copy of all the calls they reviewed. Nick and Bo are not my co-defendants but their jail calls and Kelly's friend's calls were in my discovery. All my friends use to call Kelly from jail either looking for me or just to say what's up. Lou and Kelly are friends and went to the same elementary, middle, and high school together. Twan's baby mother is Kelly's sister, so that's why my co-defendants and friends are comfortable calling Kelly.

It's truly sad that the government has to make up lies and fabricate things to get ahead, that shows that they are corrupt and can't be trusted. We all know if that lady was discussing issues related to the alleged Shropshire organization as they claimed in their affidavit to get a search warrant and their indictment, they would have locked her ass up. So if you're ever a jury at somebody's trial, don't ever listen to what the state or government say, only go off what the evidence shows, and what the government says out there mouth 50% of it is a lie, and isn't evidence.

As I explained to Kelly my concept is based on her present actions and hers is based on my past actions. According to Kelly, I "like to talk" and am "only writing this book for attention" and I'm "vindictive" and "can't wait to come home to shit on" her. I explained to Kelly that's the old me and since she's done with me I won't be wasting any more time or energy on anything concerning her, other than supporting from a distance. As I explained partly, in the last 30 months, I haven't seen Kelly and only talked to her on the phone maybe 25 times. I could have called Kelly but her actions showed me there was no need to waste my time. Trying to rebuild trust among other things is difficult through emailing and 15-minute phone calls that only lead to multitudinous miscommunication issues and misunderstandings.

Executive coach Phil Harkins hit it on the nose what me and Kelly went through stating "Clear communication that moves toward results may seem easy but it is not. In fact, communication is rarely clear, consistent and forward moving. Rather it usually suffers the pitfalls of misinterpreted emotions and misunderstood facts. Furthermore, most communication about difficult issues is characterized by circuitous argument, uncertain outcomes, lack of clarity, conflicting personalities, and misaligned goals". We all know, well we should know to "never make a decision upset." When I wrote the above paragraphs, which was late 2019, early 2020, I was upset, hurt, bitter, more so disappointed. But don't think I was just talking. That would be a mistake on your behalf. Trust me, I cut bitches off for less. Part of me still feels that way. But today, June 2021 I really don't know how to feel. Kelly still acts like she wants to be here. She hits me once a week, while sending pictures every 4-5 months and is banging this "we friends" shit. You ask me, we supposed to be in love. The last pictures I seen, I said "damn, I don't remember her looking this good." Further thinking, "friends with benefits would be right up the old Brill's alley." But Kelly makes clear she don't look at me that way. I don't know what the fuck she looking at than because I'm him! Without a doubt she tries to be here for me, but I gives her a hard way to go. She treats a nigga like I'm her first cousin or some shit. I guess that's her putting me in the friend zone and replies to my messages when she wants. Do them other niggas have to wait hours or days for a reply? Some say I'm tripping like big shoes. But you can't treat me any oh way. I'm a king, and I must be treated like royalty. If you can't give me that, then I guess I'll be on my way. Ain't no question I need her friendship and support. But I will never compromise my ethical standards for comfort. Never! It's just so much I don't understand when it comes to us. I guess prison will have a woman on to the next. I hear that "time waits for no man." It's not that I don't want to be friends. Kelly is my best friend. I love her to the moon and back. But I'm a zero tolerance type of nigga. I don't do friends with people that I feel played with me. And she definitively played with a real nigga. Furthermore, we just been through too much to do this friend thing without some professional help. Another thing about me is, I don't play with my heart. I don't see how people can play with theirs. I won't be playing with mines that's for damn sure. Anyway, we both bosses, both want shit our way, and both think we got all the sense. Which will cause resistance on trying to get this "we friends" shit going. So how can we, and why would I, try to build a friendship with her, on quicksand? Without an understanding, somebody will say or do something and the whole shit will blow like C-4. Plus, I'm still attracted to her and did not want things to be the way they are.

So how am I supposed to look at her as a friend and watch what I say? I talks a lot of shit to the ladies. You should hear Kelly trying to tell me what I can and can't say to her. What Gervonta "Tank" Davis say, "ain't no safety on this glock." So I can't stop talking shit too her. Of course it's nothing disrespectful. What fucks me up is, I'm now the man she wanted all them years. At lease I think I am. I been reading and learning how to become a better man. Ain't nobody out there reading books on communication and relationships. I don't know what she think she going to find out there. What may happen is: she going to run through 3-5 different guys, looking for lord knows what before she realize that the one, who has her best interest, is in prison, right where she left me. I will be home soon, and I don't doubt she thinks that. But the little shit she doing, and picking me up when she wants to, won't work for me. See I know my worth; I was a catch when I was home. Not saying she wasn't, because she is. In fact, shawty a badd mothafucka. What I'm saying is: It's a shortage on men, who are a catch, not women. Look around you, how many of you women, want a man, but can't find the right one? How many of you fucked 3-5 different guys, thinking you had something? Just to see you just adding to your body count. Now I'm not saying that's what Kelly is out here doing, or see will run into any of that. Honestly, I don't know what she doing, shit, we rarely talk. What I do know is, that pussy ain't vegan. Did I say something wrong? You ain't mad at me is you? You couldn't have bought this book thinking I was going to keep it any less than 100. Fake and phoney don't run in my bloodline boo! In short, all the good men are either dead, in prison, or taken. You got eyes and ears, you know this. Not to mention that Baltimore/Columbia/Towson, Maryland is number ten in the U.S for the highest women to men ratio, according to statista research department 2009, with Jackson, MS being number one. So now that I'm no longer that same ignorant nigga, who will never treat a woman the way I wrongly treated Kelly, who they call handsome now, in the best shape of my life mentally and physically, (at 6'1, 218 pounds) "I'm the one!." So I think Kelly has lost her mind not wanting me. I told Kelly home girl Ebony, (tell the kids Uncle Brill say "what's up") in July 2019, that Kelly had until I got back in court to get her act together. I'm sure she didn't get the memo, but my motion is already filed with the court, so it's really an any day thing. And guess what? Kelly been all over the United States, but haven't seen me in 3 years. But I suppose to believe that she wants to build a friendship with me. West Virginia got airports & shit right? Yea I thought so. And that right there says a lot to me. The way I carry Kelly is "fuck outta here" because her actions call for it. But after reading, studying women, and talking to some wise men, I learned that shawty don't know any better. She living life, after being in a relationship for 16 years with my lying, cheating ass. And I understand that, I also understand that life don't stop. But a hard head, make a soft ass. Just look at me, crying like shit. I don't know how she feel, but if she wanted a, "I want my cake and eat it to" type of situation, all she had to do was say that. That I can respect. I know if she don't get her act together, by the time I get back in court. What's going to happen is: she going to look up and I'm going to be home, looking like a fuck, and my feet going to hurt from walking out her life. I want nothing but the best for that lady. But, according to Baltimore statistics, it's not looking good. Every time she think she got all the sense (when it comes to how to deal with me) I think "poor Tink-Tink." At the end, I know she is a good person, and really means well. It's just I'm a different kind of nigga. Today she sticking to she don't want me and only wants to be friends, so I have no choice but to want who wants me. I been giving her the cold shoulder for two years now, and it don't seem like she will stop pursuing this "we friends" shit. So I'm going to play this "we friends" game with oh Hell Kell. I know the shit going to come crashing down like the Surfside Condos in Miami without some professional help. I tried months ago to let bygones be bygones, but my ethical standards kicked in, and wouldn't let me look pass her actions. So me being the man I am, I reached out to Kelly to let her read what I wrote and gave her a chance to tell her side. I'm not surprised she failed to address her actions, but here is what she had to say:

Kelly: "I never thought a day would come where he would be in prison doing twenty-five years and I'd be raising our son without him. From day one I've always known him. I knew he lied, I knew he was a cheater and I knew he was very immature but he grew on me. I always thought as time went on we would grow together and we would be on the same page one day but as time went on and after having repeated conversations I knew he wasn't changing for us it was just about him. Tony thinks I didn't want to be with him because he used to cheat when in fact it was just me getting tired of watching him digress. When you know a person has so much potential and you watch them grow to keep falling backwards at some point you just get tired. I've known Tony since we were kids and we had the same routine; talk for a while then he would get mad at me and we wouldn't talk for 3 months."

"So just imagine being adults still arguing but living together, so 3 months not talking, it just wasn't happening. I got pregnant and was so shocked because we were barely getting along. Man, I took 4 tests because I was shocked. 9 months of being pregnant, emotional and not having an understanding boyfriend smh. Nonetheless we can skip the small stories. I was 8 months pregnant and I was fed up so I couldn't fight him. I was too big and too far along so I brought some mace. lol He came home late drunk, gambling and he lost his money. So he came in around 3:30am which isn't unusual but he had a nasty ass attitude."

"After questioning him and him getting smart I started getting dressed and he started talking shit like yeah go to your mothers mean while I'm grabbing the mace right out the nightstand walked right up on him and sprayed him right in his face and I mean I got him good, so good that he had to call the ambulance. I ran out, jumped in my truck and went to my mother's lol. Fingers burning cause the mace got on me but I didn't care, I was just sick of his ass. I got a phone call from a good friend of ours checking on me saying Tony came walking around to his apartment building in boxers, socks and a tank top and I didn't feel bad, not even a little. Shit to be honest I might have to write my own book because all the stories I have really would be a book."

"At some point you get tired of the phone calls in the a.m. hours, having to bail him out, the late nights of gambling and the cheating. He thought because he bought me gifts I was happy and I'm sure at some point he knew the gifts couldn't make me smile but he didn't notice the smile was gone. For some reason people assumed he took care of me which I'm sure led some to believe that. When in fact he took care of his responsibilities as a man and I still work and took care of my responsibilities. I didn't think or know exactly what the outcome would be for me and him with him going to prison but I do know him going away put me a dark space and I didn't realize it until I was happy again. For some reason it felt like he was happy knowing I was living like I was in prison which I can't understand why."

"See he doesn't tell people how he went on lock up and then he refused to come out for 9 months so he can be transferred somewhere else. Imagine not talking to someone at all. You go from seeing a person every morning every night to once a month. Once lock up starts you don't talk to that person and see that person which is an adjustment. It's strange to say that once your routine changes everything changes especially when that person that was once in your life for every minute of the day to not knowing when you're going to talk to them again. November 30, 2016 my phone rings saying Kelly they got him. I'm like who got him what are you talking about and the person on the phone who was family to us name Lil Travis said it again, they got him Kelly."

"Now I'm thinking it was the police. Despite knowing at one point it was a tracker on his car I still didn't think the feds were gonna be a part of this story. I got a phone call and they said hey Kelly he will be at this address and they gave me a time he would go in front of the judge. I just knew going to the court date he would have gotten the box. I mean Tony isn't a bad person his record consists mostly of traffic charges, but the way they made him look was just crazy to me because they made him out to be a monster. Like I couldn't believe it. After that day, I knew my life was gonna be different and I didn't know if it was for the worst or better. Now I knew I could handle doing everything on my own but 16 years of having your partner there through thick and thin, I knew it was going to be different. I was depressed and I didn't even know it. It was two whole years of just not being myself and not ever thinking I was depressed; it was weird as fuck."

"I remember like yesterday me and my best friend went to Atlanta on December 3, 2018 and when I came back I kept saying to everybody I'm back y'all I'm back and I felt it I felt like myself. I felt happy. I can't explain but going to Atlanta really did what I needed it to do without me even knowing. Honestly I have been to hell and back with Tony and I wouldn't change that for the world, but he wasn't a saint, was nowhere near an angel, I guess he was just him. We grew in different ways but we had great times which I wouldn't ever want to change. It's no regrets at all. Everyone knows the stories and the lies in between a relationship of 16yrs. It wasn't perfect, not one bit of it but it was a lesson. Right now we beef just like we did as kids but these circumstances are different. I can't run into him anywhere, I can't play on his phone, we can't do anything as if it's normal because he's gone but I'd honestly rather him be in prison than a grave so one day we will get it right."

"So there's his side, my side and the truth, which is my side lol. Me and Tony never got along but it wasn't a bad thing it was just our thing. We could go about three months without talking and boom it's like we just met once we saw each other again."

Caught Off Guard

S ometime in 2014, I was listening to a police scanner that picked up a D.E.A Surveillance team. I was into all kinds of counter surveillance shit. One time I got arrested for some bull-shit and the officer found a bug sweeper that detected wireless devices and they were blown away that I had it. Anyways, I was listening to them follow a guy from some apartments in Arundel Mills which is in Anne Arundel county Maryland. They followed him up 95 North into Baltimore, and at the time I was bagging up heroin to give to my guys for distribution. I was going to be a few hours so I locked on to the channel they were on. I forgot what way the guy take to get into Baltimore but he ended up on Homewood & North Av in East Baltimore. He picked up a girl that came out of the third house from the corner and they pulled off. The D.E.A boys were on everything and they radioed back in forth everything the guy did. So me being who I was, I seen the window of opportunity to let this guy know the D.E.A was hot on his ass. A good friend of mine is from 20th and Homewood and he is the Big Homie around there without a doubt. I called him and told him what was going on, I explained that I'm trying to get in touch with a girl that left out of the third house from the corner. He said let me make a call I'll call you right back. Within minutes he called back with the girl's number. So I called the girl and told her so in so give me her number and I wanted her to tell the guy she with somebody is following him. The guy thought it was bullshit until I told her (who in turn told him) everywhere he went and what way he took to get into Baltimore. She said they were on their way to "Maryland Live Casino" Which is in Arundel Mills. I cut what I was doing short and told them I would met them there. I got on 695 East then got on 95 South. It takes me about 20 minutes to get there and I called the girl and told her I was out front, she said they were at the first set of slot machines on the right. I walked in and said "damn we live in a small ass city" It was Rico who I know from around my way. His mother lives around there and as kids we use to hang out at "The Alameda Shopping Center". Rico was from the Park Heights area in Northwest Baltimore, but it's safe to say we knew each other for 22 years. I know the girl as well, so after we laughed about all knowing each other I told him the story. From there me and Rico got close as shit. As time went on if I wasn't fucking with Rico, I was fucking with Rocko, a guy I met from hanging every damn where in Baltimore. Once me and Rocko met in 2014, we locked in from there. I thought why not introduce Rico and Rocko to each other since I was with either one at any giving moment. Rocko was from the Monroe and Mosher area of West Baltimore, but hung around Pennsylvania Ave not too far. As time went on we all got closer, and Rocko was rapping and pushing Y.F.E, which stood for Young Fly Entertainment. Now days, rappers call their group, crew, label, something. You have rapper Future who has F.B.G (Free Band Gang), Moneybagg Yo who has B.G.E (Bread Gang Entertainment) and the list goes on. In Baltimore you have many different groups, and because Baltimore has Y.G.G (Young Go Getters) I told Rocko he had to change Y.F.E. It was too much Y shit going on, Y.B.S & Y.G.G and now he was trying to push Y.F.E that wasn't going to work. So one day him and Rico called me on facetime, they both were funny as shit. "Yo how you feel about T.M.C?" Rocko said "what's T.M.C?" I said. "TOO MUCH CASH" they both said. I thought yea, Rico up the Heights getting money, Rocko over West getting money, and I'm in da north getting money, that's TOO MUCH CASH" so I said "Yea I like that shit" then we all changed our names on I.G, Rocko was Roc_tmc, Rico was Tmc_cashonly and I was and still is Tmc_yo. Our Instagram wasn't jumping, but who the fuck cared, we was getting TOO MUCH CASH. It wasn't any music being recorded but there damn sure was a lot of dope being sold. Nobody knew us as being T.M.C, but they knew we all were getting to a bag in them streets. Rocko played the studio, but not as much as he should have. His good friend/manager Manny lo was Rocko's backbone. I heard Drake's song "10 bands" and I remember we were in Norma Jeans and I pushed Rocko to get on that beat. He killed the beat than shot the video and named the song "100 bands" I broke my forearm the day before Easter/2015, so I wasn't in the video like I wanted to be but there's a quick shot of me in a cranberry hoodie. 2016 came around fast ass shit and music wasn't in the picture. It's like everything before 2016 is a blank memory, I could tell you the whole 2016 I felt something, but couldn't never figure it out. I remember me and Roc was at the bar at Ruth Chris in Dallas, I don't know where Rico was at, and it was some St. Louis girls there and they were fascinated with us. They just couldn't believe we were from Baltimore and there for the Cowgirls game. Reminded me of the time when me and Lou went to Sacramento and soon as we walked in the strip club, there was this one girl who was looking hard as shit. I walked to the bar to order a drink, just to hear the bartender say "we don't serve alcohol" I thought what the fuck, and turned around to see the girl looking at me. I walked over to her and said "what's up", her whole face lit up, and said "OMG I knew y'all was from Baltimore". I couldn't believe it, she said she been to Baltimore before and knew how we dressed and sounded. I must add Sacramento has the best Ruth Chris I ever been to, but it's one weak ass city. Anyways, Miami was the next stop for us, but I got locked up and been in ever since. That's just a long story short about how the T.M.C thing came about. Soon as I came in Rocko and Rico names were jumping, not that they weren't when I was home, but you know how niggas be in jail talking like shit. Rico was the low-key type, you know, Roley on with pockets on over load, and I was the same way, but Rocko on the other hand, bust down Roley, Big Boi AP, 4-6 chains on and the loudest in the room. But after I was in Rocko really took off and turned shit up quick! He started doing music again and dropped T.M.C, it was now 2Raw. Before you knew, everyone heard of 2raw-the-don. I heard a lot of people didn't like my man, what was there not to like? What they can't say was they ain't heard about him, and damn sure couldn't say they didn't see him in them streets. I was locked up when he turned it up, but niggas that was coming in Supermax was talking. How it was put to me, you couldn't miss him out there in the streets and he came off like the mob. According to Baltimore's Shaderoom page, which is a copycat of the real Shaderoom on Instagram, Rocko didn't fuck with me. My home girl told me she seen a picture on there of us, talking about he started getting money changed T.M.C and turned his back on me.

She said somebody commented and said the feds grabbed him why wouldn't he not change everything up, and that's exactly what it was. Rocko changed it up from Roc_tmc to 2rawthedon on I.G and turned the shit all the way up. Without a doubt Rico and Rocko supported me and I will always tilt my hat to them both. Anyways, Rocko got back on his music shit, bought a Bentley truck, did a video with Moneybagg Yo, brought him to Baltimore, shoot the video right in front of the Pennsylvania Ave market B.K.A the Avenue Market (west Baltimore) dead smack in the hood, named the song "too much money". Rocko did music with Baltimore own Benji Bo, Lor Chris, Geechie, D.C's finest shy Glizzy and Atl's Rylo.

It was July/2017 and I had a hearing to try to get home confinement before the trial started. Everybody came out to support, Rico had just started a business and told the judge if I was release he had a spot for me. Of course with my record they shot me down, but I had to try my arm. Weeks later I was on the unit most likely talking shit and guess who I seen walking in the unit? Rodriguez Moore B.K.A Rico. All I could do was shake my head, Rico was charged with conspiracy to distribute Heroin of course. He was pissed because he didn't understand how he was charged with guys he didn't even know or do business with, I thought yea that's what conspiracy is all about. Before I got arrested in November/2016 me, Rico, Rocko, Georgie, Big Head Charlie and many others use to gamble damn near every day at one of Georgie spots in Northeast Baltimore not too far from my way. I was tripping when I heard wiretap calls of me and Georgie talking shit about gambling and was fucked up when I seen pictures of us at Radcliffe when I was buying a Rolex. I thought damn, they were following a nigga like shit. One of Rico co-defendants was telling me how he heard wiretap calls of me and Rico talking about hanging out. On my unit there were two different guys from the Park Heights area (which is where Georgie is from) that was telling me the feds both asked them about Georgie. In September/2016 they grabbed Big Head Charlie, November/2016 they grabbed me and they grabbed Rico in August/2017. After Georgie got killed in September/2017 there was this article about him saying he was this infamous drug dealer in Baltimore that was under investigation when he was killed. I just use to think like damn, we all were under different investigations at the same time and was all together at some point of the day. My trial started in October/2017 and Rocko use to come until one day my co-defendant who was on home confinement (who could come and go) was in the bathroom at the court house and overheard law enforcement say "you see 2rawthedon in there?" My co-defendant told Kelly, who told Rocko, I thought damn that's crazy. Everything was just crazy, between Georgie getting killed, Lil Tay two months later Trav and them people sentencing me to 300 months, I'm surprised I ain't lose my mind. I remember during the sentencing the Marshall was taking me in the back and he said "I ain't never see the court room that packed before" everybody came out to support. I was told that I didn't even see everybody, there was more people in the hallway because they said it was nowhere to sit or stand. Next stop was F.C.I (Federal Correction Institution) Beckley in racist as West Virginia and them people had a lot of shit with them. They played with all the legal mail and all the legal documents which I needed to fight my case. Once I seen that I knew I had to get the fuck away, also Beckley was a yard full of rats. They didn't want legal documents to come on the yard so they could protect them rats, so they played all kind of games. That shit made it harder for guys (like me) to fight their case, so I started thinking of ways to get transferred. I was told to change my address to a down south one and tell them I wasn't safe on this yard. Before I could make my move, I got caught with some homemade alcohol fucking with the Baltimore homie up stairs from my unit on August 21, 2018. I was given 21 days on lock-up and they took 41 good days. When it was time for me to go back to the yard, I told them that I owed for the alcohol and I don't have the money to pay. I was told once I did that I should of be gone in 2 months. I had got into it with my unit manager right before I got caught with the alcohol about fucking with my legal documents. We all know white people don't like when we tell them about their self's, so that's a part of the reason why I was still there 6 months later. During that time, I got some pictures from my mother. I always looked at the pictures first before reading the letter, so I could know what she's talking about. So, as I went through the pictures, I said, "look at my nigga Moody, looking good shawty", then I looked at the next picture and said "DAMN!" It was a picture of him with a caption that said "REST IN PEACE". My mother was saying that she seen this on I.G and everybody was posting him and thought I might have known him. Some days later I got a letter from Kelly explaining that Moody got killed and he had just came pass her shop asking about me. Moody was from around my way and its crazy how you here one day and gone the next day. The mail was fucked up to due to the K2 problem so it took at least 2 weeks to get mailed around February-March 2019. One of my many cell buddies was Glo, he was from uptown Washington D.C. We were cell buddies for 3-4 months and he been back there a year because of a knife and end up get an extra year added to his sentence for that knife. Glo was cool as shit but he was crazy as a mothafucka, gave them people hell back there. So after Glo got his time they wanted him to go to a penitentiary but the big bosses said no, so he went back to the yard. All the officers said he will be back in 30 days. My little cousin Rod-Rod use to write me to tell me what my DM messages use to say. We only get one 15 minute call a month, so I did everything through mail. I would write little cuz and tell him to DM people for me. I told him DM Rocko just to check up on him and to tell him he has to kill that 7 rings beat by Adriana Grande and the WOW beat by Post Malone just for me. I Knew people in Baltimore wouldn't be on them songs, and Rocko would have killed them beats. A letter came from little cuz and he said Rocko said he was ok, asked did I need anything and said the beats was hard as shit. Being on lock-up 23 hours of the day there's nothing to do but send out a million letters hoping somebody would write you back and send pictures. Every time the gate opened everybody was on their door to see who it was coming on lock-up and take a guess who it was coming down the hallway? Glo crazy ass and he had this sick look on his face. Once the police left I yelled "what happen Bro" he said "I'm sick as shit, somebody told one me and they found a knife" I shook my head, he was only gone 31 days. A few days went by and on March 30, 2019 he yelled "dam Brill I meant to tell you sorry for your loss." I was confused, I didn't know what the fuck Glo was talking about, he said "your man that be rapping got crushed" I felt the hurt start at my feet than run through my whole body. I send Glo a kite (note or letter) asking was he sure and how he know. He said he was walking the yard with one of the Baltimore homies and the homie told him my man Rocko just got killed. Glo knew who he was because we were cell buddies for months, so of course I talked about Rocko. Glo didn't know the guy name who told him, just knew he was from Baltimore. I didn't know any of the

Baltimore guys from the streets but we knew some of the same people of course. There was this one kid that was there, he knew I was T.M.C and Rocko was my man. Another guy said I looked familiar than he remembered that I been to his house before. He said that I give a friend of ours dope and that friend gave it to him to sell and it was slow on his block, so I came to see what the problem was. I thought that sounded like me and that was some small world shit. Rocko got killed on March 18, 2019 and here it was the 30th, days later I got a letter from Kelly saying he got killed, the letter was dated the 18th. Being on lock-up wasn't easy, and you had your good days but not more than the bad ones. Being back there was like being in a psychological torture chamber that will have your mind doing all kinds of shit. One good thing that came out of it was that I found who I was and I had time to really read the Bible. The more and more I read, the more I started to understand a lot of things I didn't understand before. You'd be surprised about how much you would learn about yourself being back there. Can you imagine being locked in a cell 23 hours a day for 10 months? I could have went back to the yard but why go through that shit, I can't fight my case like I want to with all that playing with legal documents, plus I was trying to get somewhere that had cell phones, I could get so much more done with one and Beckley didn't have not one. After being on lock-up for the first 3 months I would have been a fool to go back to the yard. As far as Rocko goes I heard he had beef with some people and I know how beef goes in Baltimore. I was truly fucked up about what happen, that was my man and he acted like a friend. After thinking about how all my friends were either dead or in prison the hurt turned into excruciating pain for weeks. I thought and thought how things got to this point. I got word Rico took 10 years in federal prison. I use to sit there like damn I didn't see this coming. All I could do was become stronger and focus on getting home to his daughter and my other friends children to be the uncle Brill they all know; I owe that up.

To Ryan "Rocko" Brunson: I was your biggest fan and you knew that. I haven't heard none of your new music and you know I can't wait to check it out. I tell people all the time if I was home I would have got us on "love in hip-hop". I would have been pulling up on Mona Scott telling her "look, we need a slot and it don't matter which city", you already know I could talk anybody into doing something for us, who else did the talking when we were out. You know what comes after a sentence, an appeal. So I got baby girl soon as I get there, you were there for Tone so it's only right.

So when I was moved on July 1, 2019 to a prison an hour away I was pissed. Soon as they told me to pack up on that Monday morning, I knew I was going to F.C.I McDowell. Everybody in the B.O.P knows air lift (the plane ride to another prison) is Wednesday – Friday. McDowell is the fucking same as Beckley and I was pissed the whole ride there. I must say they a little better with the legal documents coming in, but I got to get the fuck out of West Virginia with the quickness. It felt good to be off lock up and I was 30 pounds lighter. I lost 30 pounds from working out before I went on lock-up, so I was looking skinny as shit when I came off 60 pounds lighter. I was getting something's in order and was glad I was off lock up, but I found out that my 10 month stay on lock up fucked up my relationship with Kelly according to her. It felt funny not having her 100% behind me and it was a lesson learned. The shit with her really caught me of guard and I wish she would have been told me that's how she felt. In the 12 days off lock up, I had to break up with Kelly and I got an email that I wasn't prepared for. Everything that happened since I been locked up caught me off guard. "Yo they killed Lor Travis down the shop today". I looked at the computer screen in disbelief and said "WOW! "It was July 12 and I was just upset about life. While on lock-up anybody I thought about I either had little cuz send them a DM message or I got their address and wrote them a letter explaining what was on my mind. April (Lor Travis's mother) crossed my mind because she always holla at me on the gram, so how could you think about April and not her son "Lor Trav". I wrote her a letter before Rocko got killed just seeing how she was doing. Me and April go way back and are good friends and went to high school together. I told April in the letter that she has to be on Lor Travis ass because we don't need any more drug dealers or killers. I explained that I was Lor Travis age before, so I know what he thought about. I watch Lor Travis grow up just as many of us did. Our youth goes through shit that leads them to a life they really don't want. I never got a letter back, but that was the case with 80% of the letters I send out. So to hear that he got killed was very upsetting and for it to happen at The Alameda Shopping Center made me feel responsible. I felt like my life was upside down, a feeling that I felt many times. It was too much going on, it been too much going on and it made me feel confused as everything else did. Lor Travis made the 5th person I lost to gun violence I cared about in the 33 months I been locked up. He was the one I cared about the most because he had a future, the other 4 people I lost made their mind up about what they wanted to do. Meek Mill said it best "when he got killed it wasn't right, but he was trying to live that life." That's how I felt about Georgie, Lil Tay, Travis, Rocko, they were all grown men. Lor Travis wasn't grown, he was a kid and had time to make his mind up. It was put to me that it wasn't for him, just wrong place at the wrong time. My love will always go out to April because I can't imagine losing my one and only.

To April: I'm sorry that things played out this way and I wish we could go back in time so you could get your baby boy back.

To Travis "Lor Trav" Chance Jr: I'm not your father but you know I wanted the best for you. I use to make sure I give you whatever you asked me for so you wouldn't get any ideas. I wish I was home, maybe things would have been different. I love you kid!

Being off lock-up was supposed to be a good feeling, it felt good but I wasn't happy. I didn't want to be in west bumble-fuck, Kelly was on some she doesn't know how to feel shit and did a good job at showing it and I was pissed somebody killed Lor Travis. The only good thing was I was able to see my family. They drove 7 hours to come see me and it made me realize they are the only ones who will always be there. Sitting on the visit with them I felt like the piece of shit I once was because I always put the streets before them. I know that ride from Baltimore to McDowell wasn't no joke, so I really appreciated them coming. For the most part I stayed focused and either was in the law room or working out to keep a clear head, but the thoughts came rushing back like a middle linebacker blitz. Before I knew it, it was now 2020 and Covid-19 was knocking at everybody's front door. Millions of Americans were out of work and record breaking people started filling for unemployment, and the B.O.P was shut down. After weeks of not coming out for nothing but a shower, we were coming out for showers, to use the computer and phone, three times a week. Shit I thought that was better than nothing. So on May 11, 2020 I came out to use the computer and I checked my emails. I had a few blues (the messages come in blue) so I clicked one and it read "Flip got killed today". I was like damn! It felt like the wind got knocked out me. It's like since I been locked up, it's been nothing but bad news after bad news. They smoked my man on Mother's Day, what the fuck they ain't have nothing else better to do? It's been nothing but shit after shit and I'm just sick of it. Flip was my man, knew him for years, but my last 8 months on the streets, we were together every day. My last birthday on the street I was with him. Flip was on his way into Family Dollar about a mile from my neighborhood when somebody ran down on him. When I heard what happened, I was like what? He was from Belair Rd in Northeast Baltimore, about 5-7 miles from where he was killed at. So I was confused about what happen, somebody had to follow him around there. Flip always wanted a little boy and just had a baby boy named Brayden Brown, weeks before he was killed. I got in the shower that day thinking "got damn Flip, you were the last Mohegan." I knew my heart hurt, but I felt nothing from being numb from lose after lose. Flip was a good dude and would give his last, he had 3 daughters that he loved to death. I always seen and heard about guys losing their friends, but to really go through it was a different kind of beast. Flip fucked with Kelly hard too, all my friends loved Kelly. A week before Flip got killed, Kelly gave me a so-called apology "I said I was sorry for how you felt." I read that and thought what kind of apology was that. She sorry for how I felt! Then said "we all make mistakes I'm sure you can understand." She followed that statement up with "what was it you were mad about?" All I did was shake my head, clearly how I felt didn't matter and she didn't feel like she was wrong. Flip your home girl is a fucking emotional manipulator. Anyways, Kelly expressed she was worried about Tone, she didn't want him to grow to be numb. Tone knew all my friends very well, Georgie, Lil Tay, Travis, Rocko and Flip. They all were like family and Tone had a personalized relationship with them all. These guys weren't just some people I seen every blue moon. So for a change I felt what Kelly was saying and the affect it could have on our son. I know losing Flip took the fight out of me. I talked to Tone and I asked him how he felt about what happen with Flip, he said "yo that's crazy." Flip fucked wit Tone too. I remember Flip was with me when I went to the studio to meet Rocko. Flip was saying he liked the beat and before I knew it, Flip had his iPhone out and had a verse done. He called me over, rapped his verse and I was impressed. I mean I ain't nobody to impress but Flip did that shit quick and his verse was hard as shit. Flip didn't know Rocko like that so he said "holla at Roc see if I can get on the song." I told Roc "let Flip in the booth". Roc came out Flip went in and killed that shit. He had everybody in the studio fucked up, and Roc had to put him on the song.

To Brandon "Flip" Brown: Man I fucking miss you. We had a lot of good ass times and I won't never forget them. Every time I talked to you since I been in, you made me feel better about my situation. It's only right I look after your kids, when I get there. Love you Bro you will be forever missed.

It was now May 17, 2020 and we now come out Monday-Friday for an hour in a half. I was waiting for the officer to open the doors so I could get my little 90 minutes, but my counselor came to my cell and said "Shropshire I need to talk to you" and he opened the door. So I followed him to his office, I thought it was my piece of shit ass lawyer calling but when I walked in he said "well I got bad news," I thought what else is new. He told me my grandfather passed, I just shook my head. I already knew he was in the hospital because he had a seizure, but for him to pass away I was like damn. I just knew he would pull through because he in and out the hospital sometimes, plus he was the toughest of the toughest. You know how older people be a different kind of tough. I'm glad it wasn't the covid-19 that took him out though. Ronald Lang Sr is his name and I'm proud to be his grandson. I watched that man take care of his family and give all his grandkids nicknames, mines was Stiffy. I remember going fishing with my grandfather and being in the boy scouts that he put me in. My aunt told me that he would always want to take me with him but my mother and grandmother said "hell no". I was the first male grandchild and my family always treated me like a Prince even though we were a low middle class family. My grandfather was real, didn't take no shit and always said what's on his mind. Once I was driving him home and we rode pass this old school in east Baltimore and he said he always wanted to go there but it was an all-white school. I could tell he was still pissed about that. After all I'm sure he went through he still was the man and started his own business Ron & Ron Handyman service. How can you not respect a man that raised all his kids didn't take no shit and didn't let nothing get in his way? After seeing how he handled things, took care of his family and how tough he was, I see where I got it all from.

To my Pop-Pop, I never thought you would have passed. You are the toughest and with all that was going on at the house, I'm just glad you at peace. I know how you didn't approve of a lot of thing when it came to your family and house and at first I didn't understand, nor agree, but now I been through some of what you been through when it comes to how you want things to go at your house, I understand now. I just wish I wasn't so blind back then so I could have gotten the knowledge and wisdom from you. There isn't a question on where I got this stubbornness from, I thought that was funny. I also never apologized for disappointing you and I'm sorry. I know this wasn't how you raised me. You made my world when you came down to the trial and gave me the thumbs up, I thought you were going to be mad at me, but you showed me to be strong. I love you and please rest up, it's that time.

My mother got in my ass because my dumb ass sitting in prison and not there with my family. I know how bad I hurt my mother with my actions, she use to tell me that all the time. I know she didn't raise me this way neither, all I can do is feel sorry about how I hurt her. She always says that this is all apart God's plan. I believe everything was already written to happen the way that it did. I now see things differently and I'm ready to serve my purpose.

WHY I CHEATED

I'm sure this chapter caught you by surprise. I thought about adding a chapter about why I cheated, just to kind of explain my actions. As I see it, cheating on the (then) love of my life was a part of my life, or should I say life style. I'm not on no Steve Harvey shit, as my D.C homie Sasso put it, but my Baltimore homie Murda told me I was. I Don't think I am, I just thought I share my point of view on how I feel, plus I ain't saying nothing that ladies don't already know. Now I'm sure its hundreds of reasons guys cheat and I know ladies have heard them all. It's a fact I was a cheater, and if you ask me it's a fact all men are going to cheat. I have talked to a lot of girls and only a handful agree, and the rest say "all men don't cheat" but haven't been with a guy that didn't cheat on their ass in the 30 years they been living. Now for the ones that think all men don't cheat and want to be optimist about that, go right ahead, but the sooner you get that guys are going to cheat, the happier your be. Good women (like Kelly) don't deserve to be cheated on. How I use to feel was that a woman should weigh the good with the bad. Meaning if he was a good boyfriend but cheated on you, you shouldn't trip. Nene Leakes said, "just because a man cheats don't mean he's not a good man" I think I was a damn good man, I just was a cheater and liar unfortunately. As I said that's how I use to view it, and I was mentally blind back then. I never said this to Kelly, but that's how I thought, I felt my good outweighed my bad. I thought and thought about why I cheated every time my dumb ass got caught, now the blind fold has been lifted, and I'm thinking clearly, I still came to the same theory of why I used to cheat. My theory is that it's just in a man's nature to cheat or be with multiple women. I told a friend of mine from Chicago that and she said "get the fuck out of here Joe". How else can you explain all your boyfriends cheating on you then? You can have the best pussy in the world, you can throw it in the air and it could turn into sunshine, he still going to cheat. Beyoncé supposed to be the baddest bitch in the world and Jay-z cheated, Offset cheated on Cardi B another bad bitch, and Niece Nash said fuck that and went and married a female so the list goes on. Being cheated on will happen, it's been in our history since forever, kings, like David and Solomon from the Bible had multiple wives, why? It may take a guy sometime to build the balls up to cheat, but it's going to happen. Many of the reasons men cheat is because of lack of sex, arguments, or his lady just don't do it for him anymore, or in my case, did it for no reason. We all know how relationships go, starts of romantic, loving, caring, fun, etc. and after a while they both get bored or just get used to each other. **They don't go out and have fun like they used to,** conversations get old and the sex gets boring. "Like every relationship, it was full-time fun at the very beginning, then more and more boring, then "how do I escape from it?" As Maurizio Cattelan put it. That goes for both women and men, so as I explain this, I'm not just talking about men. It's a never ending list of why people cheat, and it's a fact men have a way weaker will power than women. It's a lot of women that want to cheat, but it's in their nature to be caring, faithful, and loving, so it takes a lot for women to crack. Men on the other hand it takes nothing but an argument over what he think he wore last year for thanksgiving dinner, and be wrong as shit. I'm no expert on why people cheat, so I can really only speak from my point of view. As much as I tried to come up with a sufficient answer as to why I cheated, I came back to the same answer. All that, I was mad at Kelly, we were beefing, or I was drunk, was never the reason. I'm on a unit with 100 plus guys, and I don't ask every guy, but the ones I did ask all said they cheated. Most guys said they did it for the thrill of doing it, or the opportunity presented itself. One guy said it was something about fucking his girlfriend's friends that drove him crazy. Others said because they knew they could, or because all girls are different, some girls have big asses, a pretty face, big tits, etc. Females do it all the time, cheat on their boyfriend who they love but may not have the big dick they want or don't have the bag, so their side nigga will have what their boyfriend is missing. Only a few guys said because it's in a man's D.N.A to cheat or deal with multiple women and that was the answer I was looking for. I'm sure a lot of female readers will disagree, well ask yourself why your boyfriend cheated. All roads lead to a very distinct possible that it's just in a man's D.N.A to deal with multiple women. No matter how hard I think, I can't come up with a reason other than its just in my nature. For once in my life I don't have to lie about my past. I either was lying about crime or cheating, so now that I'm in the clear to tell the truth, the un-told truth, I have no reason to lie. What blows my mind is how women can deal with the shit, I don't see how they can. I dealt with some shit with Krystal, (my first girlfriend) who hurt the shit out me. I said I would never deal with no shit like that again. So I have to salute you strong women for dealing with the cheating, that includes you Kelly. It's crazy because some of the girls I cheated with wasn't shit. I had some nice girls and of course most of the time I got caught with the nothing ass bitches I was dealing with. Like why did I risk my home for a nut that I could have got at home. I'm telling you I thought of this shit all kinds of ways, and the only answer I can stand on is it's in a man's D.N.A to cheat with any kind of female, shit from what I hear niggas cheating on their girls with niggas, shit is crazy. I had no reason to cheat on Kelly, she was smart, caring, beautiful, funny, loyal, faithful, could cook her ass off, ambitious, was a lady, great mom, a family first type of woman. **She** never bitched about me coming in all different hours of the night. The best type of female a street dude could ask for, and what did I do with all I had? Cheat! Now that I'm thinking clear, I was a damn dummy, all men are dumb, because we all cheat for no reason. The last of the men I asked said something that made some sense to me. Their reason was because they were in the street light (meaning in the street and had some street fame). I guess to sum this theory up; it was the temptation that got these guys. I guess some would argue this is no different than a guy cheating with a girl with a pretty face. I would disagree because I think the big ass, pretty face thing falls in the category of lust. These guys talked about cheating because the girls came on to them, always in their face, which in turn baited them right in. As a man it's hard to turn down a beautiful woman throwing their self at you. I think women don't understand this because they turn down guys every day, but men are different than women. If a guy is in the streets and getting some kind of money, them type of girls is going to spot that guy coming from a mile away and them type of women be drop dead gorgeous. Most guys that's somebody in the streets have a girl-friend/wife, which is part of the reason why they somebody. I don't know if the guys would have cheated if the girls never came on to them, but that's what they said. I wasn't a slick cheater at all, and got caught 60% of the time. Kelly use to say "you be having some bullshit bitches." I use to laugh because she never really caught me with the bad ones. Of course I don't have no bitches now, prison will do that to you. I'm sure they all will come climbing out their holes when I give this time back and I pop up on them streets looking like a fuck. In Baltimore me and Kelly wasn't the most known. The people that knew us or heard of us knew we were together because we been together for 13 years. The name Brill made a little noise, not much at all, and if I had to guess it was because of me being with Kelly when it came to females knowing who I was. So I tried to be slick and told females my name was Tony. So on two occasions I shoot my jumper and couldn't believe the answer I got. More than half of the times I shoot my jumper I missed. I guess it was because I was too fat, wasn't dark enough, tall enough, who knows. So, I said what I said and on them two occasions I got the same answer. They both asked, "what's your name" and before I could say Tony, they said "Tony, Brill, Kelly" I damn near fell out, all I could do was smile, and say you right and pray they didn't tell Kelly because clearly, they knew her. I'm trying to tell you I can't make this shit up. That shit fucked me up because they were two different girls and they both said the same shit, blew my mind. I stopped trying to talk to girls, but it didn't last long. It's crazy because I told that girl Niesha (the one I met at Ruth Chris) my name was Tony. So after I got locked up, she asked Rocko "where your man Brill at?" When he told me that the first thing I thought about was she knew who I was the whole time. I asked her about that and she said "I met you at Norma's before". Anyways... People ask me all the time why I never married Kelly. The truth is I knew I couldn't stop cheating. I took marriage seriously and said if I ever got married I wouldn't cheat. I don't know why I hurt Kelly, and now I got my head on right I think about it often. Kelly didn't deserve me cheating, so she damn sure wouldn't deserve it as a married woman. Kelly would be a great wife, well I don't know this new Kelly, but the one I knew would have been. Since I became this new person I have apologized many of times and Kelly said "it's too late for all that." It's all good, it only takes one time for me to feel a way about something and that person don't have to worry about dealing with me again. When I told Kelly about this book, the first thing she said was what am I going to say about her. I told her I didn't call her out her name. She said "Oh ok, because I would sue your ass for defamation of character". She put laughing out loud, but she may have been serious. I laughed and told her "play if you want, I'm a real life Aaron Wallace." I then explained that "you lucky I ain't sue your ass for all the shit you put me through since I been off lock up." She hit me back and said "I ain't put you through nothing, you lucky I didn't been kill you, cut your body up, and bury your ass, the fuck! All I been through with you. One thing for sure you men cry, cry and cry when y'all think something is being done." I thought damn, she right, it's a fact men couldn't handle none of the shit they do if it's done to them. I know I can't, and I always told Kelly "If you choose to deal with the shit I do than that's on you. I'm not going to deal with that shit." I know I wish I stop dreaming about her. I been having all kinds of dreams. We all heard the saying "want who wants you." I just want to move on with my life as she did. It's funny because Kelly uses to always say she was built Ford tough; I guess that Ford broke down alone the way. I know she was in love with a version of a person she created in her head that she tried to but could not fix. She realized the only person she could fix was herself. I know she love me but enough was enough. Something's I had to see for myself to understand.

Now as far as the new me goes; I feel different. Of course, it's easy for me to feel different being in prison around niggas all day. I guess when I get home, I will have to see how I do. My cheating days are over that's for sure, I know this because my relationship days are over. I in fact believe nobody needs to be in a relationship, "this thing called life I'm learning it. The scars Kelly left on my heart is permanent, no more getting involved I'm just having my turn with it. We not doing titles, just a month by month lease." I had it coming so I'm over it, it wasn't easy. I wouldn't say she did some fucked shit up to me, I'm just talking shit, Jadakiss said that, but I am scarred because this isn't what I wanted, and I thought she would have handled it better. I know there's some good women out there but I can't allow myself to get wrapped up in love again to get hurt. That shit hurt bad, and if it wasn't for a good friend of mine who stepped up when Kelly stepped down, I might still be fucked up. I knew this girl before me and Kelly got together in 2003, we met at Chuck-E-Cheese in 2001. She used to dress up as Chuck, laugh out loud, sike naw, she was working the cash register and I had to try my arm. It was her who showed a nigga some love, when I needed it and even drove 7 hours to come see me. Got to respect a lady that's willing to deal with a nigga in prison, it's really harder than I thought it was. I ain't have nothing to offer but advice and a friendship. People I took care of on the streets wouldn't even pick up the phone. I felt like the piece of shit I was on the visit with her because I never noticed she had the most prettiest eyes I ever seen. We been around each other many of times but I never notice. I guess you can say it was her ass fault. Until this day, shawty still here for a nigga. And is still the same person, from 2001, to when I was home getting money, to me being in prison with 25 years, getting no money. Now that's a woman I can respect. Dealing with a nigga in prison isn't as easy, and I'm complicated as they come. No matter what she was here when I needed assistance so I will offer mines if it's ever needed. One thing about a nigga in prison, he won't forget who was there and who wasn't.

Anyway…Women are crazy and men are fucked up. The things I seen women/men do is a good enough reason for me not to get in anymore relationships. After what I put Kelly through and after what she put me through, why would I sign back up? I caused a lot of hurt and she damn sure hurt me, so I had enough. Men can cheat and cheat, but when that hurt comes back around they can't take it, that's a fact. It's best for me not to be in a relationship, I love women to much to just be with one, plus I don't trust anyone. It's too much shit going on now of days, look around you, nobody in a relationship is happy. I mean it's some people who are happy but how long will that last. Don't get me wrong, I loved laying up with Kelly watching Law and Order and Supernatural, but all that arguing will suck the life out a relationship. Over a ten-year period, Dr. R.C. Adams studied thousands of marriages and found that only 17 percent of the couples he studied was happy. More than 50 percent of all first marriages end in divorce. Oscar Wilde said, remarriage often is the triumph of hope over "experience." According to Robert and

Dorothy Bolton more than 60 percent of second marriages end in divorce and the divorce rates for third and fourth marriages are even higher. Another female friend said I was selfish for wanting to be in a psychological relationship with her while I'm incarcerated but wanted to do me when I come home. I explained I'm not selfish because I want a psychological relationship, am I not supposed to seek that kind of relationship? I explained to her that I'm not selling her no dreams, saying I'm going to do this and that. If we both have an understanding that we just friends and as of now it goes no further, how am I being selfish? I am being selfish in another way because I'm done with relationships for my personal reasons. In case nobody knew, because I didn't, what makes you selfish is if you do something for your own gain or personal reason. Every time I turn around, I hear about somebody breaking up, or getting divorced. Who got time for that? I'm done with it all, and I can't allow myself to hurt someone, and I damn sure don't want to feel that shit I felt. So I'm going to treat females, how I want to be treated. Despite my feelings on relationships, I know you can't achieve greatness without a thorough woman by your side. What everybody knows is it's not what you do, it's how you do it. The way I now see it is we (male/female) forgot how to be honest and transparent with our partners about what is it we want. We picked up this horrible habit of lying and being deceitful to our one true friend. What we don't realize is while being deceitful, we're being hurtful, which will in turn destroy the most important part of the relationship, the friendship! By being honest and transparent about whatever it may be, we keep that high level of respect that our partner seeks and you'll never know, you might just be able to get what it is you use to have to hide and lie about. The four greatest words in one's vocabulary are "what do you think?" -Anonymous.... I believe using those words are key, along with being honest and transparent. Instead of asking your partner "what do you think?" We do something first than lie about it later (if we got caught). By asking that question it will make your partner feel like their opinion counts, which will take you a long way. Of course, people would say "look who's talking" and I can accept that because I was a liar and a cheater. However, I'm now a different person and have been in a relationship for 16 years while living with my partner for 11 of those years. How many of you can say they have that kind of experience? So between that, me admitting my wrongs, learning from them (while paying the ultimate price) and reading countless books on relationships and communication, I think I am qualified a little to give some advice on the topic. I think I would now be a great boyfriend. However, my only fear is hurting another woman or even getting hurt myself. So I really don't know what I'm going to do. At the end of it all I can't imagine how my actions hurt Kelly and I'm truly sorry for doing so. Meek Mills said "relationships turn into situation-ships" and that's a fact. Which brings me to my next point, now as I have explained I believe I have an understanding with Allah. Yea I still curse but that don't have nothing to do with my heart. Anyways, I spend a lot of time reading the bible and the Qur'an. I want to share a few things with you. 1 Corinthians 7:26-28 says: "because of the present crisis I think that it is good for a man to remain as he is. Are you pledged to a woman? Do not seek to be Released. Are you free from such a commitment? Do not look for a wife. But if you do marry, you have not sinned; and if a virgin marries, she has not sinned. But those who marry will face many troubles in this life, and I want to spare you this." I don't know about you, but that was deep. Now Paul is speaking about not getting married because when you are married you are more concerned about your partner than the Lord to sum it all up. Now let's break down a little of what Paul said, "do not seek to be released," before that he asks "are you pledged to a woman?" I believe he is asking do you not seek to be released? Or want to be released? From what I see more than half want to be released or get out of their relationship. Then Paul says, "do not look for a wife," then says "those who marry will face many troubles in this life, and I want to spare you this." Tell me that ain't a sign to add to all the other signs we go through or see other's go through. The man said he's trying to spare you. Paul is saying not to marry so we can be more concerned with the Lord, but I take the bible a little more broader. How many people are facing many troubles? I think I'm going to listen to Paul. In 1 Corinthians 7:1-5 Paul is talking about married couples not having authority over their own body, but each other having control over the others body. Paul also is saying it's not good to have sex, but since sex is occurring, a married couple should have sex and only deprive each other to devote to prayer. Now what tripped me out was that Paul says "then come together again so that Satan will not tempt you because of your lack of self-control" Paul is talking about cheating, my opinion. 7:31 says "for this world in its present form is passing away." I don't want to waste any more time arguing about anything with anybody, especially a female. Plus, who wants to hurt someone or get hurt by someone? Signing up for a relationship is a sure way to get your feeling hurt. It's crazy it's this way, but it is what it is. The temptation will be at an all-time high for me when I get home, I know I can't stay away from women. Now before I close this chapter out, I want to share something that I read in the bible that I just couldn't believe was there, I like to fell out reading it. Ezekiel 23:20 states "there she lusted after her lovers, whose genitals were like those of donkeys and whose omission was like that of horses". So ladies, tell me you don't be lusting like shit over guys with genitals like donkeys? I'm willing to bet you have a few pictures in your phone right now. I heard many women say they not into guys whose genitals are like donkeys but still be lusting when the picture comes through their little group chats. Tell me you seen the episode of Atlanta housewives when Bolo was on there? Them women lost their damn mind. Got me thinking about going to see Dr.Miami to get a couple inches, laughing like shit. But I must say the Bible states facts and both women and men are a trip, so spare yourself the trouble, I know I will be. 8

Slick Tone

It was February 16, 2018 when I realized I messed up big time. I knew I messed up, but as a father, male parent, male ancestor, and originator that's the day I knew I fuck up! I was back at C.D.F, just came from getting a fresh 300-month sentence and the question I heard come through the other end of the phone ran through my body like melanomas. "Daddy you got 25 years?" Was the hurtful question, it felt like I was trying to piss out kidney stones when it came to answering. I didn't know what to do or say, so I did what I always did, I lied! How can a question hurt? "Who told you that?" Was my reply. I asked him that to know how he knew but also to buy myself sometime to think of a lie to tell my one and only son who was 10 years old at the time. As a baby he was always ahead, acted older than he was, make you say he has an old soul, or he's been here before. "I seen it on murder ink" was his reply. Murder ink is an Instagram page that posts pictures of victims of violence and other breaking news in Baltimore and the surrounding area. I guess because my case was on every local news and radio station in the area, they felt the need to tell their side. "No I don't have 25 years and don't believe what you see on TV or I.G" I said in my most convincing voice. I knew my son was smarter than that, that's my son, but I thought telling him the truth would break him into pieces. About 20 months later he asked me again and before I could answer, he followed up with "you been shot before?" I felt so bad about everything, my life as a whole felt over. The shit hurt because all I ever wanted was to be a father. Being fresh out of the psychological torture chamber will have you in multiple psychological states, mix that with a 25-year sentence, the death of multiple friends, learning the love of your life secretly moved on, then top it all off with knowingly lies you told your only son who thinks the world of you who is now pressing you for answers will be too much for any one man to handle. I was lost for words and my conscience told me it was time to come clean. I told him I had 25 years and that I got my ass wore-out not once, not twice, but three different times. Tone said he seen pictures of me at my grandmother's house when I was in the hospital and she told him what happen. Of course he asked when where and how. I owed up answers and I explained everything to him. I told him the truth, not only because he deserves to know, but to also make sure he knows what the streets have in store for him if he jumps out there. I told him to stay out the streets and that's the reason why he doesn't have any siblings. I'm not sure if he understood why I lied, but I explained that as his father I didn't want him to worry. One day he will be older and will understand why I lied to him. I asked was he mad at me for lying and he said "No, I knew you were lying." When I tell you them genes are a mothafucka, he sounded just like his mother saying that. You would have thought that was her on the phone. I felt so much better telling him everything and will never lie to him again. Since that day our relationship has been the best and if my situation will make him a better man, I wouldn't even be mad. Born on September 24, 2007, Antonio Shawn Shropshire Jr B.K.A. Tone-Tone, weighed 6 pounds, 8 ounces and I had to be the most joyful and proudest dad on earth. My father wasn't around so I always said that I will be the best father there is and will always be there. For nine years of Tone's life I was there and didn't miss a day, beside the 7 months I spent in prison when he was a year old. I still remember my mother use to bring him to see me and I use to hide candy in my shoe to give to him on the visit. I wasn't no weekend dad I was the real deal. When it came to being there as a father I was, picked him up from school/daycare and it wasn't a morning he didn't see my face. I loved being a father, it was the best feeling in the world. When Tone was a baby, I use to lay him on my chest, it wasn't a feeling like it. I was just happy to be a father and I took the task serious. I never could forget the birth of my son, and when we were able to take him home. Before I knew it he was walking and talking, and I was there every step of the way. I always had my vision of what I was supposed to do as a father, but as time went on I realized that I didn't know what to do. My father wasn't there so I didn't know what it was I was supposed to do. It's crazy because I'm not sure who raised my father, was his father not around and that's why he wasn't. We don't even have my father's father last name; we have a name that has no relation to us at all. It's bad enough that as black people we have our slave master's last names. It was a beautiful thing to be there with my son, to watch him grow. I don't understand how some guys are not there for their kids. Most of our father's wasn't there and I can see how that could affect them mentally when it came to being there for their children. However, on the other hand it shows me how weak of a man they are for not being there. My father wasn't there for me and I'm hurt that I'm not there for my son today. Nothing hurts more than that and it makes me feel like I failed my son. I wasn't thinking clearly when I lived the life I lived. It was that life that took everything from my son and I never looked at it that way until the blind fold came off. My son wanted a brother or sister, that life took that away from him, he wanted his father to be there and that life took that away from him. My man Bert went pass their house to drop some money off for me one day and he said he could see the hurt on Tone's face, further explaining that he thinks Tone was used to seeing me with him and Heads that it was hurtful for Tone not to see me with them. Bert explaining that to me was hurtful, because I knew Tone was hurting from my actions. The whole time I thought I was living that life for my family, but I could not have been. Anything you do that could lead to you being taking away from your family isn't being done for them. Your family would rather you be dead broke than in prison or dead. As Kelly put it "you did it for yourself" and I think she was right. I don't know if he sees it as I failed him, but I do. It was my duty to be there and I'm not, so how did I not fail him? I'm doing the best I can from prison and now that he's getting older I give it to him straight, no more lies and babying him. I tell him all the time that all that lying to him about things are over. I now treat him like the man he will be some day. He's at that age you really can't tell him nothing, every kid at 13 thinks they have all the sense, I know this because I was once that age. I explained to him that I will be there every step of the way to guide him and to let him know what's lies ahead. The way I see it is he's going to make whatever decision he wants and I just have to be there to support him and to tell him "I told you so." When I look at him I see me and Kelly when we were younger, the only difference is he's dripped in designer. I told Slick Tone my mother never bought me Jordan's, so the fact he has Gucci flip flops and Dolce Gabbana tennis, he's double blessed. We all call him Slick Tone because he always trying to be slick, or got something slick to say. Being raised by me and Slick mouth Kells, I can't say he didn't get it honest. I love talking to him because he never ceases to amaze me. One time my man Wop from Pittsburgh said let me holla at Tone. Wop said what's up and asked Tone how the ladies treating him out there. Tone knows who Wop is because I told him I hang with him and he's from Pittsburgh. Tone told Wop "you from Pittsburgh you wouldn't understand." All I could do was laugh, Wop was blown away Tone told him that. I don't think Tone was trying to dis-respect Wop, it's just he too slick. On Tone 13th birthday I crowned him "King Tone" because he is a King, his attitude, wits, his style and blood line have King written all over it. Furthermore, you call a teenager anything other than what they are they will become that, so I call it like I see it. At age 8 he came with the idea to start a kid's clothing line and said the name should be "Mucho Dinero', so that's what we did. We came out with our first set of clothing that did just ok. I had bigger plans for the kids line but needed a better quality shirt, so I put the next set off. Of course things went south with me from there. We will be coming back bigger and better, so be on the look-out for King Tone's kids line "Mucho Dinero". Overall, Tone is a great kid with the power to become whatever he wants to be. All I want is my freedom to be able to be a father to my son. My mother sends me something that said a black father is a man who had stepped up to the challenge of raising his children to be Kings and Queens. Someone who has risen above the negative stereotypes about black fathers and is a King in his own right. A provider, a protector, a lover and strong foundation. Royalty is in his lineage. I am a black father and I took proud in raising my son. Out of all the hurt and pain I felt the last four years I been lock-up, nothing hurt more than having to leave my son. I feel like nothing at times, I had one mission which was to raise my son and I failed. I will do my best from prison to teach him to be truthful, trustworthy and to always help those in need and to think before he acts. He has to understand that acting without thinking is like believing without knowing. As a father I believe he needs to know to always stand up and have morals and manners. It will be a tough journey for me to be the father he needs from prison, but I never was the give up type. Tone is amazing, funny, smart, argumentative, and always reasoning his way. If I were to ever change our names, his would be HUJJATZ, which means just that.

To my son: I am truly sorry I let you down. I have lied to you about the life I lived and I hope you can forgive me. Being in the streets will only lead you to prison or the grave yard. Your old enough to see and realize how things played out for me. The way I treated your mother is not the way you should treat a lady. I just hope your smart enough to learn from my mistakes. You have the power to become whoever you want to be, just don't waste it on something you seen me and my friends fail at. You been around to see and hear about the things we were into, don't think what happen to me and everybody we lost can't happen to you. Chris Grosser said "opportunities don't happen, you create them", so create the life you want, just do it the right way. You know I love you and everything I'm doing is all for you, stay focus Young King!

T.M.C. (TRULY MAKING CHANGE)

I remember Kelly saying to me "you act like it's the end of the world". Shit! I'm sitting in federal prison fighting like shit to give back 25 years, lost her and everything else I ever worked for, so sorry if it feels like the end of the world. Can you imagine losing everything? Imagine knowing what it is you thought you wanted, a little street fame, a little money, a family of your own and some good men around you. Now imagine losing it all. That's what I thought I wanted and that's what I was able to build. The streets gave me what I thought I wanted and the streets took it all away. When you go to prison that little fame you had goes, outta sight outta mind. The money goes for the most part and the family that you build gets dismantled. The lady that you thought wasn't going nowhere eventually moves on and your children become fatherless. Those good men that were around you, get killed, go to prison or just forget how to be that friend they once were. The hurt I feel comes and goes daily, weekly and monthly. What I'm noticing now is something will always add to the hurt or just bust them stitches open from old wounds. How the fuck did it come to this? Between the poverty in our neighborhoods across the states, racism, mass incarceration, black on black violence and now the Corona virus pandemic that claimed the lives of 530,000 plus, how can this be life? I'm not the best at delivering a message, but I'm going to try. The Prophet Noble Drew Ali said "if I can get you to think, you can save a nation" The first and only time I heard that was from a brother named Master D. Menes, from Southeast Washington, D.C. I met him at F.C.I McDowell, he follows the teachings of the Nation of Islam but he constantly evolving in his knowledge, wisdom and understanding and embraces truth wherever he finds it. He is the one who wrote the foreword at the beginning of this book. I'm sure the brother would love for me to join the Nation of Islam or even the Moorish science temple of America, which was found by The Prophet Noble Drew Ali in 1913, but never once asked me to. All the brother asks of me is to think. He also is the author of "Inside of the insides mind" and is formerly known as Tommy D. Edelin. The book can be purchased at www.istruggle360@yahoo.com his website is www.tommyedelin.com The brother has been raising a lot of great points at every service. I want to share one with you, which we all heard the story before, but for some reason, it's either ok with us, we forgot about it, or just don't give a fuck anymore. Before the epiphany I had back in December 2016, it was all three for me. This is not about black and white, it's about the foolish shit black people do to each other and why we don't have shit. But you can take it how you want, I'm just stating facts. Now I don't know how the fuck we got to the point of killing and hating each other, I would say it was all a part of a greater scheme. So called black people came from Alkebulan, known today as Afrika (Africa). Our ancestors all had an original name, culture and came from a tribe in Alkebulan. Our ancestors were brought over in enslavement ships (kidnapping is a crime here in the United States) and stripped of all knowledge of self, robbed of their heritage, put on plantations and made strictly for labor. This we all know. My opinion is that all that happened during slavery, the striping of knowledge of self-etc., and what happen after slavery, lost people who were given nothing, is a part of the reason why we hate and kill each other, which is and was all a part of a greater scheme. Which is what I call being the product of your environment. After enslavement, we were called Negroes, but before, they basically made us up, gave us new names (their names) and filled our heads with lies (Christmas, Easter etc.) which in turn, our ancestors, by no other choice, filled the next generation heads with the bullshit. Everything we now know was and/or is built on a foundation of lies. Brother Menes asked me once who was I and I had to think, was I Antonio Shropshire from Northeast Baltimore? Shropshire is a landlocked county in England, north of Staffordshire, with a population around 500,000. Can somebody explain to me where that name came from? Am I British? Oh that's right, I was a part of the royal family, but the monarch's disavowed me because the color of my ears, like they did baby Archie,

Prince Harry and Meghan Markle's son. I had to be honest with myself. I said "I don't know who I am". You could tell yourself that you are Jones, Williams, Brown, Smith, Lang, McCoy or Jackson all you want, but at the end of all that explaining, you really don't know who you are. Brother Menes explains that we need to declare our nationality. We went from nigger to negro to color people and is now known as African-Americans. Are we equal to the white race, or any other race? Yes! Do we get treated like any other race? No! Do we have a claimed nationality? If you said yes, then you're a damn fool. Every race has a claimed nationality but the so called African-American race. What you think we do because you see a box to check on your job application? Those people had us brain washed for hundreds of years. In the land of the free, where the blacks enslaved, three-fifths of a man I believes the phrase. An issue of the U.S.A Today says "Jobs losses land hard on people of color" why is that? Like Prophet Noble Drew Ali, I'm just trying to get you to think. At the end of the day, it's bigger than black and white, it's a problem with the whole way of life. I'm just a passenger. I found out my purpose was to tell the youth about what happens if they make that "Left" instead of the "Right". To tell them the feelings of hurt and pain that they will feel. I never imagined this, but I felt it. They don't know what it feels like to lose everything. What it feels like to have 25 years in prison. What it feels like to know everybody they were around are dead or in prison. They don't know what it feels like to have the love of their life move on and for their child to be lost. I bet you, they know what it feels like to be a lost child. The youth will always form new structures, define new realities, and build a new world. So, if they don't have it together today, what do you think tomorrow will be like? Back in 2017, 75% of African-American children were raised in single-parent homes. What do you think it is today? I found this to be believable. A study on Black youth suicide, found suicide attempts had risen by 73% between 1991-2017 for Black adolescents and listed exposure to racism as a factor. The youth is just one example of the future that we need to make better. Everybody has a story but, are they telling it? What good is it doing for the youth if they don't know the story? Am I the only one that is tired of the shit that is going on in Baltimore? Do you not care if your son, cousin, nephew, grandson, or godson gets killed or goes to prison? I don't hear stories about them becoming Doctors, Lawyers, Scientists, or anything other than statistics. I don't hear about what guys are doing to stop the shit that is happening to our youth. I damn sure don't want my one and only son shot dead in them Northeast, Baltimore streets or on his way to "Big Sandy" (United States of America Federal Penitentiary). The youth are young Kings and Queens and people worked hard to see to it that they don't think they are. I always looked out for the youth. Well, I thought I did but honestly I didn't. I use to give rides to school and pay for school materials (i.e. shoes, clothes, even prom stuff). I always felt responsible for the youth. When I realized what my purpose in life was, I knew it wasn't just a coincidence. I wasn't looking out for the youth like I thought. When they turned 18-20 and needed money, I didn't tell them to get jobs or go to school. I would just give them the money they asked for. I never forced drugs on anybody but, when I was asked to provide drugs, to the youth I'm speaking about, I didn't say no. Instead, I got ideas to help others help me. I knew if I said no, they would have went to someone else that wouldn't have played fair with them. Or they would have picked up a gun, rob, or kill somebody.

When I heard that my little cousin "allegedly" robbed a Baltimore City Police Commissioner, I thought "the youth is on a rise". When I hear about how my neighborhood is, I start to hate myself. I know that it's not all my fault but, I know I played a part in it. So often I get the question, "If you make it back on Appeal, are you going back to Baltimore"? For years when I was home I use to say that I wanted to move. So when I'm asked that question I say, "yes, I owe the City of Baltimore something". I like to know what the fuck I was thinking back then. I still remember when I was going to Harbor City High School, when I made the decision to drop out, to become this "Brill" character. If I could talk a grown ass man into buying dope that I turned 100 grams into 150 grams, then I could talk a high school kid into doing something other than selling dope or robbing. I believe if "The New Brill" went to the 2003 "Brill", I wouldn't be in prison today.

My plans are to hit up every high school in Baltimore to speak with the worst kids. My belief is; "If you want to attack crime, you attack where it starts". Only thing is I'm not a cop. I'm not trying to attack crime- I'm trying to attack thoughts. The same thoughts I had in 2003. I'm sure they run through the minds of the youth today. It has to be someone from amongst them to tell them what lies ahead. You think if Ironman was real and he came to the youth in Baltimore and said, "Don't sell dope", they would listen? If you said, "yes", then you never been to Baltimore. The kids would tell Ironman, "Get the fuck on Tony"! Youth crime is at an all-time high and I see why. Mass incarceration is taking their father's and women can only do so much. Thru cognizant, it's a small precedent of people that make it out that life without going to prison. So there's a high chance that you will either go to prison or get killed (usually by somebody you know). The youth follows those same actions of what got that person sent to prison or killed. So, if God is willing, I will get home sooner.

I'll start a Non-Profit Organization that will provide jobs, training, and more for the high school ages. The plan is to attack the thoughts of the youth so, they don't become the next drug dealer, killer, robber, or gang member. My plan is to try to get jobs, training, and funding to create jobs. Of course, it's going to be hard but, it's my purpose, plus you never know, the path may be already laid out for me. Plus, where there's a will there's a way. Furthermore, The Prophet Muhammad (Peace Be Upon Him) said, the first opposition to wrong is (1) hate the wrong in your heart; (2) speak out against the wrong, and (3) do something to write the wrong. I'm sure a lot of the youth will tell me "beat it" but, I'm sure I can talk a few into joining my program. I don't have plans going to them with just my story. I want to already have jobs and training for them so I can have something in hand when I pull up. I'm just glad the blindfold was lifted off me. As I explained, God will keep you blind until He's ready for you to see. People ask how I'm so spiritual but I still curse? I can't be no worse than the false prophets and pastors that trick a lot of you out of your money at a lot of the churches y'all attend. I have confessed my sins and have an understanding with God, do you? I know my purpose, do you? Have you ever heard that faith without works is dead? It is beyond true. I truly don't want the youth to feel this hurt and pain that I feel daily. If we don't do something, the youth will go through the same things and the cycles will never end. It's been going on for at least a century. When is it enough? It's not their fault that "so called Black people" were stripped of all knowledge of self. However, it will be our fault if we don't correct the youth now.

I hear the youth's actions and just telling them not to do something will not stop them from doing it. If you're not willing to really step up, then stop complaining. The way a lot of us act comes from what happened back then. Which was all a part of a greater scheme. For example, you ever seen the FX television show Snowfall? I heard that was true way before the show. So, whose fault was it that crack spread like wildfire? That was all by design. Those people never say it but, they are the reason why we act the way we do. After slavery, our ancestors were given nothing and have been denied equal liberty since forever. Therefore, not one person should think the "Black race" should have bounced back from Trans-Atlantic Enslavement Trade. If none of those things happened to our ancestors, would black people be struggling today? If your answer is, "No", then why are black people held responsible for their crimes? All that's happening today is a domino effect from what our ancestors went through. We are still being oppressed according to Robert H. Kinzer and Edward Sagrin in their book; "The Negro in American Business" (page 8). The history of America would be different today if the slaves freed from bondage had been given the famous "Forty Acres and a Mule". There is nothing that can be done about the last 400 years and if you ask me, the focus need to be the next 100 years. We have to train our youth to stop thinking the way we were brought up and lived was cool.

My focus will be the 18 and under age range. If we get to them, they will get to their children, who will get to their children and we can change the next 100 years. I once was 16 and the only thing I knew for sure was selling dope would get me rich. That was my frame of mind and look who I became (the "alleged" head of a Multi-Million Dollar drug organization) according to the Government. Our youth need to be exposed to other things. They need to hear real stories to give them a different view of life. These are young Kings and Queens and if they only know about dope, guns, and murder what are they going to gravitate to?

You have kids like Nupol Kiazolu, (The President of Black Lives Matter, Greater New York), after coming from the protests in Minnesota, running on three hours of sleep, he organized a "Non-Violent" demonstration in New York that over 1,500 people showed up to. Kiazolu felt that he was doing it for the future generations of young black people but, now feels that he is doing it for the present and the future. It is kids like him that are our future and there needs to be more of them. Our youth need to know that they have the power to do anything. They don't know this because they are being squelched and oppressed by the same kind of people that did the same things to their father's and forefather's. So sorry if I feel the focus needs to be the youth. Look at what Kiazolu was about to pull off in less than 24 hours. That's the power of our youth. Without guidance they are lost. Just as lost as I was when I dropped out of school to sell dope. I really designed myself and became who I was trying to be. So just think if I had some guidance, knew about our people and our history, who I would have become? I know once my mind is set, I can do whatever. I know I can change the thoughts of the youth. I hear young guys say, "Four years of prison ain't shit". I think, "Wouldn't four years of college be easier"? It's the mindset of the youth that is the issue. They follow behind the generation before them and so forth. When will we step in and say, "That's enough"!

I haven't been on the streets in four years so, I don't know what all is going on out there. But, I don't hear about people doing anything to stop the youth in Baltimore from following the wrong path. It's so many things that these kids can do. So many things they can become. Every young male/female I hold a conversation with, I make it my business to see what they are into, what they doing. I then explain to them that it's better to struggle 4-8years of college than to not go and struggle the rest of their lives, as their families most likely are. I don't remember anybody coming to my high school explaining a "like mines" experience or offering me a job and training. I might not be in prison today if somebody pulled up and really ran it all down to me and offered me training or a job. As I learned, kids want two things: (1) money and (2) knowledge. There's nobody really offering them a way to get both.

The Government claimed that the "Shropshire organization" operated from 2010-2017, sold Heroin, carried guns, worked from "secret stash" houses (to cut and package Heroin), discarded cell phones to evade detection, and were the main Heroin Trafficking Organization for customers in Harford and Baltimore counties. I'm disputing a lot but, what I am really disputing is that I didn't work with, nor did I conspire with any of the guys I was charged with during 2010-2017. Therefore, there was no "Shropshire

Organization" by law. "THE REAL SHROPSHIRE ORGANIZATION" will spend it's time attacking the thoughts of the youth. The name won't be "The Real Shropshire Organization", even though it has a nice ring to it. But it will be "TMC" (Truly Making Change). It's a better fit and has a real story behind it, with real people with real purpose. Founded by Rodriguez "Rico" Moore and I, in the name of Ryan "2RAWTHEDONE" Brunson. It's time we do something other than sell dope.

MORPH

M orph/ Morf/ vb: to change the form or character of: transform

What makes a person morph? Do people just wake up and are different? I guess nobody can answer the question of why people change. I would guess people change for multitudinous reasons and as hard as it is to morph, it's even harder to convince people you have. I guess that comes from so many people faking, acting like they Morphed, most likely for a personal gain. Of course people can Morph for the worse, but I'm talking about people changing for the good. The most people you would hear changed would be guys in prison, everybody call it jail talk. "Yea baby I ain't that nigga no more, I'm different" I'm sure every female who dealt with a guy in jail heard that before. Then the guy comes home and does the same thing he told the lady he wasn't going to do. That's also called selling dreams, and I see why people have to jump through rings of fire to prove they Morphed. Growing up in Baltimore you don't see too much of anything change, it's like if anything it gets worse. Remind me of the saying "the game don't change just the players." The game is just a metaphor used to describe something, more so used as a verb. The game could be anything, the dope game, the basketball game, a relationship, the judicial system, the prison system. Those things don't change only the players. You always see a different dope boy whose name wasn't ringing last week, you hear about the newest NBA Star, he cheated so she with him now, 20 years ago that judge's father did the same thing and the young replaced the old in prison. It's the same game just different players, when will change come? I guess that's why they say "change is good" because you don't see it that often. If I told you I Morphed would you believe me? If no, why? Of course the people that know me personally would say no. Is it because your life experience allows you to believe changing is unrealistic? Is it because I said nigga, talked ignorant and called women bitches in this book? I use to think a lot of things just wasn't possible, I now believe anything's possible. My cell buddy seen I ordered a book named "Listen up or lose out", a book on how to avoid miscommunication and said "them shepherds made you change your life slim." (Shepherds to him are white people that oppress the black race.) I laughed because it was funny, I then explained to him that it wasn't the shepherds that made me Morph, it was Allah. Yes, you heard right I Morphed, I changed the form of my character. I get the question often, "what's different about you Brill?" Well for starters, Brill isn't based off the character Brill off the movie "Enemy of The State" anymore. All Brill means is to Be-Real-In-Live-Long. Of course I made it all up, but according to Lolly Daskal "life is not about finding yourself, life is about creating yourself" and I agree. I still have a sense of humor and still find everything funny, still got all the jokes, still good looking, that's not going anywhere and I still curse sometimes. "Well what's different Brill?" The way I think! I don't think the same way I use to and I learned how to be patient. I was ignorant, selfish, a drug dealer, childish, vindictive, a womanizer, cheater, liar and manipulator. I learned not to raise my voice, but to improve my argument. Everything I explained in this book was from the way I seen things then. I made sure I talked the way I did then because it was a then thing, a then mind set. Today, I try not to use the word nigga, call women bitches and curse because that shows a level of ignorance. I now spend my time seeking knowledge, reading and writing. I don't see the need to lie, I don't have a reason to. Now that I think about it, why lie about something? Things go a lot smoother in the long run when you tell the truth. I didn't use to understand how I was selfish, I do now. Being selfish is when your reason for something is only based on your own personal reasons. What was so hard for me to realize that? The manipulating Brill was nothing more than the selfish Brill, I use to help people help me get what I wanted. The only thing I will have to see how I do is with women. When I heard the word womanizer, I thought it was something super crazy. Womanizer just means to pursue casual sexual relationship with numerous women. Some women are mananizers, I don't think that's a word but it's true. As far as my drug dealing days, they are over and I never thought about the life's I helped ruin until I ruined my own. I always were a nice guy, kind hearted and helped people in any way I could. When the people I sold drugs to talked to me about getting help, I told them I would help them get help. I never forced anybody to use/sell drugs, and never put them in a situation that left them no choice like I seen other dealers do. When people didn't have money and asked me for drugs, I never said no. This don't make it right, but it's says a lot about who I was. So now that I consider myself a morphed person that wants to do good, I'm not surprised that I want to help others. Whether you agree or not I been helping people in my own little way my whole life. I feel strongly about helping the people in Baltimore because I feel like I owe them. I took and took from Baltimore and now it's time to give back. I was once this vindictive person that would wait to that particular time to strike. I want to use that same vindictive energy to pay up what I owe the city that reads. I used to want to be a father, hang in the hood all day and party all night, then do it all over again the next day. Now it's like, I just want to go for a walk daily and watch the moon nightly. Feeling different about life is a different feeling, and I didn't use to care about nothing but my family. Now I see that was the selfishness in me and it's all most like I grew a conscious, or maybe I just grew up. I know it was Allah who Morphed me because soon after I felt that supernatural like epiphany, I viewed everything differently. The lawless way I seen life was gone and all I wanted was knowledge. I always believed in Allah, but used to feel like why was life the way it was. However, after reading and studying the bible and Quran, I now understand why and what Allah wants from us. So as life started to change in front of my eyes, since I been in, I see the bigger picture and now I realize what my purpose in life is. How did I miss all the signs that the life I was once living was coming to a screeching halt? As I had time to piece everything together it all made sense, I was blind and the supernatural like experience was Allah taking the blind fold off my mind. It's like when everybody is telling you your wrong, but you think you were right, then realizing you were wrong, why didn't you see it at first? You were blind and it took something to happen to you to see you were wrong. That something was a higher power, Allah! I can't really explain it but all the signs are always right there. Albert Einstein said "If you can't explain it simply, you don't understand it well enough" well maybe I don't understand it well enough or maybe like Lil Poppa say "what's understood ain't for everybody to understand". Never the less, It's a lot of smart, caring, passionate, successful people in Baltimore and with the right person leading by example, Baltimore can be one of the most palpated black cities.

It's amazing that former officer Derek Chauvin thought it was ok for him to knee on George Floyd's neck. Was it no different than the officers of the L.A.P.D Beating Rodney King? Those four officers thought that was ok and that happen in the 90's. It's no reason why similar things are happening today. It's crazy how they did Colin Kaepernick for taking a knee. Those same people should feel stupid because Kaepernick told you so. As breath taking as it was to watch the video of Floyd being killed, it had the same effect of the video of Ahmaud Arbery being ambushed by two white men. As I explained, that kind of thing is taught not learned. It was father and son who gunned down Arbery, who was just going for a jog less than 2 miles from his house. The last time I checked, the nation's prison population was 2.2 million with blacks making up 34% of all inmates. Which led me to believe that's why black people only account for 13% of America's population. I come to realize that black people are forced to sell drugs and to commit crime. It's not just about not having the resources and the opportunities as others, its psychological as well. So when I say black people are forced, I don't mean they don't have a choice, I'm saying psychologically, a lot of us don't have a choice. This is simple, it isn't marine biology. If parents are supposed to teach the children, but don't know or aren't able to teach the children because of our past history, what will the child learn? Nothing is the correct answer. So if one generation has nothing, what will the next generation have? Nothing! If that generation has nothing to give the next generation what will that generation have? Nothing! Do I have to say how long this has been going on? I think I do, it's still going on today, it never stopped. A study done by the Brookings Institution published in February/2020 found that in 2016 white families net worth was estimated at $171,000, which was 10 times greater than black families. Alisha Moreland -Capuia of Oregon Health & Science University said that "the persistent pandemic is racism, that's the pandemic, recent deaths of individuals of color stems all the way from 1776." Many researchers say that racism is associated with a lot of psychological consequences like depression, anxiety, or past traumatic stress disorder. Danielle Jackson a psychiatry resident and board member of the American Psychiatrists said "Perpetrators of racial violence may have changed uniforms, speech, and coded messages, but the message remains the same" Black people "are other, you are less than." It's impossible to imagine, but just try to imagine what so called black people's ancestors went through them 400 years. "Racism is traumatic for people of color" said Monica Williams, a clinical psychologist and professorate the University of Ottawa in Canada who studies African American mental health. If Williams studies led her to believe that, what do you think black people ancestors went through? Your answer said be unimaginable hell! Now if researchers say racism and watching the 8-minute video of a white officer kill a black man is associated with a host of psychological consequences, what do that say about former slaves trying to raise their children without nothing? It says that you had 500 years of black people going through psychological consequences right? It's called "Racial Battle Fatigue", a term used to explain the psychological stress response-frustration, shock, anger, disappointment, resentment, anxiety, helplessness and fear-experienced by people of color in historically white spaces says Roberto Montenegro, an assistant professor in Child and Adolescent Psychiatry at the University of Washington school of medicine who studies the biological effects of discrimination. Long story short, It's my opinion that our ancestors raised our great grandparents suffering from a severe case of "Racial Battle Fatigue." Not just that, our ancestors were not only treated worse than animals, but was miseducated and stripped of all knowledge of self. Which in turn was handed all the way down to the generation today. I believe that our parents suffered from "Racial Battle Fatigue" raising us, which caused our parents and us to suffer mentally. So mentally, we are focused to sell drugs and commit other crimes. Think about it, how long has drug dealing, drug use, and crime been a part of black people's culture? Mentally, a person is going to mimic what they see for the most part. You hang around a person long enough you will start to act and talk like that person unconsciously right? It's the same for most black people who grow up seeing crime, who was raised without a pot to piss in and a window to throw it out. It's called cause and effect. There will always be an effect from a cause. What happened back then, (the cause) had an effect on today. The sooner people realize that, the sooner they can help fix the effect. So ask yourself, whose fault is it that some of the black race lack knowledge of self and that crime is mentally a part of our culture? Which makes the crime we commit, not our fault.

It was so hard for me to open up about my life's story. I ran into many road blocks when it came to writing this book. I didn't know how to write a book or what to say. I just wrote it all the way I seen it. I wasn't getting money like Big Meech. However, I did in fact live that life and by the rules. I always stood on all ten and to me that outweighed the life I didn't live and the money I wasn't getting. Of course it's so much I'm forced to take to the grave and I talked to Allah about it all, in shaa Allah (God Willing) he'll drop all the charges. It's a fact I write this book to share the pain and hurt my erstwhile life brought me. Also to show my growth and vision of the next chapter of my life. I'm sure a lot of people went through more than I did, but what good will come out of the bad if nobody knows? This book is nothing more than the life and thoughts of a once blind/unconscious man who Morphed into a knowledge junky/activist that has plans on starting a non-profit organization that will attack the thoughts of today's youth, which is all known to me as The Real Shropshire Organization. I'm no longer the un-conscious person I once was, thanks to Allah. I'm now able to tap into my higher self, which in turn Morphed my morale way of ruminating. These last four years of me being in prison have been tragic. Oscar Wilde said "what seems to us as bitter trials are often blessings in disguise" If I got a year off my sentence every time somebody told me prison saved my life, I'll be home already. As emotional and abreast the ride has been, I can't say I disagree with Oscar and others. I was able to build a stronger relationship with my mother and now have a truthful one with my son, something I don't think would have happen had I never came to prison. Finding your new purpose in life is a good feeling, mix that with no longer hiding who you were is a great feeling. Blessed are those who have found their purpose in life and are doing it. Says The Honorable Minister Louis Farrakhan. It's like "when you stop chasing the wrong things, you give the rights things a change to catch you" -Lolly Daskal. One of the many lessons I learned was not to stress over the things I can't control because they always turn into enigmas, and postponing the inevitable will only postpone the eventuality. Over all I feel this chapter of my life is closed and I'm eager to start the next. As of 2021 my mission is only to get home to my son, educate myself and to build new relationships. The old way thinking is out and its time for people to meet the new Brill. I have a 28 U.S.C 2255 (motion to vacate, set aside or correct sentence, that I prepared) pending in the court on Fifth, Sixth and Fourteenth Amendment violations. God willing I'll be home sooner than later, so wish me luck. Well until then my friend, take care of yourself and "don't be afraid to give up the good to go for the great" -John D. Rockefeller.

Acknowledgements

I could have not written this book without the blessings, knowledge and strength given to me by Allah. Without a doubt this book would not have happen without the support and help from my family and others. My Grandmother Marie, my Mother Deneen, Aunt Monica, Uncle Rodney, and Cousins Rod-Rod, Askyia, and Sharonda. BIG SHOUT to my Cousin Ranard, you came through for me cuz, I won't forget it. Double salute to my son Tone-Tone, you're my one and only and I love you with all my heart. You also are one of a kind, don't forget that! If you don't listen to nothing else I have told you, please never let your emotions over power your intelligence. S/o to Rico at Real Savage Publications, you already know what's up slim, from Baltimore to Southeast D.C (S.W.A.B). Brother Menes double salute sir! Thank you for the knowledge and your assistance, we locked in. S/o to Strivin Artist Graphic Design, Dynasty's visionary design, Elite Authors, and Shardae at L.A Management on the editing. S/o to Baynard Woods, Justin Fenton, Tim Prudente, D. Watkins, and Ty (North Danville, VA) thank y'all for the assistance.

BIG SHOUT to the Lang Family as a whole, the support y'all gave me was truly felt. Big thanks to my grandmother Margurite and Pop-Pop Bill for the support through this troubling chapter of my life, I love y'all. Double salute to my mother and cousin Rod-Rod, y'all both really stepped up and without a doubt it wouldn't be a me today without y'all help and support. I love you both. I'm really blessed by the best because he gave me a mother who has supported me every step of the way. Auntie (Moni) I know I drove you crazy lol, but I know it did nothing but make you stronger. Meona (Big Face)

I appreciate your support and assistance. Rae-Rae, cousin Tony loves you! Dame, you already know you family.

S/o to my co-defendants Munch, Lou, Omari, and Twan, make sure y'all hold it down for Northeast. S/o to everybody I grew up with, y'all know who y'all are. S/o to everybody I can't mention, you all know who you are. Who I deal with isn't for everybody. S/o to Bert, Tom-Tom, Darryl & Chelse, Mike Huff, Monique, Hue, Ros'e D, Samos Ty, Dj Manny, Shotgun (Shawnta), Amy, Smitty, Mal the general, Zebee, Hfranks, Ahri the honor is all mine, Manny Lo, James Jones, Sean P, Head, Sasso (Southeast D.C), Bullhead Mo, Dovell, Y.B.G Ty, Tayrock, lom_Jada, E-Watts I heard you holla at me, Westport Moonie WYA? Jazzy what up fam, I can't wait to dead broke you lol, Moneyjake I hear you doing your thing and Doodah that was some real shit, I won't forget it. Chicken (Greenmount) I heard you were home, stay focus. Terrance you already know where we stand, nothing but love. BIG SHOUT TO: my Cedonia family, y'all already know "C.A SPORTS, WE IN THE GAME!", S/o to Nick G and my Ramblewood family what up! The whole Curbeam family, (Furl you know where we stand) and the Jeffries family, Hood (Justin) I love you bro and I'm sorry I wasn't there for you like I should have been. I didn't know any better. S/o to Joe, Dina, Bryona I love y'all. John (Cashland), Pam from X'cetra salon, Kings & Queens hair palace, what's up! C.C you already! S/o to Ms. Lorna and Rayshawna y'all supported me and I will never forget that. Certified Fly Guy (Danny) you are certified! You stepped up for me and my son, so you already know. Ranisha what up slim, you a real one. Big Head Bogie you already know what it is, and I always have appreciated our friendship, tell Brandy I said what's up. If you're in Baltimore go to "Studio Fix Salon" for all your hair needs. Ask anybody that knows, they about that hair life for real. My T.M.C brother Rico what's up! We will be there soon to do it the right way this time. Chenellnicole what's up sis! Shamir I didn't forget your assistance love. To the whole Alameda, York Rd and Northeast Baltimore, may they never say we didn't live! Redz what's up family, thanks for the push! Worm (20th) you already know where we stand, you a real nigga. S/o to Jacqueline (gracias por siempre chekiando como estoy!) Bo & Ryan I'm glad y'all home, without a doubt the kids need y'all, so stay focus. S/o to Old York & Willow, Fresh, Hott, Row, Nico, Davon Lay what up! S/o to Ms. Williams at "The 24 Hour Secretary" S/o to my father Shawn, I love you Mo! April W, you know my heart goes out to you. Snoop (Chris) you already know what's up, I love that our sons are click tight, reminds me of when we were that age. Lisa (Macon G.A) I hope your able to read this, thanks for the push. S/o to all the kids and their mother's, y'all know Uncle Brill love y'all, this includes you Rae (Rae_z) and Nae (Truulyb). S/o to my IG family and everybody that helped me promote the book, I be seeing the comments. To my guys in the mix, get it together before it all fall apart. BIG SHOUT to those who left my side since I been gone and under stress. You turned your back and counted me out so I know you ain't shit. If I forgot you, charge it to my mind not my heart. Most of the people I named I don't even talk to. I know what our relationship was when I was home, so I feel no way about not hearing from you. As I said, I don't talk to a lot of niggas but they still the bro's. The same goes for my so called home girls, I ain't made at y'all.

Kelly, Kelly, Kelly! Without a doubt I have to say sorry for EVERYTHING I did in the past, I wasn't careful and I took you for granted. I never once thought about how the life I lived would someday effect you, which in turn affected us. Being a FOOL was what led me to the decisions I made, LOVE was what brought me to the bitter place I was at and it was KNOWLEDGE that led me to realize it all. It's crazy where we are, we use to hit each other about everything, and now it's like we don't even know each other. All you do is ask do I need anything, I don't need your money, I needed you, the old you. I guess sometimes love last, and sometimes it hurts instead. I can say I'm glad we are doing much better than we were when I wrote this book. Anyway... You're doing a great job at raising our son and I wouldn't ask for Tone to have a different mom. I hope that you know I hate the fact I'm not able to produce, due to my situation. You know I always took pride in taking care of our family, and the shit hurt that I'm not able to do so today. So double salute to you for holding shit down to the ground when it came to what we will forever share together (our son.) Thank you for everything you do. S/o to the crew, Volante, Theresa, Ebony, Trina, etc. Thank y'all for the support. Nimya hey baby, please stay focus. Ms. Tammy you will forever be my second mother; how could I forget where I started. S/o to Nicole (Boo), Dominique, Dj, Peyton, Tray and Baby Creed.

BIG SHOUT OUT: to all the men behind the wall, free da guys! What up to the home team (Baltimore/D.C) at all the federal prisons. S/o to the guys I was at Supermax (C.D.F), Beckley and McDowell with. S/o to my guys Wop (North Pittsburgh), T.C (Lorain, Ohio), yall my brothers for real. S/o to Mass (Newark, New Jersey 6th Ave), Bo (East Oakland), Big G (Charlotte, NC), Homi (North Philly, Erie Ave) aint no question you my nigga and you are one slick talking/rapping mothafucker, can't wait until we fucking them streets up together. Ty (Norfolk, VA Uptown), Trip (Chi-Town, Rack city), Black Byrd aka Dre (Chattanooga). Saquann "Say" Harris (Southeast D.C), Author of "What We Chatting Bout". My Baltimore guys Slice, Rizzy, Cheeks y'all already know Northeast to Hoffman street. Cheeks you already know OPERATION SHUT THE WHOLE SHIT DOWN, Big Head Charlie, MBK Barney, Chuck b.k.a G.O, West Baltimore Kim, Oaky, Park Heights Dre, Lil Wop, Wan, Gee, Los, Boo-Boo, D.J, Man-Man, Dirty, Twan, Josh, Ail (Big Bunk), Murda, Southside, Richie Rod (Lil Rod), Blue-Black, Pipe and Dorsey. Shout to "The Great Billy Guy" (Baltimore OG) who said: "Not only do I get money; I take the hardest hits on the chin from the opposition (law enforcement). I bring class, flair, and dignity to a game that is now full of gutless-hateful-jealous niggars. I rest well at night due to the real men of the game who know who I am and what I stand for." I couldn't agree and relate more, because I took a lot on the chin and even though this is a nightmare vacation from hell, I sleep well at night knowing I always stood on all ten and played the game by the rules. So it's a must each and every one of you salute the real and never the fake. FREE DA GUYS!!!

BIG SHOUT OUT: to everybody we lost to Covid-19, police brutality (SAY THEIR NAMES), and the senseless violence etc., REST IN PEACE: Ronald Lang Sr., Darryl Lang, Mr. Jeff, Ms. Karen, Georgie, Lil Tay, Travis, Moody, Rocko, Lor Travis, Flip, B (Oliver St), Fat Relly, Lil Meat, LT, Zora, JJ, Sean b.k.a Layedbackjack, Baby J, Uncle Nicky, Cousin Ashley, Uncle Danny, Bernard, Danny (hermosa_danny) Uncle Bubbles and anybody I forgot.

About the Author

Antonio "Brill" Shropshire, a Baltimore native, co-founder of Mucho Dinero kids clothing line and Entrepreneur, who is now serving a 25-year sentence. Besides focusing on being a great father from prison and getting Mucho Dinero back up and running with Tone (his son and Founder of Mucho Dinero), Brill or Tony as his family calls him, spends his time studying federal law and educating himself for his return to society. While standing on morals and principles from prison to the street, he tries to maintain a level of respect from his peers. Now that Brill sees life through a different lens, he fights only to return to his son and to start a non-profit organization to give back to the city of Baltimore that he so vigorously took from. Also once released he will join the fight against police brutality, for equal rights and prison reform. Feel free to contact Brill on any topic or issue, he would love to hear from you.

I.G: TMC_YO
FACEBOOK: ANTONIO SHROPSHIRE
EMAIL: antonioshropshire85@gmail.com
WRITE: #62637-037@bop.gov

Made in the USA
Middletown, DE
01 September 2021